The COURSE OF HISTORY

Ten Meals That Changed the World

STRUAN STEVENSON

RECIPES BY
TONY SINGH MBE

BIRLINN

First published in 2017 by
Birlinn Limited
West Newington House
10 Newington Road
Edinburgh
EH9 1QS

www.birlinn.co.uk

Text copyright © Struan Stevenson 2017
Recreated recipes copyright © Tony Singh 2017

ISBN 978 178027 491 1

British Library Cataloguing in Publication Data
A catalogue record for this book is available
from the British Library.

Designed and typeset by Mark Blackadder

Printed and bound by Gutenberg Press, Malta

The
COURSE OF HISTORY

'Statistics show that of those who contract
the habit of eating, very few survive'
GEORGE BERNARD SHAW

CONTENTS

LIST OF ILLUSTRATIONS

Prince Charles Edward Stuart ('Bonnie Prince Charlie')

Old Culloden House

The Battle of Culloden

Major-General Edward Braddock

The Battle of Monongahela, 1755

Carlyle House, Alexandria

Thomas Jefferson

Alexander Hamilton

James Madison

Francis I, Emperor of Austria

Prince Charles-Maurice de Talleyrand-Périgord

Ministers, diplomats and statesmen at the Congress of Vienna

Archduke Franz Ferdinand and his wife, Sophie

Franz Ferdinand and Sophie arrive in Sarajevo

The Hotel Bosna, Ilidža

Achnacarry Castle

William Larimer Mellon of Gulf Oil

Henri Deterding of Royal Dutch Shell

Sir John Cadman of BP

Walter Teagle of Standard Oil

Kurt Von Schuschnigg, Austrian Chancellor

Hitler's Berghof mountain retreat on the Obersalzberg

Hitler arrives in Vienna, March 1938

Stalin, Roosevelt and Churchill at the Tehran Summit, November 1943

Churchill presenting the Sword of Stalingrad to Stalin

Churchill's birthday banquet, 30 November 1943

President Richard Nixon meeting Mao Zedong

Nixon with Zhou Enlai at the banquet in the Great Hall of the People, Beijing

Egyptian President Anwar Sadat, US President Jimmy Carter and Israeli Prime Minister Menachem Begin

Sadat, Carter and Begin at Aspen Lodge, Camp David

INTRODUCTION

There is a famous Spanish proverb that says 'The belly rules the mind'. This is a clinically proven fact. Food is the original mind-controlling drug. Every time we eat, we bombard our brains with a feast of chemicals, triggering an explosive hormonal chain reaction that directly influences the way we think.

Countless studies have shown that the positive emotional state a good meal induces naturally enhances our receptiveness to be persuaded. It triggers an instinctive desire to repay the provider. This is why executives regularly combine business meetings with meals, why lobbyists invite politicians to attend receptions, lunches and dinners and why major State occasions almost always involve an elaborate banquet. Churchill called this 'dining diplomacy' and sociologists have confirmed that this principle is a potent motivator across all human cultures. As a lifelong politician, I have witnessed 'dining diplomacy' at first hand, sharing meals with royalty, presidents, diplomats and business leaders across the globe.

This book will take you on a journey to discover how food has transcended its primal role as life-giving sustenance to become a weapon of unimaginable power, used throughout history as a means of persuasion. We will explore how eating and drinking have been at the epicentre of some of history's most momentous events. We will look at its role as a key influence on those events and not just its place as an intriguing historical footnote. We will examine the many ways it has been used, consciously, or unconsciously to persuade, coax and cajole major historical figures into epoch-changing decisions.

From the Last Supper and Jesus' betrayal, right up to Tony Blair and Gordon Brown's notorious 'Granita Pact' formed at the eponymous Islington restaurant, tales of historically significant meals have always fascinated me. Could a lavish dinner washed down with gallons of wine hours before the disastrous Battle of Culloden have clouded Bonnie Prince Charlie's judgement and led to the defeat of the Jacobite cause? Could Archduke Franz Ferdinand and his wife Sophie have avoided assassination if they had dined quietly the evening before their fateful visit to Sarajevo rather than indulging in a nine-course banquet accompanied by some of Europe's finest wines? Could Austria have dodged absorption into Hitler's Third Reich if the pompous Austrian Chancellor Kurt von Schuschnigg had declined an invitation to lunch in Hitler's Berghof in February 1938?

The list of variables leading to the outcomes of these events is of course endless, but what cannot be denied is that each situation had one thing in common. Food. And what better way to step into the shoes of these historical figures than to taste the meals they ate for yourself? This is why I have collaborated with one of the UK's foremost chefs, Tony Singh, to refashion each recipe into an accessibly modern style, so you can bring history to life in your own kitchen.

All of the meals in this book have been intensively researched and, wherever possible, based on actual menus or historic records of the food that was served. In a very few cases, the information is limited or absent and in these instances the authors have sought to reproduce as authentically as possible the dishes that most likely were consumed.

So next time you have friends or family over for dinner, why not dip into this menu of momentous meals and share with them some of the food that changed the course of history?

Bon appetit!

Struan Stevenson
October 2017

ACKNOWLEDGEMENTS

With great thanks to the incomparable Wendy Brown, who introduced me to the amazing celebrity chef Tony Singh. Also to my publisher Hugh Andrew at Birlinn, who has shown profound faith in this book from its earliest days and has patiently guided me through its lengthy gestation. My gratitude, as always, to my long-suffering wife Pat, who saw me typing away in my study hour after hour, day after day, for wearying months and years. Her patience, support and forbearance are forever my inspiration.

One

BONNIE PRINCE CHARLIE ON THE EVE OF CULLODEN

14 April 1746
Culloden House,
near Inverness

THE GUESTS

PRINCE CHARLES EDWARD STUART
'Bonnie Prince Charlie'
son of James Stuart, exiled claimant
to the British throne

His Jacobite leaders:
LORD GEORGE MURRAY,
JAMES DRUMMOND, DUKE OF PERTH
LORD JOHN DRUMMOND
WILLIAM DRUMMOND, VISCOUNT STRATHALLAN
LORD KILMARNOCK, LORD BALMERINO,
LORD PITSLIGO, LORD ELCHO

Highland clan chiefs

Officers of the Irish Picquets and
several French commanders

Bonnie Prince Charlie stared across the battlefield in shock and dismay, his handsome face spattered with flecks of blood and mud. His horse had been shot through the shoulder and was staggering between groups of fallen Jacobite soldiers, blood pumping from its wound. The prince could hear the screams of his dying soldiers above even the bitter wind howling off the Moray Firth. All around him the British Redcoats, commanded by the battle-hardened 'Butcher Cumberland', were taking a full and brutal revenge for the prince's previous victories against them. The Redcoats' blood was up and they hunted down the fleeing High-landers, pausing only to shoot, behead and bayonet the wounded as they found them. It was said that every single British sword and bayonet was encrusted with Jacobite blood.

It was just after midday on Wednesday 16 April 1746 and this was the aftermath of the Battle of Culloden, the last pitched battle fought on British soil and a bloodbath. The battle had lasted less than an hour. Cumberland's Hanoverian army lost just 50 men, while the kilted, blood-stained bodies of more than 1,200 Jacobites, their broadswords, muskets and leather targes (shields), lay scattered like confetti on the boggy moor.

The Jacobite dream lay dead in the mud and with it a Royal Stuart era that had lasted for more than 400 years. The defeat must have been twice as crushing for the prince because only two nights previously, at a lavish dinner for his officers in nearby Culloden House, he had toasted his loyal commanders in Bordeaux wine as they talked of their coming victory. They feasted on lamb, cheese and cream crowdie while Prince Charles Edward Stuart boasted that his very presence would strike fear into the hearts of the English soldiers. The Jacobite rising of '45 would soon achieve its goal with a decisive military victory and his father, James Francis Edward Stuart, son of James VII and II, would be named King of Scotland, England and Ireland.

Yet while the prince and his lords feasted, his foot soldiers starved. Their dinner was very different indeed, and unknown to the laughing, drinking prince he was presiding over the final Jacobite banquet on British soil. He could barely have imagined the horrors that would engulf his army and change Scotland forever on Drummossie Moor within the ensuing 48 hours. History was quietly being written during that meal and soon this charismatic champion of a cause, this man who would have been king, would be a failure on the run.

*　　*　　*

In August 1745, Prince Charles Edward Stuart stepped out of a small rowing boat and onto the Scottish mainland. He was met by just a few loyal MacDonalds, but word of the Young Pretender's arrival fired through the glens of the West Highlands and the clans came flocking to his cause. As his army swelled he raised his standard amid the glowering hills of Glenfinnan on 19 August. Within months his victorious army had swept into Edinburgh, crushed the Hanoverian forces at Prestonpans and marched on into England, reaching Derby by 4 December 1745. Bonnie Prince Charlie and his Jacobite army were within 114 miles of London and the fulfilment of his dream. But news had arrived that the Duke of Cumberland, youngest son of the Hanoverian King George II and Charles' own cousin, had been recalled from Flanders and was now in England, having brought with him 25 battalions of infantry, 23 squadrons of cavalry, and four companies of artillery. Major-General Wade's Hanoverian army was ensconced in Scotland and there were strong rumours that a third, large government force was defending London. In fact this was untrue, and had Charles forged on to London it is possible the capital could have fallen and the Stuarts could have reclaimed the British crown. However, Lord George Murray, one of the prince's senior commanders, argued in favour of a retreat to Scotland and won the support of the majority of the officers. Charles was outraged and told them they were about to snatch defeat from the jaws of victory, denying the Stuart restoration. Charles proclaimed: 'You ruin, abandon and betray me if you do not march on.' Nevertheless he reluctantly agreed to the Council's decision to retreat.[1]

So began the long march back to Scotland. The demoralised Jacobite army was exhausted, cold and hungry. In early February, Prince Charles fell ill with flu and stopped to recover in Bannockburn House near Stirling. Here he took a lover, the pretty and youthful Clementina Walkinshaw, who nursed him back to health.

On 20 February 1746, the Jacobite army occupied Inverness and laid siege to Fort William. By now, 9,000 government troops under Cumberland's command had advanced as far as Nairn, only eight miles east of Inverness, and Charles' army, short of food, ammunition and other vital supplies, started to form up on the high ground at Culloden Moor, then known as Drummossie Moor, to defend Inverness. The boggy ground of Drummossie Moor had been selected by Charles as an ideal battlefield as he thought it would hinder any charge by Cumberland's cavalry. Murray pointed out the unsuitability of the ground for his own Jacobite troops, as the flat, boggy turf would slow the charge of his foot soldiers and make them sitting ducks for the Hanoverian artillery and muskets. But Charles, who mistrusted Murray following his decision to retreat from Derby, refused to listen and insisted on the choice of Drummossie Moor as the battlefield.

Bonnie Prince Charlie had requisitioned Culloden House as his head-quarters, and it was here on the evening of Monday 14 April that he invited his officers to join him for a fateful banquet. This was the home of Duncan Forbes of Culloden, Lord President of the Court of Session. Forbes was a devout Protestant and Hanoverian loyalist who had tried desperately to dissuade many Highland chiefs from supporting the upris-ing. As an ardent government supporter, he had even raised a small force of 2,000 men to fight for King George. But as the Jacobite army moved towards Inverness, he retreated, first to Ross-shire and then to Skye, aban-doning his beloved home to the Jacobites. Prince Charles had chosen his billet well. Culloden House was renowned for its hospitality. The Lord President was known to keep casks of claret in the main hall from which guests could literally help themselves by the 'pailful'. The chairs surround-ing the large oak table in the main dining hall at Culloden House had been specially designed with grooves into which poles could be inserted so that servants could carry drunken guests more easily to bed.

Captain Edmund Burt (an English military engineer), in his *Letters from the North of Scotland*, wrote that

> It is the custom of that house, at the first visit or introduction, to take up your freedom by cracking his nut (as he terms it), that is, a cocoa-shell, which holds a pint, filled with champagne, or such other sort of wine as you shall choose. You may guess that few go away sober at any time; and for the greatest part of his guests, in that conclusion, they cannot go at all. A hogshead of fine claret was kept in the hall, so that guests or even passer-bys could refresh themselves with a pint of claret. As the company are disabled one after another, two servants, who are all the time in waiting, take up the invalids with short poles in the chairs as they sit (if not fallen down), and carry them to their beds, and still the hero holds out.

And in a pamphlet entitled *Memoirs of the life of the late Right Honourable Duncan Forbes, Esq; of Culloden; Lord-President of the Court of Session of Scotland*, published some years after his death, the author states: 'He and his elder brother whose generosity was as extensive as his genius, obtained the designation of being the greatest bouzers [sic], i.e. the most plentiful drinkers in the North.'[2]

While the Young Pretender was presiding over what proved to be the last gathering of his loyal officers, the Duke of Cumberland camped only eight miles away in Dalcross Castle, had settled down to a more modest dinner to celebrate his 25th birthday. The rotund Cumberland, who had the bulging eyes of his Hanoverian ancestors, was not a man easily given to frivolity. Nevertheless he had ordered four gallons of brandy, plus a 'Sufficient quantity of Biscuit and Cheese' for every man, to be distributed to each battalion as part of his 15 April birthday celebrations. A strict disciplinarian, Cumberland ordered his officers to ensure that there was no drunkenness.

Lord George Murray, aware of the fact that the Hanoverian army would be joining in the duke's birthday celebrations, suggested to Prince Charles that they should mount a night attack on the enemy encampment at Nairn, believing he'd catch the Redcoats drunkenly napping. 'This is Cumberland's birth day, they'l all be as drunk as beggers,'[3] he reportedly said. Bonnie Prince Charlie was enthusiastic about this plan and it was agreed that the Jacobite army would set off at dusk the following evening. In the meantime, Charles insisted that news of the proposed night attack should remain a closely guarded secret to ensure that Cumberland was caught off guard.

Buoyed by this inspired idea and convinced that the night attack would lead to his ultimate victory, Prince Charles was in great spirits as he took his seat at the head of Duncan Forbes' table in the main dining hall at Culloden House. Nothing was allowed to dent his optimism. As the night wore on and the prince's confidence soared in line with his consumption of claret, he became more and more garrulous. When one of his officers suggested that they might be wise to designate a place of rendezvous in the event of a defeat, the prince quickly rebuked him, remarking 'only those that are afraid can doubt my coming victory'.[4]

Gathered around the great dining table in Culloden House were the cream of the Jacobite leadership and clan chieftains including Lord George Murray, Lord James Drummond, Duke of Perth and his younger brother Lord John Drummond, as well as William Drummond, Viscount Strathallan, Lord Kilmarnock, Lord Balmerino, Lord Pitsligo, Lord Elcho and the many clan chiefs including: Glengarry, Clanranald, MacDonald of Keppoch, who had arrived that same day with 200 men, Chisholm, Maclean, Mclachlan, Mackintosh, Fraser, Farquharson, Lovat, Lochiel, McGillivray and Stewart of Ardshiel (who commanded the Appin Stewarts). They were joined by the officers of the Irish Picquets and some French commanders. These were men who were willing to risk everything to see Prince Charles' father restored to the throne. They knew that victory for Bonnie Prince Charlie would see their fortunes soar. Supporters of the Hanoverian King George II would surely flee the country and their castles, mansions, land and estates would be handed out to loyal Jacobite supporters by a grateful monarch restored to his kingdom.

But they also knew the penalty for defeat. They realised that their own homes and estates would be forfeit and they would most probably end their days on the scaffold. They were gamblers playing for the highest possible stakes, and with a decisive and potentially final battle against the Hanoverian army imminent they were determined, in a mood of soaring confidence, to enjoy the lavish food and wine on offer. The grand oak dining table in the great hall at Culloden House was crowded with crystal glasses, silver cutlery and white porcelain crockery emblazoned with the coat of arms of the lord president. Delicately embroidered lace table-mats from Forbes' renowned collection had been carefully placed in front of each of the guests. It was truly a setting fit for a prince.

As they chatted effusively about the prospects of defeating the Hanoverian army and reminisced over past exploits and victories, teams of servants supplied them with a magnificent feast which began with mussel brose, followed by a rack of lamb wi' a skirlie crust, dished up with peppered turnip, potato and cabbage cakes. An intermediary course of Dunlop Cheddar with bannocks was followed by cream crowdie – a compote of berries macerated in whisky, with toasted oatmeal, heather honey and whipped cream.[5] This extravagant banquet was washed down with copious servings of champagne and French claret from the absent lord president's abundant cellar and numerous casks. Toast after toast was proclaimed by the various clan chiefs, praising 'His Royal Highness The Prince Regent and his illustrious father the rightful King James VIII of Scotland and III of England.' The feasting and drinking went on into the wee small hours, with ever-more extravagant boasts and discussions about the forthcoming

Jacobite victory over the Duke of Cumberland and the certain restoration of the Stuarts to the throne of England, Scotland and Ireland.

Bonnie Prince Charlie's sumptuous banquet contrasted sharply with the meagre fare dished out to his soldiers. That same day, he had ordered provisions to be brought from Inverness to feed his men, as they had eaten nothing for 24 hours. There was enough oatmeal stored in Inverness to have fed his army for a fortnight, but due to the incompetence of his quartermaster, none of it had arrived at Culloden. Only one biscuit per man could be distributed to the starving Highlanders. Lord George Murray blamed the lack of proper provisioning on John Hay of Restalrig, who had been given this task by the prince. But provisions and money were running dangerously low and the Jacobite soldiers were starving and disgruntled as they had been given neither adequate food nor pay for weeks. It was also seeding-time in Scotland and many of the prince's disillusioned followers had deserted and slunk back to their farms and crofts to plant their spring crops. The Duke of Cumberland's army meanwhile had been constantly well provisioned by the British Navy, which had followed them up the east coast of Scotland.

It was against this background that Charles and his officers arose early on the morning of Tuesday 15 April, perhaps suffering from little sleep and the excesses of a long, wine-fuelled night. The weather had taken a turn for the worse and a cold, rising wind was driving rain and sleet across the nearby Drummossie Moor, when news came that some scouts had spotted Redcoats on the move in the vicinity. Believing Cumberland's entire Hanoverian army was now on the march and that the decisive battle they had all been anticipating was imminent, Charles and his commanders formed his men into two battle-lines facing east on the boggy moor. But as the day progressed and the evening sky darkened, it soon became clear that the scouts had been mistaken and that Cumberland's men were not on the move from their camp at Nairn after all. And now the well-kept secret of the proposed night assault began to have unintended consequences, as several thousand starving Jacobite soldiers headed off towards Inverness in search of food and somewhere dry to sleep. Some even tore leaves off cabbages growing in farm fields in an attempt to quell their hunger pangs. The prince's troops had no idea that they were about to be summoned at dusk to begin the eight-mile trek towards the slumbering Hanoverian army camp at Nairn.

Realising that his numbers had been seriously reduced, in panic

Murray sent many of his officers to find the missing men, but it was an impossible task. Dismayed at this setback, Murray now had second thoughts about the night attack, but Prince Charles was adamant it must go ahead. The night march to Nairn must begin. Lord George briefed his officers on the plan, insisting that the much-diminished army should set off around nine o'clock and that the march had to be undertaken in 'the profoundest silence'. In order to maintain an element of surprise on the slumbering enemy it was agreed that the Jacobite army would stay clear of the roads and instead traverse fields and moorland on their way to Nairn. Lord George told his officers that they were to 'give no quarter to the Elector's Troops, on any account what so ever'.[6] Murray even instructed his officers on how their men should cut the guy-ropes of the enemy tents and stab and shoot with pistols anyone seen to be struggling within.

The much-depleted Jacobite army left Culloden in two columns as dusk fell on Tuesday 15 April. The front column was led by Murray and the second column by the prince himself and the Duke of Perth. The prince remained on foot throughout the night march. They left behind huge bonfires burning at Culloden to fool the Hanoverians into believing they were quietly encamped for the night. As they set off, Bonnie Prince Charlie walked up to Lord George and hugging him said: 'Yu cant imagine, nor I cant express to yu how acknowledging I am of all the services yu have rendered me, but this will Crown all. You'l restore the King by it, you'l deliver our poor Country from Slevery, you'l have all the hon(ou)r & glory of it, it is your own work, it is yu imagined it, & be assured that the King nor I, will never forget it.'[7] The prince walked alongside Murray for some time, neither of them speaking, before Charles stopped and said, 'Well, God blesse yu. Il go and see if all follows.'[8]

The Jacobite army made slow progress over the heavy ground in the dark. When finally they were within two miles of the Hanoverian camp, it was already almost dawn and there were signs of Cumberland's army beginning to stir. The English sentries could be heard calling to each other. The smell of roasting meat from the previous evening's feast drifted across to the starving Jacobites, who had only been provided with a single biscuit to eat over the previous 48 hours. Murray's fleet-footed Highlanders had made good progress on the night march, but the gap between Murray's column and the one led by the prince had continued to widen, forcing Murray to stop several times to enable them to catch up. The delays had a fatal impact on the timing of the assault and Murray realised now that it was too late to achieve surprise. He sent back for permission from Prince Charles to abort the mission. But as dawn began to break, he grasped that he could no longer risk waiting for the prince's answer and commanded his troops to wheel round and begin the long march back to Drummossie Moor.

*　　*　　*

It was around four a.m. when the prince got the news that Murray had aborted the intended night attack and had begun marching back to Culloden. Charles was appalled. He could not believe that Murray had disobeyed his express orders and began to suspect he had been betrayed. He ordered John Hay of Restalrig to ride with all possible haste to the front of the column and order Murray to resume the attack. He even commanded two Irish soldiers to keep a close watch on Murray and to shoot him if they caught him in any clear act of treachery. Reaching the front of the column, Restalrig told Murray that it was the prince's explicit command that he should resume the agreed attack on the Hanoverian camp, but Murray, who blamed Restalrig for the fact that his troops were exhausted and starving and that this had clearly slowed their pace, chose to ignore him. Murray proceeded to organise the withdrawal back to Culloden. Furious at the snub from Murray, Restalrig rode flat out back to Prince Charles, telling him that Murray was blatantly refusing to obey His Royal Highness's orders. The exasperated prince, seeing some officers from the Duke of Perth's battalion, angrily demanded to know what had gone wrong and why the assault had not taken place; he was heard to shout, 'Where the devil are the men a-going?' When an officer explained that they had been ordered to return to Culloden by the Duke of Perth, the prince shouted, 'Where is the Duke of Perth? Call him here!'

Soon the Duke of Perth himself arrived and informed Bonnie Prince Charlie that Lord George had aborted the night assault and wheeled his column around 'more than three quarters of an hour agoe'. 'Good God,' the prince was heard to yell. 'What can be the matter? What does he mean? We were equal in number and would have blown them to the devil. Pray, Perth, can't you call them back yet? Perhaps he is not gone far yet.'[9] But the Duke of Perth explained that it was too late to reverse the decision. Restalrig pled with the prince to take a horse and ride to the front of the column where he could confront Murray in person. The prince set off at speed, soon bumping into Murray and his retreating troops. The fuming prince was heard to shout at Murray, 'I am betrayed,' which must have been deeply hurtful to one of his most loyal and dedicated commanders. But it was now too late to overturn the decree.

As dawn broke, Murray and his Atholl Brigade arrived back at Culloden House, sullen, perplexed and worn out. It was around six a.m. Prince Charles arrived shortly afterwards. By the time the starving Jacobite soldiers, half dead with fatigue, reached the lord president's house, they began to disperse, many heading to Inverness to forage for food, while most of the others who had participated in the abortive night march collapsed asleep on the lawns and grassy banks surrounding the mansion. The tide had turned and with it, the sudden realisation that the Jacobite army, starving and exhausted after their futile night march, could face the might of the Hanoverian army within a matter of hours in a full-scale pitched battle. It was the first time that the normally confident prince began to fear defeat. He could hear the grumblings and protests of his dispirited men and this further depressed him.

But even now he failed to hold a war council to decide what action to take. Instead he ordered officers from each of his regiments to go into Inverness to buy or commandeer supplies of food for the troops, telling them to threaten to destroy the town if anyone refused to hand over provisions. As he was doing so, the Marquis d'Eguilles, French ambassador at the court of Prince Charles, asked for an audience with the prince and kneeling before him, begged him not to fight a battle that day, but rather to retreat to Inverness or further into the Highlands, where the Jacobite troops could be fed, rested and reinforced before facing the might of the Hanoverian army. But the Young Pretender, his judgement certainly now clouded by exhaustion, would not listen to reason. He insisted that the battle should be fought on Drummossie Moor, although he and most of his officers thought it unlikely that they would face Cumberland's army that day. They had, after all, been within just two miles of the Hanoverian camp at Nairn and had seen no signs of activity that might have signalled preparations for a major assault. Dismayed, the French ambassador hurried back to his house in Inverness and began to burn his papers, convinced that the Jacobite army was facing imminent defeat.

It was around 8 a.m. when Charles, after grabbing some bread and a glass of whisky, finally threw himself onto a bed, fully clothed, with his boots still on. He fell instantly into a deep sleep, but barely 20 minutes later, a guard rushed in to waken him, stating that Cumberland's army had been seen on the march. They were heading towards Culloden. A bewildered prince, reeling from disrupted sleep, lurched outside to a scene of bedlam. Men, staggering from lack of sleep and unappeased hunger, were standing shivering in groups, wondering what to do. Others lay sleeping where they had fallen to the ground in exhaustion, the noise and clamour of the startled camp unable to wake them. Officers were shouting orders and trying to rouse their slumbering troops. Some leapt onto horses and galloped off towards Inverness to sound the alarm and gather up the missing men who had gone in search of nourishment. There was no time now to prepare food, even if any had been available. The Young Pretender decided to forego some proffered porridge, in solidarity with his starving troops. He decided to face the enemy, like his men, on an empty stomach.

Lord George Murray, Cameron of Lochiel and the other chiefs advised the prince that his army was in no fit state to face the might of the Hanoverian army and instead should retreat across the River Nairn from where they could be fed and rested before confronting the enemy. But the prince's close adviser Sir Thomas Sheridan and some of his Irish and French officers were of the opposite opinion. They felt that the prince should stand his ground and fight. Still smarting from what he regarded as Murray's betrayal, Charles decided to ignore the advice of his most experienced commanders. The die was cast. The battle would go ahead on Drummossie Moor.

Prince Charles was only three months older than his cousin and adversary, the Duke of Cumberland, yet they were both courageous leaders. It was the English duke, however, who had been hardened by military involvement in Flanders. Cumberland's army rose early on 16 April and began their march to Culloden. Well fed, rested and provisioned from ships of the Royal Navy, the 9,000 troops were in good spirits and ready for the fray. An advance reconnaissance party consisting of Campbell Highlanders and Kingston's Light Horse startled the slumbering Jacobites who fired artillery pieces to summon the clans to their battle positions. Unfortunately, many of the starving and exhausted men were scattered so widely across the area that they failed to hear the guns. Others slept through the tumult. Again Murray complained to the prince about his choice of Drummossie Moor and again the prince, who by now was deeply suspicious of Murray's motives, rebuffed him.

The Jacobite army of around 5,000 men was assembled into two hastily constructed lines on the moor. To their front, the heather-covered Drummossie Moor stretched away in the distance, interspersed with patches of bog. To their left, a morass, impenetrable for either cavalry or infantry, stretched almost all the way to Culloden House and the shores of the Moray Firth, while on the right, within 300 yards, a stone dyke provided the boundary of a field which sloped down to the River Nairn. Around noon they caught sight of the duke's army for the first time, spread out in a great formation that extended well beyond both flanks of the prince's front line. Cumberland's well-trained Redcoats moved forward slowly and methodically until they were within 300 yards of the foremost Jacobite columns, the fixed bayonets of the infantry and the drawn sabres of the cavalry glinting occasionally in the watery sunlight that appeared from time to time through the heavy clouds. Regimental colours fluttered in the breeze and the pipes and drums of the Campbell Highlanders, who had joined the ranks of Cumberland's army, resounded in taunting waves across the moor.

It was the defining battle that Bonnie Prince Charlie had long sought, and yet he now faced his enemy in the most inauspicious circumstances. His ranks were depleted by desertion, his men were almost fainting from hunger and exhaustion after their abortive night march, and his key commanders were in open disagreement on his choice of battleground. Waves of nausea engulfed Charles as he gazed at the formidable array of scarlet-coated and white-gaitered regiments facing him across the boggy moor. It was too late to change his plans. It was a case of fighting as bravely as possible and leaving the outcome of the battle to God. A cold drizzle had now turned into a freezing sleet, pelting into the faces of the Jacobite ranks. A shot thundered out from one of the Jacobite cannon and the Hanoverian artillery responded. The Battle of Culloden had begun.

Cumberland's artillery was accurate and efficient, their guns pounding the Jacobite ranks. A blizzard of iron shrieked through the air. The grapeshot and musket balls cut swathes through the Jacobite ranks, scything down men where they stood. A cannonball decapitated one of Prince Charles' grooms, Thomas Ca, knocking him from his horse immediately behind the prince and splattering the Young Pretender with blood and mud. A nearby officer's horse had its leg almost severed by another explosion and the prince's men urged him to pull back out of harm's way, but he refused, riding forward, sword in hand urging his loyal troops to have courage.

A Jacobite charge was met with bayonets by the Hanoverians. Cameron of Lochiel led his men forward and got close enough to fire his pistol at the Redcoats, before a musket ball shattered both his ankles; the seriously wounded clan chief was carried from the field by survivors of the ill-fated charge. They propped him against the inside wall of a nearby bothy and left to rejoin the battle. A group of English dragoons was about to enter the bothy when they were suddenly called away by a Redcoat officer. The wounded Lochiel had narrowly escaped capture and certain death.

Within 45 minutes it became apparent that the battle had been lost. Orders were given for the Jacobites to pull back and leave the field. The heather of Drummossie Moor was stained red with Highland blood. The prince took flight on horseback, while those of his troops who could, split up and headed for the hills. The Duke of Cumberland ordered his men to kill every wounded Jacobite soldier they found on the battlefield. The Hanoverian troops carried out this task with enthusiasm, beheading and butchering many of the wounded Highlanders. With their bloodlust up they set off for Inverness, raping and ransacking in a savage and uncontrollable rage.

The killing frenzy went on for three days. Wounded Highlanders were thrown onto horse-drawn carts and taken to a nearby bothy where they were hauled from the cart, forced to sit with their backs to a wall and mercilessly shot and clubbed to death. A column of English dragoons discovered around 30 wounded Jacobites hiding in a barn. They locked the barn door and set fire to the building, burning alive all of the men inside. The extent of the butchery of the captured and wounded Jacobites was such that the Provost of Inverness made his way to Cumberland's headquarters and interrupted the duke's victory celebrations to plead for mercy for the defeated Highlanders. His appeals were met with guffaws of laughter and for his trouble the provost was assaulted and unceremoniously kicked down the stairs.

The aftermath of the battle was grim and became a milestone in British history. The carrying of weapons, the wearing of tartan and Highland dress, the playing of bagpipes, were all banned under strict new laws from London. Leading Jacobites who had supported the Young

Pretender such as Lord Balmerino, Lord Kilmarnock and Lord Fraser of Lovat – 'The Old Fox' – were beheaded. James Drummond – the Duke of Perth – managed to board a French vessel in May 1746, but suffering from wounds sustained during the battle and the privations and hardships he had endured during his escape, he died on board.

Meanwhile Bonnie Prince Charlie made his famous escape to the Isle of Skye in an adventure that has become the stuff of legend and was immortalised in the popular folk refrain 'The Skye Boat Song'. He has been helped by Flora MacDonald who took the young prince on a rowing boat to Skye, disguised as her Irish housemaid 'Betty Burke'. Charles' escape was aided and abetted by a great many Highlanders, despite the fact that there was a massive £30,000 price on his head (around £6 million today). For months he criss-crossed between the Scottish islands with government troops in hot pursuit until finally he made it to Loch nan Uamh in Arisaig, very near where he had so optimistically stepped ashore the previous year. Here, two small French ships rescued him and his colleagues and took them back to France. Charles never returned to Scotland. Other rebel commanders like Lord George Murray, Ardshiel and Cameron of Lochiel, fled to the continent. Murray was welcomed by the Old Pretender in Rome, but shunned by Bonnie Prince Charlie, who never spoke to him again. Back in Britain hundreds of less prominent Jacobites were hung, drawn and quartered for committing acts of high treason against the Hanoverian crown.

Prince Charles was joined in France by his mistress Clementina Walkin-shaw. The Aix-la-Chapelle treaty, which ended the war between Britain and France, led to his expulsion from France and return to Italy. He took up residence in Rome and in 1753 Clementina gave birth to the Young Pretender's illegitimate daughter, Charlotte. But Charles' drunken, abusive behaviour and his constant womanising caused Clementina such distress that she was forced to seek the help of the prince's father, the Old Pretender. James agreed to pay her an annual stipend and help her and her daughter find refuge in a convent, all of which he kept secret from Charles. When Charles' father died in 1766, the Young Pretender discovered Clementina's secret hideaway and, furious, cut her stipend in half, forcing his mistress and daughter into virtual penury.

Charles married Princes Louise of Stolberg-Gedern in 1772, living first in Rome then moving to Florence in 1774. It was here, in 1777, that he purchased the Palazzo di San Clemente, now fondly referred to as the Palazzo del Pretendente. In Florence he also began to use the title Count of Albany as an alias. Bonnie Prince Charlie died in Rome on 31 January 1788 at the age of 67. It was said he died of liver failure caused by years of excessive drinking. His final Culloden dinner may have set the seal on his fate in more ways than one.

The loyalist troops of the Hanoverian King George II could not rest on their laurels for long. By 1754, 2 million British settlers had occupied large tracts of land in North America. The French, meanwhile, had only around 60,000 settlers in their own North American colonies, and they relied heavily of the support of the Native Americans in what was rapidly becoming an escalating conflict with their old enemies from Britain. As we will see in the next chapter, attempts by the British to raise taxes on their American colonies to pay for the war against the French and their Indian allies, sowed the seeds of rebellion and led ultimately to the American Revolutionary War and to the creation of the United States of America.

MENU

Mussel Brose

Rack of Lamb wi' a Skirlie Crust
Neeps and Tattie Cakes

Dunlop Cheddar with Bannocks

Cream Crowdie

Champagne
French Claret (red Bordeaux wine)

MUSSEL BROSE

SERVES 6

1 kg mussels, washed and de-bearded
100g butter
1 medium onion, finely chopped
2 sticks celery, finely chopped
4 bay leaves
10g fresh thyme
6 large cloves garlic, finely chopped
400ml dry white wine

Use a large pan with a tight-fitting lid. Melt the butter. Soften the onion, celery, bay, thyme and garlic in the hot butter. Pour in the wine and bring to the boil. Add the mussels, pop on the lid; keep on full heat. Cook until the mussels have all opened. Pour into a colander over a bowl as you want to keep all the stock the mussels have given up. Take the meat out of all the shells and keep aside. Strain the stock through a sieve and keep to one side.

FOR THE BROSE

100g butter
100g plain flour
150g fine oatmeal
salt and white pepper
100g onions, finely chopped
250ml milk
80ml double cream
70g curly parsley, chopped
1 bunch spring onions, finely sliced

FOR THE BROSE BASE

Melt the butter on medium heat in the washed-out mussel-cooking pan. Stir in the flour and cook for 2–4 minutes. Take the pan off the heat and gradually stir in the mussel stock to get a smooth soup. Return to the heat and stirring all the time, bring to the boil. Simmer gently for 8–10 minutes and season with salt and white pepper. Add oatmeal and chopped onions, stir and simmer for a further 10–15 minutes. Add the milk and cream and bring to the boil, season, stir in the mussels and parsley. Take off the heat and add mussels. Serve and garnish with spring onions.

RACK OF LAMB WI' A SKIRLIE CRUST

SERVES 6

3 racks of lamb, French-trimmed
(try to get 8 rib racks for 4 ribs per person)
80g lamb dripping
1 large onion, finely chopped
80g butter
2 sprigs of rosemary, finely chopped
180g pinhead oatmeal
salt
black pepper
½ nutmeg, grated

Place a heavy-based frying pan over a medium heat and soften the onions, with the rosemary, in the dripping to a golden colour. Add in the oatmeal and stir thoroughly; coat with the onions. Add a large pinch of salt and lots of black pepper and nutmeg and stir for a couple of minutes. Then turn the heat down as low as it'll go. Keep cooking for around 10–15 minutes, stirring regularly until the oatmeal has softened to give a toasty bite when tasted. Adjust the seasoning and then put onto a tray and flatten out and let cool.

Preheat the oven to fan 200°C/400°F/gas 6. Season the lamb generously with salt and pepper. Heat a large, heavy frying pan over a moderately high heat and brown 2 of the racks well on the meaty sides for about 1–2 minutes, then turn and brown the other sides for a further 1 minute. Finally, brown the ends briefly so that all of the exposed meat is seared. Remove and repeat with the remaining two racks. Put racks in a large roasting tin, standing them in pairs with their bones interlinked. Roast for about 4 minutes. Take all the racks out of the oven and pat on the skirlie crust covering all the fat. Place them back in the oven in pairs just in the roasting trays with the crust facing up and cook for 15 minutes or more.

NEEPS AND TATTIE CAKES

SERVES 6

400g turnip or swede, peeled and cut
into cubes roughly the same size
400g floury potatoes, peeled and
cut into cubes the same size
100g butter
150g dry cured bacon, chopped into small dice
rapeseed oil
salt and black pepper

Boil the turnip or swede in salted water for about 20 minutes until completely tender, then drain well. Boil the potatoes in salted water for about 20 minutes until completely tender, then drain well. Return both into the same pan under a very low heat for a few minutes to dry out. Heat butter in a frying pan and fry off bacon till coloured, then pour into the neep and tattie pan. Bash the veg into a chunky mash with a touch of salt and lots of pepper.

Heat oven to 220°C/425°F/gas 7. Grease an ovenproof frying pan with a splash of rapeseed oil. Press the mashed mixture into the dish and bake for about 40 minutes until crisp and golden. Remove from the oven, turn out onto a board and cut into wedges.

DUNLOP CHEDDAR WITH BANNOCKS

SERVES 6

TRADITIONAL AYRSHIRE DUNLOP CHEDDAR

Traditional Ayrshire Dunlop is a hard-pressed cheese not unlike cheddar, but moister. When young it is mild with a nutty flavour and smooth, close texture. As it matures it develops a good strength with a slight sharpness. The cheese is quite mild at 6 months, maturing at 12 to 14 months. This cheese is named after the village of Dunlop in Ayrshire, Scotland and is made with the milk from Ayrshire cows. The making of Dunlop cheese dates back to the 1700s when Barbara Gilmour, a farmer's wife, started making a cheese at the Hill Farm, Dunlop.[10]

FOR THE BANNOCKS

250g fine oatmeal
250g wholewheat flour, plus extra for dusting
1 tsp salt
1 ½ tsp baking powder
100g cold unsalted butter, cut into very small pieces
355ml buttermilk
1 ½ tsp baking soda

In a large bowl, whisk together the oatmeal, flour, salt, and baking soda. Add the butter and rub or cut in until the mixture resembles coarse meal. Mix the buttermilk and baking soda together. It should foam a little. Add to the flour mixture and mix gently and quickly until a dough forms. If needed, add a little extra buttermilk or flour to adjust the consistency; it should look very wet, but not soupy. Turn the dough out onto a work surface, heavily floured with wholewheat flour. Dust the top of the dough with additional wholewheat flour and pat into a flat disc, about 2cm thick. Fold the dough in half over itself. Pat until flat again, dusting with flour if necessary. Continue folding and patting flat until the dough is firm enough to move. Heat a large non-stick pan or griddle over medium-low heat. Transfer the dough carefully into the pan. Using a knife, score the top of the dough with a cross, taking care not to cut all the way through the dough.

Reduce the heat to low. Cook over low heat for 7–10 minutes or until the bottom begins to brown in spots; carefully flip over and cook the top-side for 7–10 minutes, or until it begins to brown in spots. Flip the bread over if it begins to brown too much on one side and cook until the interior has cooked through, about 14–20 minutes total. Do not cook too quickly, lest the outside burn before the interior is fully cooked.

CREAM CROWDIE

SERVES 6

80g pinhead oats
600ml double cream
100g honey
whisky (to taste)
700g raspberries

Lightly brown oats in a pan over a medium heat until a light brown colour with a lovely nutty aroma. Remove from heat and allow to cool. Beat cream until soft peaks form. Add honey and then whisky. Fold in the toasted oats. Layer in a tall glass, beginning with a small number of berries, then whipped-cream mixture, laying alternate layers of berries and cream and ending with a few berries on top.

Two

SOWING THE SEEDS OF THE AMERICAN REVOLUTION

14 April 1755
The Home of John Carlyle,
Alexandria, Virginia

THE GUESTS

GENERAL EDWARD BRADDOCK,
*Commander-in-Chief of
King George II's Forces in North America*

WILLIAM SHIRLEY,
Governor of Massachusetts

ROBERT MORRIS,
Governor of Pennsylvania

JAMES DELANCEY,
Governor of New York

HORATIO SHARPE,
Governor of Maryland

ROBERT DINWIDDIE,
Governor of Virginia

JOHN CARLYLE,
*host, merchant, landowner and
Keeper of the King's Storehouses*

GEORGE WASHINGTON,
future first President of the United States

Major-General Edward Braddock sat proudly on his horse with Britain's 13 colonies of North America at his feet. He wore the distinctive uniform of a senior officer of the Coldstream Guards: a long red greatcoat with wide black lapels edged with gold braid; a black, gold-trimmed tricorn hat atop a curling white ponytailed wig; a white waistcoat, white lace shirt and cravat; and white breeches tucked into knee-length black leather boots. An exquisitely curved sabre hung in a scabbard at his side, attached to a broad, yellow sash.

If Braddock looked magnificent, he surely felt even grander. In his pocket was a letter signed by King George II, authorising him to take swift and ruthless military action. At his back were the 1,500 men of two British army infantry regiments, fresh off a ship and hungry for action. At Braddock's command they would soon unleash a campaign of deadly retribution against the French and native American forces that were threatening British colonial interests and subjects. Ahead of him, Braddock had a very special dinner to savour. That night he would meet with the most powerful men in America to appraise them of his strategies and detail their part in his plans. He could look forward to respect, cooperation – ideally, gratitude – and some of the finest cooking that this new world had to offer.

All these things Braddock would get. But the decisions taken at this meal would trigger other events that the proud general could not foresee. These included one of the most disastrous engagements in British military history; the flaring of a local tussle into an international conflict; and Braddock's own bloody, agonising death. Perhaps most dramatically of all, it would spark revolutionary fire in the mind of a young and then-loyal British colonial officer: George Washington.

*   *   *

In the 1750s much of North America east of the Mississippi was in the hands of either Britain or France. There were around 75,000 French colonists, living mostly along the St Lawrence River valley. They were outnumbered 20 to 1 by the 1.5 million British settlers who lived mostly on the continent's coastal fringe, from Newfoundland in the north to Georgia in the south. In between these colonial settlements, various native American tribes held patches of territory. In 1753, trouble began to brew in 'Ohio Country', the rich lands of the upper Ohio River. British traders were keen to expand west, but the French maintained an earlier claim to the land. In spring 1753, 2,000 French troops moved into the Ohio valley to protect French interests. They established forts and drove off British traders, eventually seizing a stronghold the British were building at the strategically important confluence of the Allegheny and Monongahela rivers (this spot is now in downtown Pittsburgh). They strengthened this outpost and called it Fort Duquesne.

Meanwhile, Governor Robert Dinwiddie of Virginia had sent 23-year-old Lieutenant-Colonel George Washington to assist the British fort-builders, and when Washington discovered they had been driven off there was a brief battle. Washington had the best of the skirmish before pulling back and establishing a secure position called Fort Necessity. In July this was surrounded by French troops and Washington was forced to surrender. He later safely withdrew, but news of these two clashes reached England in August and the government promptly appointed General Braddock as leader of an expedition to dislodge the French.

Braddock landed at Hampton in Virginia in February 1755, and sailed into Chesapeake Bay and up the Potomac River to reach Alexandria (which is just south of modern-day Washington, D.C.). This town was barely five years old, having been built up from the tiny settlement of Belhaven that had grown around a tobacco warehouse on the Potomac riverbank. The arrival of General Braddock and his troops, with kilted bagpipers and Redcoats, was a shock to the town. This large force had been cooped up in uncomfortable transport ships for a tempestuous four-month voyage from Ireland and they were wild in their enthusiasm at being on shore. This was the largest military force ever assembled in North America at that time and they set up camp in fields on the outskirts of Alexandria. General Braddock was forced to issue daily orders warning against unruly behaviour and 'overindulgence in liquor',[1] but relations between the townspeople of Alexandria and the English soldiers, who had now been joined by 700 colonial militia recruits, quickly began to deteriorate. The troops pillaged the local town, taking anything that wasn't nailed down, and drunkenness and brawling between English soldiers and local townsfolk became an everyday occurrence.

General Braddock's aide-de-camp, Lieutenant Robert Orme reported in his journal: 'The general was very impatient to remove the troops from Alexandria, as the greatest care and severest punishments could not prevent the immoderate use of spirituous liquors, and he was likewise informed that the water in the place was unwholesome.'[2]

General Braddock himself was billeted in the home of John Carlyle, a Scottish merchant who had emigrated to Virginia, and it was here that the dinner would be held to thrash out Braddock's military manoeuvres. Carlyle certainly had the resources to make sure the meal did honour to the importance of the occasion. He was very wealthy, having become a major landowner and prominent social and political figure. Carlyle's extensive business activities included import and export trade to England and the West Indies, retail trade in Alexandria, an iron foundry in the Shenandoah valley and a blacksmithing operation. Carlyle and his wife Sarah had constructed a grand stone-built mansion, which was the largest in Alexandria. For the most part, houses in Alexandria were simple wooden log cabins. The roads were unpaved and muddy in winter. But John Carlyle had gone to great lengths to build a large, impressive home in the style of mansions from his native Scotland, filling it with sumptuous furnishings and fittings as a clear statement of his wealth and importance.

The Carlyle household had nine slaves, although there were no sleeping quarters provided for them. The groom slept with the horses in the stable, while the cooks slept in the kitchen, a small building constructed in the yard beside the mansion house. Carlyle's personal slave, Moses, slept in the corridor outside his master's bedroom. John Carlyle employed slave labour in all of his landholding and business ventures. Slaves toiled in the fields of his three plantations. Skilled craftsmen worked in the blacksmith shop. Enslaved carpenters, masons and joiners laboured in his construction enterprises, including building Carlyle House itself. In Carlyle's merchant business, slaves served in numerous capacities.

When he died, Carlyle's probate inventory names his nine slaves from his mansion house in 1780 as Moses, Nanny, Jerry, Joe, Cate, Sibreia, Cook, Charles and Penny. The arrival of General Braddock and his followers must have tested even these nine slaves, accustomed to looking after the welfare and comfort of the Carlyle family. The disruption to Carlyle's household must have been considerable, although he, his wife Sarah and their small son remained in residence throughout the general's stay. But Braddock's fondness for food and spirits would have kept the kitchen staff in the house busier than usual, and his love of female companionship would have been a constant source of gossip throughout the township.

Carlyle's own letters describe General Braddock's stay in an uncomplimentary way: 'The General and his aide-de-camps, secretary and servants lodged with me. He took everything he wanted, abused my home and furniture and made me little or no satisfaction. Tho' expressed a great deal of friendship for me and gave me a commission as Keeper of the King's Storehouses and paid me £50 for the use of my house for a month.' In another letter, he describes General Braddock as 'A man (if I am a judge) of weak understanding, positive and very indolent, slave to his passions, women and wine, as great an epicure as could be in his eating, tho' a brave man'.[3] George Washington later described him as 'Generous, disinterested, but plain and blunt in his manner, even to rudeness'.[4]

Carlyle noted in writing to his brother the friction that had arisen between the local citizens and soldiers of Braddock's force: 'By sum means or another came in so prejudiced against us, our country etc that they used us like an enemy country and took everything they wanted and paid nothing, or very little for it, and when complaints was made to the comdg officers, they curst the country, and inhabitants, calling us spawn of convicts, the sweepings of the gaols etc, which made their company very disagreeable.'[5]

As Keeper of the King's Storehouses, Carlyle had been required to purchase supplies for the incoming British forces. In a letter he received from Sir John St Clair – General Braddock's Deputy Quartermaster General for North America – Carlyle was instructed:

> As His Majesty's service requires it that two months corn and hay be laid in here for four hundred horses for sixty one days, you are hereby empowered to buy up at the market price 198,400 lb (88 tons) of hay or Corn Blades, and 4,600 Bushells of corn or oats; you are to be very secure in making your contracts, that what is agreed for may be delivered by the time appointed. The sooner the whole is got together it will be the better, and on its being brought to this place you are to prepare proper magazines for its reception. You are from time to time to give me an account of what provender you have got, and what you have in view. Given under my hand at Alexandria this 3rd day of February 1755.[6]

In due course Carlyle reported to St Clair that he had only been able to source 10,000 pounds of hay and 1,200 bushels of oats, as none of the surrounding farmers had anticipated such a large military force arriving on their doorstep and had consequently fed most of their hay and oats to their own cattle and horses during the winter. This was the first ominous sign of the misfortune that would plague Braddock's ill-fated venture. Nevertheless, Braddock intended to live in some style during his stay in Alexandria. Thirty soldiers in full dress uniform, including tall black leather boots and white breeches, were permanently stationed on guard duty outside Carlyle House, offering a drum roll and salute on the approach of the general or any prominent visitors.

*   *   *

Braddock had been instructed by King George II to meet with the royal governors of the colonies to discuss plans for mounting three major military campaigns, together with the improvement of relations with the native Indians and the establishment of a common fund to defray the cost of war with the French.

This was no mean undertaking. It was to be the first major meeting of its kind ever held in America, and indeed there would not be another of such importance until the Founding Fathers met 20 years later to write the Declaration of Independence.

Even with good steeds riding at an easy trot, covering around six miles per hour was the norm over rough terrain, where there could be fallen trees on the road and other hazards. On a journey of several days, it was normal not to push horses further than 25 miles a day, with a rest every two or three hours. As a result, four of the governors arrived in Alexandria on 13 April; the next day, Governor Dinwiddie of Virginia joined them. The scene was set for one of the most historic meals in American history to take place on 14 April 1755.

Described by John Carlyle as 'The Grandest Congress ever held in America', the menu for the supper consisted of clam chowder, potted woodcock and 'delicious cakes'[7] prepared by Carlyle's cooks, washed down with copious volumes of beer, cider, wine and spirits. During the supper, General Braddock read out his letter of authority from King George II, in which he outlined the plans for the special council meeting that they were now attending and its agenda, detailing the strategies for an assault on the French at Fort Duquesne in Pennsylvania and other key military objectives.

*   *   *

Breakfast and lunch (known as dinner) were the main meals of the day in colonial America. Supper was generally taken in the early evening and consisted of a light repast. Breakfast for the 18th-century settlers usually consisted of an alcoholic drink, such as cider or beer (water was often too risky to drink) and a plate of porridge, which would have been bubbling away on the stove all night, or cornmeal mush and molasses. Fresh breads were also common and becoming more and more popular at breakfast time.

Dinner would be eaten around noon, and for a merchant family like the Carlyles would usually consist of two courses. The first course would include meat dishes and deep-filled, spicy meat pies, with typical side dishes of sauces and pickles. The second course would involve puddings including fresh, cooked, or dried fruits, custards, tarts and sweetmeats. Salads, known as 'sallats', were seasonal and generally more common at supper, sometimes even used as a table decoration. As always, copious draughts of cider or beer would accompany the food.

Having a big meal at suppertime was relatively unusual, but John Carlyle's cooks and household slaves were more than ready to take up the challenge. Twelve people sat around his table that evening in Alexandria, including the five colonial governors, General Braddock himself, the young George Washington, Augustus Keppel (who commanded the little naval squadron that had brought Braddock and his troops from England), Colonel William Johnson and General Braddock's two aides-de-camp, Robert Orme and Roger Morris. The dining room in Carlyle's home was not large, but big enough to accommodate the twelve guests around a mahogany table with matching chairs, positioned on a wooden floor. A large fireplace dominated one wall, while two windows provided light and delivered an uninterrupted view down tree-covered banks to the wide Potomac River.

The five governors were a formidable bunch and each carved a prominent place in American history. William Shirley, the King's Governor of New England was born in Preston, England, where he trained as a lawyer. He came to Massachusetts in 1731 to seek his fortune and set up a law practice in Boston. In due course he was appointed as 'Surveyor of the King's Wood'[8], a post that necessitated wide travel around the woodlands and forests of New England. During the course of these travels he would frequently come into contact with frontiersmen who would tell him tales of butchery and savagery by the native Indian tribes, which were mostly allied to the French. Shirley built up a considerable hatred for these Indians and for their French masters, particularly those located in Nova Scotia known as the Acadians. In 1741 Shirley was commissioned as the Royal Governor of Massachusetts. An adventurer with an insatiable appetite for glory and a strong belief in his own skills as a military strategist, he was ready and willing to offer his support for the plans to attack the French.

Governor of Pennsylvania from 1754 to 1756, Robert Hunter Morris was born into a wealthy family in 1700 in Trenton, New Jersey. He received a classical education, qualifying as a barrister. He later became chief justice of the New Jersey supreme court. He gained notoriety for his many battles with Benjamin Franklin over attempts to levy taxes on the lands of the Penns in Pennsylvania. Morris defended the Penn family against the imposition of taxes, while Franklin said he spoke for the people of Pennsylvania and demanded a tax on all personal estates and property as a way of raising money to pay for the defence of the citizens against the French and their Indian allies.

James DeLancey, the Governor of New York, was born in New York City in 1703. He was educated in England and attended Corpus Christi College, Cambridge, before studying law at the Inner Temple, London. He was admitted to the bar in 1725 and returned to New York to practise law and enter politics, becoming a member of the New York Assembly, and in 1731 he was appointed as second justice of the Supreme Court of New York. Two years later he was appointed as chief justice of New York and served in that role for the remainder of his life. He is renowned for presiding over a famous case that many say provided the basis for press freedom in America. In 1754 he granted a charter for the creation of King's College (now Columbia University).

Governor Horatio Sharpe of Maryland was born in England in 1718. He was commissioned in the king's forces in 1745 as a captain and saw action against the Jacobite rebellion. He arrived in Maryland in August 1753 and was appointed by King George II as Royal Commander in Chief of all British forces and commander of colonial forces for the protection of Virginia and the adjoining colonies, a post he held until the arrival of General Braddock. He was known as an efficient civil and military administrator as well as being a renowned host, gentleman farmer and fancier of fine horses. He was a close friend of George Washington.

The last of the five governors present that evening was Robert Dinwiddie, a British colonial administrator who served as Governor of Virginia from 1751 to 1758.

Another serving soldier, Colonel William Johnson, later to become Sir William Johnson, 1st Baronet, was also present at the historic supper. Born in 1715 in County Meath in Ireland, Johnson was an Anglo-Irish official of the British empire. As a young man, he moved to the province of New York to manage an estate purchased by his uncle, Admiral Peter Warren, which was located amidst the Mohawk Indians, one of the six nations of the Iroquois League. Johnson learned the Mohawk language and Iroquois customs and was appointed British agent to the Iroquois. Throughout his career as a British official among the Iroquois, Johnson combined personal business with official diplomacy, acquiring tens of thousands of acres of Indian land and becoming very wealthy.

This was an impressive gathering of America's colonial leaders. George Washington later wrote: 'Alexandria has been honoured with 5 Governors in consultation; a happy presage I hope, not only of the success of this expedition, but for our little town.'[9]

*   *   *

The evening began around 4.30 p.m. with John Carlyle's liveried slaves serving the assembled governors with a choice of rum punch, beer, cider, rum and whisky. His household slaves were generally selected from those who had been born and raised in Virginia, as the ability to speak English was important when working in a large household such as John Carlyle's. Carlyle, like many other wealthy merchants at that time, had a paternalistic view of his slaves, whom he referred to as 'famely [sic]'.

The pre-supper drinks were typical of the time. Rum was king of the colonies before the Revolutionary War. It was made from molasses imported from Caribbean sugar plantations. Sometimes the raw material arrived legally; sometimes it was smuggled. American rum was inferior to the Caribbean variety, but the domestic stuff was cheap and available. For example, a gallon of American rum cost 1 shilling and 8 pence in Philadelphia in 1740. The smoother, better Caribbean variety went for 2 shillings and 5 pence. With prices for domestic alcohol so low, it was estimated that the average adult male in British North America may have consumed as much as three pints of rum a week.

There was no doubt that the rum on offer at John Carlyle's house that evening was the smoothest Caribbean vintage available. Whiskey, on the other hand, was not yet so common. Although George Washington himself in his later years became one of America's biggest whiskey distillers, producing over 4,000 gallons a year in stills at his Mount Vernon home on the Potomac River, in the 1750s its production was largely limited to farmers who had surplus grain. However, John Carlyle's Scottish antecedents had given him a taste for good whisky, and drams from several bottles of quality Scotch were available for the assembled guests.

Following the pre-supper drinks, General Braddock and John Carlyle then invited the company to take their places at the lavishly decorated table, set with the best imported, cutlery, crockery and linen that money could buy. The Negro cooks had been busy in the kitchen all afternoon preparing the evening's delicacies. There were no cookbooks to work from in colonial America, and even if there had been, few if any of the slaves could read. The cooks were usually trained by the slave owner's wives, the best cooks soon building up a substantial repertoire of tasty recipes that they could readily prepare from memory.

Carlyle's slaves served the first course, a rich clam chowder made with milk, chopped clams, potatoes, onions, celery, parsley and garlic and fortified with a generous slug of sherry.[10] The pioneer women learned to go out at low tide to gather the large geoduck clams, which they often sliced and fried like chicken, or in this case chopped, for making the rich chowder. (Geoducks are massive clams that flourish in Washington State's Puget Sound. They can weigh up to 15 pounds each and can live for up to 160 years. They burrow down into the muddy seabed and breathe through a long, fleshy syphon that extends from their body up to the sea floor.) This rich chowder got the discussions off to a good start. As the wine flowed, the five governors eagerly swapped news of the latest political and social events in their provinces and questioned the young George Washington at length on his military exploits. Tales of Colonel William Johnson's adventures amongst the Mohawk Indians also fascinated them.

The soup was followed by a local delicacy much favoured by General Braddock – potted woodcock and colonial 'pyes'. The game dish involved the plucking, singeing and drawing of several small woodcock, prior to them being seasoned and baked with a quantity of fresh butter and spices, after which the meat was packed into earthenware pots, heated, cooled and then sealed with a layer of clarified butter. Potting various kinds of meat was a common practice at that time, before the arrival of refrigeration. Sealing meats in fat or butter prevented their exposure to air and subsequent spoilage. However, it was not uncommon for newly opened potted game birds to smell bad because the butter used as a sealant had gone off. In such cases, the birds would be removed, dipped for half a minute in boiling water to remove the old butter, then returned to the pot and re-sealed with fresh, clarified butter. The colonial pyes prepared by Carlyle's cooks were a rich mixture of chicken, shrimp and vegetable filling, covered in a crusty pastry.

The preserved potted meat was then served with fresh-baked bread, boiled potatoes and spring vegetables, including cabbage and turnip, and accompanied by several glasses of rich French claret. Vegetables included beans, peas, turnips, parsnips, carrots and potatoes. The 'delicious cake' referred to in a subsequent letter from George Washington to his neighbour and muse Mrs George William Fairfax (Fort Cumberland, 14 May 1755), was Buttermilk Pye, a sweet concoction of buttermilk, sugar, lemon, eggs, melted margarine and nutmeg.[11] Carlyle's servants proffered glasses of madeira and port to accompany the cake and the meal ended with more rum punch, whisky and wine being served to those who wished.

During the course of this substantial repast, which lasted until almost 9 p.m., General Braddock outlined details of the plan prepared by the government in London. The plan focused on three military objectives designed to wrest control of the Ohio valley from the French. The first involved an expedition against Fort Duquesne, which Braddock himself vowed to lead. The second was the conquest of Crown Point and Fort Niagara, and this was delegated to Colonel William Johnson. The third military objective, the capture of the Fort at Oswego, was given to Governor William Shirley, the self-proclaimed military strategist and glory hunter with a visceral hatred of the Indians and the French. General Braddock immediately conferred the rank of Major General on Shirley so that he could undertake this spring offensive with maximum authority.

As the evening wore on, the assembled company turned their attention to the need to raise money for a common fund to defray the costs of the war with the French. Braddock asked each of the governors to 'raise forthwith as large a sum as can be afforded as their contribution to a common fund, to be employed provisionally for ye general service in

North America'. The governors' response to this was to complain that it had been extremely difficult to obtain funds from their colonial legislatures, so they suggested that His Majesty's ministers should come up with the cash themselves.

In a letter written to London several days after this meeting, General Braddock stated, 'I cannot but take the liberty to represent to you the necessity of laying a tax upon all of His Majesty's dominions in America, agreeably to the result of the Council, for reimbursing the great sums that must be advanced for the service and interest of the colonies in this important crisis.'[12] Braddock's letter, arising from the discussions with the five colonial governors over supper in the home of John Carlyle, contains the first known recommendation for British taxation of the colonies. His radical idea ultimately led, years later, to the Boston Tea Party and the American War of Independence.

*   *   *

The next day, 15 April, the five governors, together with Braddock, Carlyle, Washington and Johnson, discussed the detailed implementation of the plans that had been outlined the night before. The governors finally departed for home on 17 April. News of the great meeting in Alexandria spread rapidly. Public demands for something to be done about the French appeared to have been met, and the governors returned to their respective provinces to be hailed as heroes. When Shirley of Massachusetts and Morris of Pennsylvania arrived in New York City, the *Pennsylvania Gazette* recorded that they were met with a salute of cannon, welcomed by the Governor of New York, members of his council, the mayor and principal gentlemen of the city:

> They passed through streets lined with uniformed militiamen at parade rest. Governor DeLancey and the other gentlemen passed on into the Fort where his Majesty's and all the Royal healths, with success to the North American enterprise, being first drunk, they proceeded through the line still formed by the militia, to the New York Arms in the Broad-Way, where an handsome entertainment was provided for the purpose, and where the aforesaid healths were repeated and went round with great cheerfulness and alacrity. The militia were discharged between two and three in the after-

37

noon; and the several Governors, we are told, expressed great satisfaction on the appearance: the doors, windows, balconies, and the tops of the houses, being particularly decorated with red cloaks etc, added no small beauty to the same, and diversion of the time.[13]

Meanwhile, Braddock's force remained encamped in Alexandria for another three days before setting out to march to Fort Duquesne in Ohio on 20 April, where the general expected to engage and expel the French. However, prior to their departure Braddock made the first of several major strategic blunders. Convinced that his troops' heavy equipment would hinder their march in the spring heat, he ordered his men to leave behind their jackets, shoulder-belts, waist-belts and swords, as well as many of their flintlock muskets and half-pikes. Attired only in their waistcoats and breeches, they set off with around 1,500 men, 400 wagons and over 1,000 baggage horses on 20 April, crossing the Allegheny Mountains heading for Fort Duquesne.

*   *   *

Braddock had spent 45 of his 60 years in the British Army, having joined the Coldstream Guards at the age of 15. Yet he had seen little actual fighting despite having served in several European campaigns. His nickname, 'The Bulldog', was based on bluster and aggression rather than ferocity and tenacity in battle. He believed his trained Redcoats to be innately superior to the French colonials and their native American tribal allies. He did not acknowledge the danger of the locals' knowledge of the territory and their guerrilla tactics, and thought the fear that the native Americans instilled in the colonial settlers was exaggerated.

Braddock and his regiments set out from Alexandria on 20 April 1755 on a tough trek over 110 miles of heavily wooded and mountainous territory, hauling all of their necessary cannons, ammunition and provisions with them. Braddock decided that it would be wise to build a road across the Allegheny Mountains into western Pennsylvania in order effectively to supply the fort he intended to capture, so he split his expedition into two columns, a 'flying column' of 1,350 men, which he commanded and, lagging well behind, a supply column of 750 men with wagons loaded with most of the baggage, commanded by Colonel Thomas

Dunbar. Among the wagon-masters were two young men who would later become American legends in their own right – Daniel Boone and Daniel Morgan. Braddock had procured the wagons and provisions with the help of another soon-to-be-legendary figure – Benjamin Franklin. Braddock took 23-year-old George Washington along because he was familiar with the territory following the battle at Fort Necessity, the ruins of which they passed on their march.

In comparison, the French garrison at Fort Duquesne consisted of only 250 regular troops and Canadian militia, with around 640 native Indians camped around the stronghold. When Claude-Pierre Pécaudy de Contrecœur, the French-Canadian commander, received reports from Indian scouting parties that the British were on their way to besiege the fort, he immediately realised that he could not withstand an assault by Braddock's cannon and decided to mount a pre-emptive ambush.

By 9 July 1755, Braddock's men had slogged their way over 100 miles of mountains and forests, had crossed the Monongahela River and were within 10 miles of Fort Duquesne. However, the trek had shattered his men's resolve. They had run out of virtually all of their provisions and many were suffering from scurvy and fever. All were starving and exhausted. About 1 p.m., as they were plodding along the 12-foot-wide track that their engineers had cut through dense woodland, shots echoed out. From the trees on their flanks, a force of 300 Indians (Ottawas, Miamis, Hurons, Delawares and Shawnees) led by 30 French officers and men were firing at will into the leading British units.

Although Braddock's force hugely outnumbered his French and Indian enemy, the general's insistence on deploying standard British army fighting tactics proved disastrous. The British infantry were more accustomed to fighting *en masse* in formation in open fields and were not prepared for this type of encounter. They could not tell where the enemy was or how many of them they were up against. The enemy's first volleys had slain many of their officers riding near the front of the column, and soon the leading elements started to fall back through those bringing up the rear, causing confusion and panic.

The fleeing Redcoats collided with the main body of Braddock's force, which had rushed forward on hearing the first salvo of gunshots. The 500 colonial militiamen, who were more accustomed to this type of warfare, quickly took cover in the woods themselves, mimicking their enemy, from where they tried to snipe at the French and the Indians.

But meanwhile Braddock, instead of telling his soldiers to take cover and shoot from behind the trees like the Indians, was trying to resolve the disorder in his ranks by ordering his men to form up into regular units on the narrow forest track, where they provided an easy target for their concealed enemy. In the confusion, many of the Redcoats mistook the colonial militiamen as enemies and began firing back at them in the woods.

The fighting raged on for several hours. Four of the general's horses were shot out from under him during the course of the battle. But when he rode out on the fifth, Braddock was shot off the horse and George Washington, whose hat had been knocked off his head by a bullet, took command of the beleaguered troops, forming an effective rearguard which enabled the remnants of the force to disengage and retreat. Washington later wrote to his mother:

> We marched to that place, without any considerable loss, having only now and then a straggler picked up by the French and scouting Indians. When we came there, we were attacked by a party of French and Indians, whose number, I am persuaded, did not exceed three hundred men; while ours consisted of about one thousand three hundred well-armed troops, chiefly regular soldiers, who were struck with such a panic that they behaved with more cowardice than it is possible to conceive. The officers behaved gallantly, in order to encourage their men, for which they suffered greatly, there being near sixty killed and wounded; a large proportion of the number we had.[14]

Of the 1,350 men General Braddock had led into battle, 456 were killed and 422 wounded. Out of 86 officers, 26 were killed and 37 wounded. The French and Canadians reported only 8 killed and 4 wounded, while their Indian allies lost 15 killed and 12 wounded.

Washington described the scene: 'At length, in despight of every effort to the contrary, they broke and run as sheep before the hounds, leaving the artillery, ammunition, provisions and every individual thing we had with us a prey to the enemy; and when we endeavour'd to rally them in hopes of regaining our invaluable loss, it was as much success as if we had attempted to have stop'd the wild bears of the mountains.'[15]

Washington gained the reputation of a hero when, despite being horribly ill with dysentery, he helped to organise the withdrawal of the survivors to safety over a 40-mile trek, including the fatally wounded Braddock, who had been shot in the lung. He continued: 'The shocking scenes which presented themselves in this night's march are not to be described. The dead, the dying, the groans, lamentations and crys along the road of the wounded for help, … were enough to pierce a heart of adamant.'[16] Luckily, rather than giving pursuit, the Indians lingered behind, busying themselves by scalping the dead and wounded. Twelve British captives were taken back to Fort Duquesne, where the Indians burned them alive. When General Braddock finally succumbed from his wounds four days later, Washington helped to bury his body and conceal the grave to ensure the Indians did not dig him up and defile his corpse. Before he died, Braddock presented his battle sash to Washington, who continued to wear it after the end of the Revolutionary War and even after he became the first President of the United States. Braddock's batman, Thomas Bishop, attached himself firmly to Washington and continued to serve as his valet and personal factotum for more than 30 years.

Benjamin Franklin later said of General Edward Braddock:

This general was, I think, a brave man, and might probably have made a figure as a good officer in some European war. But he had too much self-confidence, too high an opinion of the validity of regular troops, and too mean a one of both Americans and Indians … I ventured only to say, '… The only danger I apprehend of obstruction to your march is from ambuscades of Indians, who, by constant practice, are dexterous in laying and executing them …' He smiled at my ignorance, and replied, 'These savages may, indeed, be a formidable enemy to your raw American militia, but upon the King's regular and disciplined troops, sir, it is impossible they should make any impression.'[17]

The Braddock Expedition, or as it is more accurately known 'Braddock's Defeat', was one of the British army's worst losses in the 18th century and it confounded the British. It had other consequences as well. The French had won a temporary victory in their struggle for control of the Ohio valley and Virginia's frontier. Soon these two nations, which had up to now been skirmishing in a colonial locale, would be fighting in an intercontinental conflict – the Seven Years War, known in its American theatre as the French and Indian War.

The disaster also had very deep impact on Lieutenant-Colonel Washington. He realised that the British military was not the invincible force that everyone had previously imagined. Indeed he had learned at first hand its incompetence and ineffectiveness. He had been at that grand gathering in Alexandria, where a British general had sat down to dinner in full control of his destiny, with a royal mandate, resources, a strategy and powerful friends. That same general now lay dead in the dirt. Furthermore, it was at that fateful meal that Braddock had informed the assembled governors of the need to raise taxes to pay for the war against the French and their Indian allies. This was the first time that taxes levied by a British king on his American colonies – 'taxation without representation' – had ever been mooted. The dinner and its aftermath helped sow the seeds of future revolution in the mind of the young George Washington.

In later years Washington was to serve as a formidable commander-in-chief of the Continental Army during the American Revolutionary War. As one of the Founding Fathers, he subsequently presided over the convention that drafted the American Constitution, which replaced the Articles of Confederation and created the post of president, a position to which he was duly elected as the first President of the United States and, as we shall see in the next chapter, he would rely on his closest associates, Thomas Jefferson, Alexander Hamilton and James Madison to sort out the settling of the crippling Revolutionary War debts and to decide on the site for the new US capital city.

MENU

Aperitifs
12-year-old Caribbean rum
12-year-old malt and 12-year-old blended Scotch whisky
Rum punch
Beer
Cider

Clam Chowder

Colonial Pye
Potted Woodcock

Buttermilk Pye

Imported French red and white wine
and local Virginia wine
Madeira and port

CLAM CHOWDER

SERVES 6

1 kg clams, washed and sautéd open,
with all juice kept and meat taken out of shells
100g unsalted butter
150g white onion, finely diced
3 celery sticks diced into 1 cm pieces
75g plain flour
1 litre fish stock
300ml double cream
2 bay leaves
70g fresh thyme, tied up with string
300g floury potatoes, cut into 2 cm cubes
salt and freshly ground black pepper

Heat the butter in a large pot over medium-high heat. Add the onion and celery and sauté until softened, mixing often. Stir in the flour to distribute evenly. Add the stock and juice from clams. Reserve clams for garnish. Add cream, bay leaves, thyme and potatoes and stir to combine. Bring to a simmer, stirring consistently (the mixture will thicken) then reduce the heat to medium-low and cook for 20 minutes, stirring often, until the potatoes are nice and tender. Then add clams and season to taste with salt and pepper. Cook for another 2 minutes. Take out bay and thyme and serve.

COLONIAL PYE

SERVES 6

800g boneless, skinless chicken thighs cut into 5cm bits
400g king prawns, peeled and de-veined
220g unsalted butter
500g onions, finely chopped
8 cloves garlic, peeled and finely chopped
2 bay leaves
2 sprigs fresh thyme
130g plain flour
150ml white wine
1 litre chicken stock
150ml cream
150g diced red pepper
150g frozen peas
100g frozen pearl onions
70g curly parsley, finely chopped
salt and pepper to taste
500g frozen puff pastry, thawed
1 egg yolk mixed with 1 tbsp cream, for egg wash

In two sauté pans, over medium-high heat, melt 60g unsalted butter in each. When hot, add the chicken to one pan and the prawns to the other. Season and sauté the chicken till barely cooked and take off the heat. Do the same with the prawns until just barely cooked. Remove to a large baking tray to cool.

In a large pan, over medium-high heat, melt the rest of the unsalted butter. When hot add the onions, garlic, bay and thyme and season. Cook until the onions are soft but not brown. Sprinkle in the flour and continue to cook for 5 minutes. Raise the heat to high and add the wine, stirring constantly. Add the chicken stock, reduce the heat and simmer for 5 minutes. Add the cream and simmer for another 5 minutes. Check the sauce for seasoning and set aside to cool.

Preheat an oven to 200°C/400°F/gas 6. In a large bowl, combine the cooked chicken, shrimp, peppers, peas and pearl onions. Pour the cooled sauce mixture over and test for seasoning. Stir in the chopped parsley. Fill 6 deep-dish pie containers or bowls with the filling. Roll the puff pastry out to 5cm thickness. Cut 6 circles that will fit around the rim of the baking container. Egg-wash the edges of the rounds of puff pastry. Place the pastry over the top of the containers and press down on the edges to seal. When ready to bake, egg-wash the tops of the puff pastry. Place the pies in the preheated oven and bake for 1 hour or until the pastry is golden and the filling is bubbling. Remove from the oven and serve.

POTTED WOODCOCK

SERVES 6

6 woodcock breasts removed and skin taken off, all skin removed from legs and then meat taken from legs minced, weighed and topped up with pork mince to make 300g
100g unsmoked streaky bacon, rind removed and minced
½ medium leek, finely chopped
4 cloves garlic, finely chopped
1 tbsp thyme, leaves only
small handful of parsley, finely chopped
2 tbsp cream sherry
salt
freshly ground black pepper
freshly grated nutmeg
100g clarified butter

Set the oven to 170°C/325F°/gas 3. In a large bowl, mix together the pork, bacon, leek, garlic, thyme, parsley and sherry. Season well with salt and freshly ground black pepper and add a grating of fresh nutmeg. Spread half the pork mixture evenly across the bottom of individual ramekins. Put one piece of the woodcock breast on top and then cover with the rest of the mince mixture. Press down firmly, making sure it is all tightly packed. Cover the pot with some greaseproof paper then some foil and stand in a roasting tin. Fill the roasting tin halfway up with hot water and place in the oven for 1 hour, until hot in the centre and firm to the touch. Remove from the oven and leave to cool. Cover with melted clarified butter and set in fridge. Serve directly out of the ceramic pot.

HISTORICAL NOTE

No matter what type of meat was being potted, the method was always the same. The meat was cut into pieces, baked with a quantity of fresh butter or other fat (usually with spices and seasonings added), pounded with a mortar and pestle (or ground), packed into earthenware pots, heated, cooled, and then sealed with a layer of clarified butter. Small birds, like woodcock, were sometimes potted whole.

Very little water was used in cooking the meats and they were baked at high temperatures to kill any organisms that could cause spoilage, or at least capture them underneath the layer of hard fat where they were not exposed to the air. The layer of fat also prevented the entry of airborne contaminants that could cause spoilage.

Many early recipes specify using fresh butter because if the butter was on its way to going bad prior to being used to seal the pots of meat or cheese, the quality of the ingredients was affected and their shelf life was much shorter. Prior to covering with butter the meat was re-seasoned and packed into pots in the usual manner. Some cooks would then place the pots in the oven for a few minutes to condense the meat as much as possible by excluding air.

The early American colonialists commonly potted beef, venison, ox-cheek, tongue, rabbit, ham, veal, chicken, salmon, mackerel, trout, eels, pike, smelts, pigeons, lamprey, char, moor-game, hare, oysters, ducks, herrings, and a variety of small birds. Game birds were also routinely potted included woodcocks, partridges, ortolans, grouse, quails, etc.

WINE

Imported French red and white wine, and local Virginia wine.

BUTTERMILK PYE

SERVES 6–12

225g plain flour
110g butter, cold and cut into cubes
80g icing sugar
1 large egg

Sieve flour and icing sugar into a large mixing bowl. Using your finger-tips, gently work the cubes of butter into the flour and sugar until the mixture resembles breadcrumbs. Add the egg to the mixture and gently work it together using your hands until you have a ball of dough. Sprinkle a little flour over the dough and on a clean work surface roll out to about 2.5cm thick and pop into the fridge to rest. Line a 25cm non-stick loose-bottomed tin. Using a splash of vegetable oil on a piece of kitchen paper, lightly oil the inside. Carefully roll out your pastry, turning it every so often, until it's about ½cm thick and line the tin. Line the tart shell with baking parchment and baking beans, pop in the fridge for 1 hour whilst you preheat oven to 180°C/350°F/gas 4. Bake the tart for 15 minutes then take it out, carefully take out the baking beans and then re-bake for 10 minutes till golden and dry all over. Leave to cool.

FOR THE PYE FILLING

3 large eggs, lightly beaten
150g plain flour
200g caster sugar
360g buttermilk
175g butter, melted and cooled
1 scraped vanilla pod
½ tsp ground nutmeg

Preheat oven to 200°C/400°F/gas 6. In a bowl, whisk together eggs, flour, and sugar. Whisk in buttermilk and butter in 4 parts, alternating between the two. Whisk in vanilla. Pour filling into crust; sprinkle with nutmeg. Bake for 15 minutes. Reduce heat to 150°C/300°F/gas 2. Cover pie loosely with foil. Bake until filling is set, 35 to 40 minutes. Transfer to a wire rack and let cool. Serve at room temperature.

WINE

Madeira and port: rich, sweet fortified wines from Portugal.

Three

HOW WASHINGTON D.C. BECAME AMERICA'S CAPITAL

20 June 1790
Thomas Jefferson's Residence,
57 Maiden Lane,
New York City

THE GUESTS

ALEXANDER HAMILTON,
*a Founding Father of the United States
and the Treasury Secretary*

JAMES MADISON,
*a Founding Father, the leader of the
House of Representatives, and future
fourth President of the United States*

THOMAS JEFFERSON,
*a Founding Father, the Secretary
of State, and future third President
of the United States*

The young republic that had so triumphantly freed itself from colonial rule was now one step away from tearing itself to pieces. In June 1790, just 14 years had passed since the signing of the Declaration of Independence, the United States was in a precarious position. George Washington had only been president for a year and he was finding it difficult to unite the country. Congressmen from the northern and southern states were at each other's throats over the huge $25 million Revolutionary War debt (around $1 billion today), incurred while the country won its independence from Britain.

One faction, led by Secretary of the Treasury Alexander Hamilton, wanted the federal government to assume liability for the debt. Hamilton knew that there were thousands of American soldiers who had fought in the war but who had still not been paid. Furthermore, the outstanding loans from countries such as France and Holland must be settled if America was to establish international credit.

But the Leader of the House of Representatives, James Madison, had recently defied Hamilton, blocking his bill in Congress. Madison argued that sharing the debt across all the American states was unfair to the poorer southern states, which would end up subsidising rich northern states like Massachusetts. Newspapers in the southern states were calling for the Union to be dissolved rather than countenance such an act. The debt question had been deadlocked in Congress ever since and Hamilton was angry and frustrated.

There was also the thorny question of where the proposed new US capital should be located. Hamilton favoured a location in the north; Madison wanted it to be in the south, to placate the southern states and bring the country together. He was deeply frustrated that of the 16 locations currently under consideration, most were in the north, with Philadelphia as the main contender. Again, there was deadlock and uncertainty. Improbably in such a torrid, adversarial atmosphere, these issues would be decided, these bitter enemies reconciled and the young republic set on a firm footing over one delicious and artfully conceived dinner.

*   *   *

It was a sultry late afternoon on 19 June 1790 as Alexander Hamilton was ushered out of the front door of President George Washington's home at 39–41 Broadway, New York City, by a liveried black slave. The treasury secretary had been to visit the president to discuss the looming debt crisis. Washington had appointed a handful of key advisers, principal amongst whom was Hamilton. Today, such a group would meet as a cabinet, but in those days Washington preferred to consult his advisers individually about their specific policy areas.

Hamilton was a tall, slim figure. He had a long, slightly upturned nose and dark, penetrating eyes. In the fashion of the time, he wore his brown, curly hair long, tied in a ponytail by a black ribbon. He wore a long black coat and a white lace cravat, knotted at the neck. He was aged only 33 in 1790, but already one of the most powerful men in the country; a rapid ascent for a man born out of wedlock in the West Indies to a married woman of French descent. His father was the fourth son of a Scottish laird. He became a courageous senior military commander during the Revolutionary War and a close aide to General George Washington. As treasury secretary, Hamilton became the author of the key economic policies of Washington's administration and the founder of America's national bank – the government-owned Bank of the United States. Now, as Hamilton strode down Broadway that warm June afternoon he saw the distinctive figure of another great man, and one of his fiercest adversaries, approaching: Thomas Jefferson.

Jefferson had been the principal author of the Declaration of Independence and was then the US secretary of state. He was the third child of ten born to a planter and surveyor who had emigrated from Wales to Virginia. He was 47 years old in 1790. A talented linguist and academic, Jefferson had returned only the previous year from a five-year posting in Paris as US minister to France. He intended to live away from politics, running his sprawling Virginian plantation, Monticello in Charlottesville, before Washington persuaded him back into office.

Jefferson had assumed many of the affectations of the European political classes during his sojourn in Paris. He was wearing a well-cut jacket with pearl buttons, offset with a cravat of fine silk, a red waistcoat and matching breeches. As he trod purposefully along Broadway, straight-backed and easily distinguishable from the lumbering gait of other New Yorkers, the tall, thin, white-haired Jefferson was the epitome of flamboyant elegance, a fact that irritated Hamilton. The secretary of state was heading to Washington's house for a meeting with the president. Although he had heard of Hamilton by reputation, Jefferson had only met him for the first time when he had arrived in New York in March. They were colleagues in Washington's team of close confidantes, but in the few short weeks of their acquaintance they had already clashed fiercely on the issue of the war debt and the location of the new capital. Jefferson was convinced that Hamilton was a ruthless, aggressive political predator who would be a dangerous enemy if opposed.

Hamilton may not have liked Jefferson, but he seized the opportunity on that hot New York afternoon to speak to him about the brewing crisis. He offered his hand and Jefferson shook it warily, enquiring whether or not Hamilton had met the president and whether they had discussed the debt crisis and the location of the capital. Hamilton confirmed that they had and said that he would very much enjoy an opportunity of sharing his views on these matters with Jefferson. He considered that nothing less than the future of the Union was at stake and felt that they should both work towards the common cause of supporting President Washington's fledgling administration. Jefferson immediately suggested that Hamilton should join him for dinner the following evening and said that he would also invite James Madison, his close friend, adding that it would be a small and intimate meal with only the three of them in attendance.

James Madison was renowned as the 'Father of the American Constitution'. In 1789 he had become the leader of the new House of Representatives. Initially in favour of a strong federal government, by 1790 he had changed his position and now favoured strong state governments. Thirty-nine years old at the time of the dinner, Madison had been born into a rich tobacco plantation family in Virginia. A small and slight man, he wore his straight, prematurely white hair swept back across his head, exposing a distinctive widow's peak.

Hamilton readily agreed to the offer of dinner. Later that evening, Jefferson wrote a formal invitation to Madison and Hamilton, inviting them to his temporary home on Maiden Lane the following day. It was to be a dinner that would have a huge impact on the future course of American history.

*   *   *

As a former ambassador to France, Jefferson was a connoisseur of good food and wine. Even before leaving for France, he had been renowned for throwing lavish dinner parties at his 5,000-acre Virginian plantation, Monticello. Jefferson had more than 100 slaves at Monticello, where his beautiful housekeeper, the 'almost white'[1] slave Sally Hemings, together with his faithful butler Burrell Colbert, ruled over the 15 house slaves, almost all members of the Hemings family. As a teenager, Sally had accompanied the newly widowed Jefferson to Paris when he served as US ambassador. She became pregnant by Jefferson at the age of 16 in Paris and she eventually bore him six children, four of whom survived into adulthood. Jefferson also had six legitimate children by his wife Martha, who died, aged only 33, shortly after giving birth to their last child. Only two of his legitimate children, both girls, survived into adulthood, and both always denied that their father had sired any children by Sally Hemings.

While in France, Jefferson's duties had involved the negotiation of commercial treaties with several European powers. His predecessor in the role had been the elderly Benjamin Franklin, whom Jefferson greatly admired. When Franklin decided to retire from the post at the age of 80, after 10 illustrious years, Jefferson was asked if he was to become Franklin's replacement. He replied, 'No sir, I succeed him; no-one can replace him.' Though struggling financially, Jefferson was nevertheless able to take up residence in an imposing villa in the Champs-Élysées in Paris, complete with stables and a large garden where he grew American crops like corn, sweet potatoes and watermelons. His daughter Patsy was sent to a convent school, while his slave James Hemings was taught French culinary skills.

Jefferson's initial attempts at diplomacy in France were not easy. Many European states regarded the US with scepticism, believing it to be a breakaway phenomenon from the British empire that could never prosper economically. This opinion was bolstered by the fact that 85 per cent of goods sold or traded in the United States came from Britain. Even so, Jefferson scored a major diplomatic coup in 1785 when he secured a trade agreement with Frederick the Great of Prussia. This threw open the doors for further agreements with smaller European sovereignties like Denmark and Tuscany.

After succeeding Franklin as American minister at Versailles, Jefferson had witnessed the first chapter of the French Revolution. As a rebel

for dinner on 20 June 1790. To ensure that his two dinner guests could converse in absolute privacy, Jefferson instructed James Hemings that each course should be served quickly and discreetly and on no account should they be otherwise disturbed during the course of the dinner. It was the custom to eat only two meals daily at that time, involving a hearty breakfast and a substantial dinner taken in the late afternoon. Jefferson had arranged for his guests to arrive at four p.m., and as he waited for them he reflected that a migraine that had troubled him throughout that hot day had begun to subside. He was looking forward to a fine dinner and a robust debate.

*　　*　　*

Madison was the first of the guests to arrive. Jefferson told him that they had to try to persuade Hamilton to accept their proposition that the new capital should be located in the south. As they also wanted to resolve the issue of the war debt, although they distrusted Hamilton's motives for seeking to have the federal government assume this liability, believing that it would dramatically shift the balance of power from the states to the centre. Both men were aware of the fragile nature of the new American republic. Uniting the former competing and adversarial states was no easy task, and they feared that Hamilton's federalist approach could upset the applecart and tear the states apart. They had to find some way of reaching a compromise with Hamilton. Jefferson knew that Hamilton had a sharp mind and would proffer strong arguments to bolster his case. But he looked forward to hearing Madison's counter-arguments, as good food, great wine and the cut and thrust of intellectual debate were Jefferson's favourite pursuits. Hamilton, meanwhile, had calculated that if he could get Jefferson and Madison alone over dinner he might be able to persuade them to his point of view. This was why he had readily accepted Jefferson's invitation.

When Alexander Hamilton arrived, James Hemings showed him into the drawing room; he shook hands with Jefferson and Madison and thanked Jefferson for his kind invitation. Hemings withdrew and quietly closed the door. The three towering intellects were now alone together. The atmosphere was tense. Hamilton knew that Jefferson and Madison disliked and distrusted him, but surely here was his chance to convince them by the articulacy and logic of his arguments.

Jefferson poured each of his guests a glass of dry, white wine, explaining that it was Hermitage,[3] made from the Roussane and Marsanne grapes, from the hills surrounding the town of Tain-l'Hermitage in the Rhône region of France, south of Lyon. Jefferson prided himself on an intensive study of plants and viniculture and there is no doubt that he was a considerable wine expert, enjoying three or four small glasses with his dinner every day but 'not a drop at any other time'.[4] Jefferson led his two guests through to the dining room where Hemings had laid out a generous quantity of food on the table, sideboard and 'dumbwaiters', small movable tables that were positioned next to each guest. Jefferson explained that he had come to admire these dumbwaiters while he was in France and being unable to source any in America he had one of his slaves, who was an expert joiner, construct several. Jefferson told Madison and Hamilton to sit where they pleased and invited them to help themselves to salad, accompanied by another white wine. This one, he explained as he filled each of their glasses, was a 1786 Bordeaux from Graves. Dry white wines from this region on the left bank of the Garonne River are a blend of the Sauvignon blanc and Sémillon grapes, he explained, his knowledgeable small talk soothing the animosity of the rivals.

Two servants now brought in the main dishes. The first was a capon stuffed with Jefferson's favourite Virginia ham and cooked with chestnut purée, artichoke bottoms, truffles, cream, white wine and chicken stock. This was a specialty of Jefferson's Paris-trained slave. It was served with a rich Calvados sauce made from the famous French apple brandy from Normandy, which Jefferson explained he had brought back from France. He served this with a glass of rich, red, aromatic Vino Nobile di Montepulciano, one of the great Sangiovese wines from Tuscany. The second hot course that evening was another favourite at Monticello: *Boeuf à la Mode*. This was served with a glass of delicious dark-red Chambertin from the village of Gevrey-Chambertin in Côte de Nuits, one of the finest French Burgundies. By now Alexander Hamilton would have been mightily impressed by the hospitality on offer. Sensing this, Jefferson would have curtailed his small talk and guided his relaxed two guests towards the key purpose of the evening: a compromise on the debt and the location of the new capital.

An attractive range of meringues, macaroons, bell fritters and other small sweets had been set in front of each person to be enjoyed before the dessert and all three gentlemen now picked at these greedily, as the two houseboys entered with the main pudding, a Baked Alaska or vanilla ice cream encased in warm meringue, a classic from Monticello that always amazed guests. Jefferson served this with an unusual still or *non-mousseux* wine from the Champagne region of France. He was the only person importing this type of wine into America at the time and had already persuaded President Washington to purchase a quantity. His favourite was imported from a Monsieur Dorsay in the village of Ay.[5]

As they sipped this unusual cloudy wine, Madison fired the first salvo of the discussion, stating that Hamilton's plan for federal 'assumption' of the war debt was a bitter pill for southern states like Virginia to swallow, because they considered that they had already paid most of their own war debts. Hamilton said that he understood this problem but that maybe a special adjustment could me made for Virginia and the other southern states. The seeds of a compromise were already being sown.

Jefferson now threw in his own proposal, asking Hamilton to consider locating the new capital city on the banks of the Potomac, as a sop to the southern states. Hamilton's spoon, heaped with Baked Alaska pudding, hesitated on the way to his lips. He stared across the table at Jefferson. After a moment's hesitation he said he could agree to the Potomac idea, provided it was delayed for 10 years, during which time Philadelphia would take on the accolade of being the temporary capital. He reminded Jefferson and Madison that the citizens of Philadelphia had been promised that their city would become the new capital, and all three knew that there were enough Pennsylvania votes in Congress to block the entire deal.

Madison thought about this for a few moments, sipping some of the champagne from his glass, before finally nodding his head in agreement and announcing that in this case the question of the debt assumption should be brought before the House again and that this time he would abstain rather than vote against it. He also said he would lobby hard to ensure there was enough support for the bill to pass. Hamilton said that he would likewise lobby the Pennsylvanians to support the idea that Philadelphia would be only the temporary capital for the next 10 years, with the Potomac site being voted through as the permanent capital.

To seal this historic compromise, Jefferson now poured some fine French cognac into three balloon glasses and offered a toast to the success of their agreement. The three men clinked glasses. There was a general discussion then about the key congressmen that would have to be won over for both the debt assumption bill and the Potomac site for the American capital. Madison, as floor leader in the House, suggested that several congressmen who owned property on the banks of the Potomac could be persuaded to support the assumption bill if they were gently reminded that they would profit hugely from the building of the new capital city on their land. Hamilton said that he would invite some of the Pennsylvanian congressmen to dinner the following week to win their support for the temporary capital plan.

As the three men rose to their feet around 8 p.m. on that sultry evening, they were all smiling. Hamilton in particular was overjoyed that finally, after repeated defeats in Congress, he could now look forward to his historic assumption bill being approved. He considered this as a critical step towards saving the Union and turning the US dollar into a credible currency, respected internationally. Jefferson and Madison were also happy, knowing that their deal had secured the construction of a new capital city on the banks of the Potomac, straddling the southern agrarian states of Virginia and Maryland. They had also secured a promise from Hamilton that he would reduce Virginia's contribution to the war debt, a deal that in fact saved the state an estimated $1.5 million. The bargain represented a massive victory for the southern states. It was an elegant covenant and one that had undoubtedly been assisted by the liberal application of copious quantities of good food and fine wine. As James Hemings showed Madison and Hamilton out to their waiting carriages, Jefferson wished them goodnight and turned to go back inside. Pausing on the top step, he pondered on the fact that although his dinner had accomplished everything he had set out to achieve, he and Madison had also had to surrender to Hamilton on the question of the federal debt assumption. Which side had won he wondered? Was everyone a winner or had no one really emerged victorious?

In the days that followed Jefferson's historic dinner things began to move quickly. Hamilton, through his close working relationship and friendship with Washington, knew that the president favoured the Potomac site, not least because he himself owned large tracts of land on the banks of the river and had reminded Hamilton in one conversation that the value of this land would increase 1,000 per cent once the decision to build the capital there was announced. So Hamilton knew that Washington would be overjoyed and would certainly approve the secret deal.

Madison meanwhile, true to his word, persuaded four southern congressmen who owned land on the banks of the Potomac to switch their support and back the deal and only one month after the dinner party Congress passed the bill for the siting of the new capital in Virginia and Washington signed it. Five days later, the debt assumption bill scraped through the House with a majority of one vote. In 1791, Congress agreed to name the new capital city Washington, and as a pacifier to Philadelphia, they declared that the main thoroughfare would be named Pennsylvania Avenue. The dinner-table bargain had succeeded, although the brief rapprochement between Jefferson and his arch-enemy Hamilton did not last for long. One year after the dinner party, Jefferson resigned as Washington's secretary of state, frustrated by constant defeats at the hands of Hamilton. Nevertheless, he went on to serve two full terms as president from 1801 to 1809, the second of which was in the capital city that he had helped to secure over his momentous dinner in New York. Thomas Jefferson lived to the ripe old age of 83, dying in Virginia in 1826. He is buried at Monticello.

James Madison later became secretary of state during the presidency of his lifelong friend Jefferson, eventually succeeding him to become America's fourth president in 1809. Madison lived to the age of 85 and died and was buried at the family plantation, Montpelier.

Alexander Hamilton died in 1804, at the age of 49, fatally wounded in a duel with the US Vice President Aaron Burr. The duel was triggered, somewhat ironically, by an insult at a dinner party.

As president, Jefferson would have watched with interest the rise to power in Europe of Napoleon Bonaparte, whose path to glory had been forged by the French Revolution. As we shall see in the next chapter, Napoleon's eventual abdication and exile to Elba in 1814 paved the way for a major peace conference in Vienna at which Jefferson's old adversary, Prince Charles-Maurice de Talleyrand-Périgord, would conspire to dominate the proceedings. During Jefferson's presidency, Talleyrand, as a key advisor to Napoleon, had first encouraged the French emperor to invade America to consolidate France's territorial ambitions on that continent. This had become a major concern for Jefferson and he was therefore greatly relieved when Talleyrand ultimately negotiated a treaty with the US which passed ownership of the territory of Louisiana to the Americans for the sum of $11,250,000. Subsequently France retracted its interest in America and concentrated its efforts on Napoleon's expansionist European strategies. As Jefferson knew only too well, Talleyrand was a slippery character and his ambition to carve out a key European role for the defeated French nation following Napoleon's abdication was soon to be realised at the dinner tables of the Hofburg Palace in Vienna.

MENU

Aperitif
Hermitage

Mixed Salad

Capon Stuffed with Virginia Ham
Boeuf à La Mode

Baked Alaska

Digestif
Cognac

Graves
Vino Nobile di Montepulciano
Chambertin
'Non-mousseux' (still) white wine from Monsieur Dorsay
in the village of Ay in the Champagne region of France

APERITIF

Hermitage, the delicate white wine made from the Roussane and Marsanne grapes, from the hills surrounding the town of Tain l'Hermitage in the Rhône region of France, south of Lyon. These white wines, which have aromas of honeysuckle, tropical fruit and earthy minerals, may be cellared for up to 15 years.

MIXED SALAD

SERVES 6

½ head romaine lettuce
½ cucumber, peeled and sliced
2 tomatoes, cored and cut into small wedges
1 small onion, sliced thin
¼ watermelon, deseeded and cut into cubes
1 pepper, cut into thin strips

FOR THE DRESSING

½ tbsp English mustard
150ml peanut oil
50ml red wine vinegar
salt and pepper to taste

Whisk all the ingredients for the dressing together. Cut the lettuce into bite-sized pieces, place in large bowl and toss with all other prepared ingredients and serve.

WINE

Graves. From the heart of Bordeaux, just outside the city of Bordeaux itself, dry white wines from this region on the left bank of the Garonne

River are made from a blend of Sauvignon blanc and Sémillon grapes, producing a lively and structured wine with a hint of oak from the cask.

CAPON STUFFED WITH VIRGINIA HAM

SERVES 6

1 2.7kg capon
200g fresh bread, cut into 2cm cubes
150g butter
190g shallots, diced
100g garlic, chopped
200g wild mushrooms, cleaned and chopped
150g chicken liver, cleaned and chopped
250g Virginia ham, chopped
1 egg, lightly beaten
200ml double cream
150g parsley, chopped
2tsp thyme leaves
½ tsp fine sea salt
¼ tsp freshly ground white pepper
1 litre chicken stock boiled down to 300ml
500ml red wine
2 tbsp cornflour

Preheat the oven to 180°C/350°F/gas 4. Spread the bread on 2 large baking sheets and bake for 10 minutes, until dry. In a heavy-bottomed pan, melt the butter. Add the shallot and garlic, cook over low heat until softened for 5 minutes. Then add wild mushrooms and cook till soft. Add the chicken livers and cook for 5 minutes. Stir in the Virginia ham. Remove from the heat and let cool.

In a large bowl, toss the bread with the Virginia ham mixture. In a bowl, beat the eggs, cream, salt and pepper and herbs; pour the mixture over the bread and stir to thoroughly combine the ingredients. Lower the oven temperature to 165°C/325°F/gas 3. Cut the tips off the capon wings and place in a large roasting pan with the neck. Put the capon in the pan, breast side down and fill the neck cavity with stuffing. Pull the skin over the stuffing and secure with a skewer. Turn the capon breast side up and fill the cavity with stuffing. Wrap any leftover stuffing in foil. Rub the butter over the capon; season with salt and pepper. Roast the capon for 1½ hours, rotating the pan once. Roast for about 1 hour longer, rotating the pan once.

Meanwhile, add the stock and wine to the saucepan and bring to boil. Add a pinch of salt and simmer over low heat for 45 minutes. Remove the capon from the oven. With a large spoon, scoop the stuffing from both cavities into an ovenproof bowl; cover with foil and keep warm. Tilt the capon to release any juices into the roasting pan. Transfer the capon to a carving board and let it rest for up to 20 minutes. Pour the pan juices into the wine and stock pan and bring to boil. Mix the cornflour with 150 ml of cold water, and whisk into the boiling liquid. Bring back to boil and simmer for 5 minutes; adjust the seasoning and strain and serve with the capon.

WINE

Vino Nobile di Montepulciano – one of the great Sangiovese wines from Italy. It comes from the vineyards that surround Montepulciano, a picturesque hill town 25 miles southeast of Siena in southeastern Tuscany. Full of summer fruits, strawberries and rose essence with a sumptuous palate and exceptional balance.

BOEUF À LA MODE

SERVES 6

800g chuck steak, cut into 5cm dice
3 tbsp beef dripping
2 medium white onions, finely chopped
75g plain flour
700ml red Burgundy
200ml beef stock
10 cloves garlic, chopped
4 sprigs fresh thyme
2 bay leaves
400g small shallots
200g single piece smoked bacon, rind taken off,
chopped into cubes
200g button mushrooms, wiped clean
2 carrots, peeled and diced
2 sticks celery, wiped, peeled and cut into cubes
100ml cognac

Bring the dripping to just under smoking point in a casserole or pan and sear the beef, a few pieces at a time, to a rich, dark brown on all sides. Using a slotted spoon, transfer the meat to a plate as it browns. Next add the chopped onion to the casserole and brown that a little too.

Now return the meat to the casserole or pan and sprinkle in the flour, stirring around to soak up all the juices. Then gradually pour in the Burgundy and beef stock, again stirring all the time. Add the chopped garlic, herbs and seasoning bring to the boil, then turn down to the lowest heat possible, put the lid on and cook very gently on top of the stove for 2 hours. Then, using a bit more of the dripping fry the shallots and bacon in a small frying pan to colour them lightly. Add to the casserole, together with the mushrooms carrots and celery; add the cognac then put the lid on and cook for a further hour.

WINE

Chambertin, from the village of Gevrey-Chambertin in Côte de Nuits. One of the finest French Burgundies. Gevrey-Chambertin is the largest wine-producing village in Burgundy's Côte d'Or. Located in the far north of the Côtes de Nuits above Morey St Denis, classic Gevrey-Chambertin is typically deeper in colour, firmer in body and more tannic in structure than most red Burgundy. The best can develop into the richest, most complete and long-lived Pinot Noir in the world.

BAKED ALASKA

SERVES 6–12

To assemble this recipe, you'll need a bowl that holds 4 litres. The exact size of every bowl will vary, so it helps if you're flexible during the assembly process! Line the bowl with cling-film, extending up and over the sides of the bowl.

2 swiss rolls
1 litre strawberry ice cream, softened
1 litre vanilla ice cream, softened
1 litre chocolate ice cream, softened

Use a sharp serrated knife to cut the swiss roll into slices 1–2cm thick. If you're using a smaller bowl, you can make thicker slices, but if you're using a larger bowl, you'll need more pieces so you should err on the side of thinner cake slices. Press the slices into the bowl, right up next to each other, covering the bottom and sides of the bowl. The cake slices can be squished together and manipulated a bit to get the most even coverage – the goal is to have as few gaps between cake slices as possible. When you get to the top of the bowl, you can cut the slices to fit the top of the bowl, re-roll them so they're smaller, or otherwise manipulate them to get an even layer at the top of the bowl. Spread the ice creams in layers in the bowl, trying not to damage the wall of swiss rolls covering the bowl. Once this is done, place in the deep freeze for 24 hours so it really hardens.

FOR THE MERINGUES

240g egg whites at room temperature
pinch of cream of tartar
227g caster sugar

Whip the egg whites and cream of tartar in a large bowl with a mixer on medium-high speed until foamy, about 2 minutes. Gradually beat in the sugar on high speed until the whites are glossy and hold stiff peaks. Remove the top layer of cling-film then invert the cake onto a parch-ment-lined baking sheet. Remove the rest of the cling-film and cover the ice cream bombe completely with the meringue, making the dome-shaped top slightly thicker than the sides. Form swirly peaks in the meringue using the back of a spoon. Freeze for at least 3 more hours.

Preheat the oven to 260°C/500°F/gas 9. Bake the cake until the meringue peaks are golden, about 4 minutes, or brown the meringue with a blowtorch. Let the cake soften at room temperature for 5 to 10 minutes before slicing.

WINE

Bubble-free, or 'non-mousseux' (still) white wine from Monsieur Dorsay in the village of Ay in the Champagne region of France. This was an unusual wine even in the 18th and 19th centuries and is virtually unheard of today. George Washington was so impressed with the wine that he asked Jefferson to import some for him.

HISTORICAL NOTE

On 16 November 1805 Thomas Jefferson wrote to the wine merchants Barton & Guestier[34] as follows:

> Sir,
> I thank you for the communication respecting the wines of Mr Guestier. Of Bordeaux wine I have a plentiful store. So I have of Champagne of middling quality. Still if Mr Guestier has any of first quality I would take some boxes. If he should have broken a box, perhaps he could send me a bottle or two by the stage so safely packed as not to break. The quality preferred is what we call the silky or soft, meaning a little sweetish but very slightly so. Whether it is mousseux or non-mousseux is unimportant. The only objection to what I have is that it is entirely dry without any softness. Accept my salutations & respects.
>
> Th. Jefferson

DIGESTIF

COGNAC

This is a grape brandy produced in the French region of the same name in the Charente-Maritime and Charente departments and in a few areas in Deux-Sèvres and the Dordogne. The permitted grape varieties include Ugni Blanc (predominantly), Folle Blanche and Colombard. According to the appellation regulations, Cognac must be distilled twice in traditionally shaped Charentais copper pot stills and aged at least 2 years in French oak.

Four

FORGING A HUNDRED YEARS OF PEACE AT THE CONGRESS OF VIENNA

2 October 1814
Hofburg Imperial Palace,
Vienna

THE GUESTS

EMPEROR FRANCIS I *and*
EMPRESS MARIA LUDOVIKA OF AUSTRIA

PRINCE KLEMENS VON METTERNICH,
Austrian Foreign Minister

PRINCE CHARLES-MAURICE DE TALLEYRAND-PÉRIGORD,
French Foreign Minister

ROBERT STEWART, VISCOUNT CASTLEREAGH,
British Foreign Secretary

TSAR ALEXANDER I,
Emperor of all the Russias

PRINCESS LOUISE OF BADEN,
wife of Tsar Alexander

COUNT KARL NESSELRODE,
advisor to Tsar Alexander

KING FREDERICK WILLIAM III OF PRUSSIA

CHANCELLOR PRINCE KARL VON HARDENBERG OF PRUSSIA

WILHELM VON HUMBOLDT,
Prussian Ambassador to Vienna

KING FREDERICK VI OF DENMARK

… among thousands of others.

The masked ball held in Vienna on 2 October 1814 was possibly the most spectacular party ever held. The ball and banquet were hosted by Emperor Francis I and Empress Maria Ludovika of Austria; they had invited over 10,000 guests to the Hofburg imperial palace in Vienna, including the leading statesmen and diplomats from virtually every European nation, together with two emperors and empresses, four kings, one queen, four heirs to thrones, two grand duchesses and countless princes and princesses. The cream of European society – the rich, the powerful, the great and the mighty – were there that night.

To feed this vast army of distinguished guests, Europe's finest chefs, led by Marie-Antoine Carême, had prepared a staggering array of dishes based on a catering list which included no fewer than 300 hams, 200 partridges, 200 pigeons, 150 pheasants, 60 hares, 48 *boeufs à la mode* (pot roasts), 40 rabbits, 20 large white young turkeys and 12 medium-sized wild boar. There was an assortment of roasted, baked and cold meats, including 600 pickled and salted ox-tongues. There were pastries and pies and pistachio, almond, chocolate and Seville orange gateaux. There were 3,000 litres of soup, 2,500 assorted biscuits, 1,000 *Mandl-Wandl* (oval-shaped pastries with an almond filling), 60 Gugelhupf sponge cakes, as well as many other cakes and sweets. Soft drinks, lemonade, chocolate milk, tea, almond milk and some of Europe's finest wines were available in abundance.[1]

But this was not just a gargantuan gastronomic symphony; it was also one of the most important political gatherings in history. For the great and the good that dined in Vienna were the conquerors of Napoleon. They had gathered together to thrash out a lasting peace, to carve up Europe and share the spoils of war. The delights of the overloaded dining tables helped create relationships and stage negotiations that over the next eight months would change the history of Europe and, ultimately, secure peace for 100 years.

*   *   *

Francis I, head of the Habsburg family and Emperor of Austria, was the last person ever to be crowned emperor of the now defunct Holy Roman Empire, dismantled by Napoleon in 1806. Although Austria had been impoverished by years of war, Francis I and his wily Foreign Minister Prince Klemens von Metternich had calculated that Austria might snatch more than its fair share of the spoils at the negotiating tables, if it lavished hospitality on its important international guests. The imperial palaces and grand mansions of the Austrian capital were made ready and by the time the congress began in the Autumn of 1814, the 250,000 population of Vienna had been swollen by as much as a third, with the arrival of lobbyists, vendors, tradesmen and assorted hangers-on, attracted by the lure of Europe's glitterati.

Europe had just emerged from years of revolution and bloody war. An estimated 5 million people had been killed and millions more had been maimed and disabled. Millions had been displaced. The continent had been ravaged and ripped apart by Napoleon, who had raised the French tricolour everywhere from Madrid to Moscow, placing his family members and friends on thrones across his gigantic empire.

Total war had come to Europe for the first time, with armies numbering hundreds of thousands clashing in devastating blood-soaked battles that left entire cities, towns and villages in ruins. Napoleon's ruthlessness and his propensity to strip his conquered territories of paintings, statues, jewels and anything of value left Europe as a smouldering and bankrupt wreck. But in 1814 the whole edifice came tumbling down. Despite having captured Moscow in 1812, the Russian winter finally overwhelmed him, driving him into headlong retreat by December that year.

This proved to be a turning point in the Napoleonic wars, with France's key allies, Prussia and Austria, switching sides. Even Napoleon's brilliant advisor Prince Charles-Maurice de Talleyrand-Périgord, had resigned in protest at his ruthless subjugation of his enemies. Talleyrand began spying on behalf of the Allied powers, sending secret messages that exposed Napoleon's weakness. By 1814 his Grand Armée was over-stretched, exhausted and dwindling in size.

Napoleon was defeated and his empire shattered. He was sent into exile on Elba and the victorious Allies agreed that the time had come to regroup and rebuild. After months of wrangling, the Treaty of Paris was signed in May 1814. It was generous to the defeated French. In a bid to assist King Louis XVIII to re-establish the Bourbon monarchy, the Allied powers had allowed France to retain a few of her conquered territories like the former papal enclave of Avignon and some colonies in the New World. The Allies even agreed that France could keep most of the treasures looted by Napoleon, which included priceless works of art by Raphael, Michelangelo, Titian and Rembrandt. They hoped that these generous terms would enable the French to reintegrate peacefully into the community of nations.

The Treaty of Paris also decreed that there should be a major congress or summit meeting where the Allied powers could decide on the fate of the vast territories that had been captured and governed by Napoleon and his family. When Emperor Francis I of Austria offered Vienna as the venue for the summit, it was readily agreed. Geographically, Vienna lay at the heart of the European continent, and as the third biggest city after London and Paris, it was regarded as a place of sophistication and culture, adorned with graceful parks, elegant squares and a multitude of palaces and grand baroque mansions.

The four major victorious powers, or 'the Big Four' as they were known, Austria, Great Britain, Prussia and Russia, had been brought together a full week before the official conference began by the scheming Austrian Foreign Minister Klemens von Metternich, who was president of the congress. At 41 years of age, the thin and stylish Metternich was well known for his sophistication and high intelligence and for his scandalous love affairs, which kept tongues wagging in Vienna that autumn.

Great Britain was represented by its foreign secretary, the tall, thin and ascetic Robert Stewart, Viscount Castlereagh. The 45-year-old diplomat invariably dressed in black, which many said suited his sombre state of mind. He was rarely seen to smile. Russia sent Count Karl Nesselrode, a German citizen and former sailor in the Russian navy who had risen dramatically through the ranks to become Tsar Alexander's trusted advisor. Prussia's representative was the oldest of the group, the white-haired 64-year-old Chancellor Prince Karl von Hardenberg. He was almost completely deaf and for that reason was usually accompanied by the Prussian ambassador to Vienna, Wilhelm von Humboldt, brother of the famous explorer and naturalist.

Together, the ministers and diplomats representing the Big Four had plotted to carve up the spoils between them, presenting the other countries attending the congress with a *fait accompli*. Their plans were to be shattered by the cunning French foreign minister, Talleyrand, sent by King Louis XVIII to represent his defeated nation in Vienna. Described by Napoleon as 'the shit in silk stockings', Talleyrand was feared and revered in equal measure and his presence in Vienna proved to be pivotal for the outcome of the summit.

By the time Talleyrand arrived in Vienna, the Big Four had agreed that they would form themselves into a central committee which would control the agenda, the programme of meetings and the final outcome of the congress. They argued that this was fair because their nations had borne the brunt of the fight against Napoleon and therefore it was their right to decide Europe's future. The other attending nations could voice their opinions, but could not alter the decisions of the Big Four in any way. Clearly this view was unlikely to be met with general acclaim by the 200 smaller nations, protectorates and principalities who had come to Vienna expecting to play a part in deciding Europe's future. Nor was Talleyrand prepared to accept this diktat. Indeed Castlereagh had been pressing the others to include France in their discussions, as he had heard that Talleyrand was already fomenting opposition to the Big Four's plans amongst the other participating nations.

Metternich decided to confront Talleyrand, and on 30 September invited him to a conference of the Big Four. At the meeting, Talleyrand objected to their dominance of the congress. He demanded that France should have equality with Austria, Prussia, Russia and Great Britain. At one point, Talleyrand was handed a protocol that had already been signed by the four powers. Deeply disgruntled, he read it and asked why it referred repeatedly to 'allies'? 'Allies against whom?' he enquired. 'Not against Napoleon, he's on Elba. Not against France, peace has been made. Surely, not against the King of France, he guarantees the durability of this peace. Gentlemen, let's speak frankly,' he concluded. 'If there are still Allied Powers then I don't belong here.'[2]

Talleyrand had put his finger on the key flaw in the Big Four's plans. How on earth were they going to persuade the other nations attending that their views didn't matter? Indeed the ever-tetchy Talleyrand pointed out that there were only two dates of importance: 30 May, when it was agreed to hold the congress, and 1 October, when it was scheduled to open. Nothing that had been decided between these dates was valid, in his opinion. Talleyrand's withering assessment was met with a stunned silence, broken by Castlereagh, who quickly agreed that the protocol should be withdrawn. Talleyrand had won his first major skirmish and the scene was now set for the opening of the congress.

But by 1 October, such was the consternation caused by Talleyrand's intervention that no official invitation or proclamation had been made signalling the opening of the congress. It was now certain that the first major event would be Emperor Francis I and Empress Maria Ludovika's magnificent banquet and ball on 2 October. The top table for this event included almost all of the greatest and most powerful emperors, kings, queens and leaders of the day.

Forty-six-year-old Emperor Francis I of Austria had already been on the throne for 22 years. He was frail and white-haired, looking older than his years. His wife, Maria Ludovika, Empress Consort of Austria and Queen Consort of Hungary and Bohemia, was only 27 years old; tall and pale with a long, aquiline nose and black curly hair, she had fled to Austria when Napoleon invaded her homeland in northern Italy in 1796. She hated Napoleon and despised Metternich, whom she accused of attempting to discredit her.

As a ruler of one of the Big Four great powers, Tsar Alexander I, Emperor of all the Russias, cut a dashing figure at the ball. He was tall, blond and handsome and had an insatiable sexual appetite that already rivalled that of his grandmother, Catherine the Great. She had doted on Alexander to the jealous disapproval of her own son, Alexander's father, Tsar Paul I. Alexander came to the throne in March 1801 following the murder of his father, and it was rumoured that he had played a part in the assassination, a rumour strengthened by his subsequent appointment of some of the assassins as his personal advisors. His wife was the stunningly beautiful 35-year-old Princess Louise of Baden. Tsar Alexander had for a time been an ally of Napoleon, even waging a small-scale naval war against Britain. But he and Napoleon could never agree on key issues, particularly on the fate of Poland, and their alliance finally collapsed in 1810. Napoleon's ill-fated invasion of Russia two years later effectively sealed the French emperor's fate and turned Alexander into one of the great conquering heroes of Europe.

The angriest and most aggressive delegation in Vienna was undoubtedly the large entourage from Prussia, led by their king, the volatile and eccentric Frederick William III. The Prussians were determined to win compensation for the damage they had suffered at the hands of Napoleon, and Frederick William saw himself as one of the great powers, although the much diminished state of Prussia barely justified this allusion.

Last and certainly not least of the Big Four was Great Britain, represented by the aloof and peculiar Viscount Castlereagh, who had caused a scandal in London by challenging a fellow minister to a duel. Castlereagh had come to Vienna determined to ensure the Royal Navy maintained its position as the dominant sea-going force in Europe. He was also unique in the company of the Big Four in that Britain had always regarded Napoleon as an enemy and had never forged any alliance with him. Together with King Frederick VI of Denmark, Klemens von Metternich and Prince Charles-Maurice de Talleyrand-Périgord, this was the volatile company who took their seats at the top tables for the great banquet in Vienna that evening.

The emperors, empresses, kings and queens were welcomed into the grand hall by a loud trumpet blast. A specially constructed raised dais adorned with large white and silver silk hangings had been prepared for the royals, so that they were visible to all. The Empress of Austria sat at the front together with the Empress of Russia. Next to them were the queen of Bavaria and the Russian grand duchess Catherine, Alexander's sister.

The hall was lit by a dazzling array of crystal chandeliers bearing over 8,000 candles, creating a stunning and disorientating effect in the huge, white-and-gilt-panelled ballroom. Exotic plants and flowers decorated the central stairway, which led to the upper galleries and balconies that in turn were draped with red and gold velvet. The tables for the royals and senior diplomats had been set with polished and shining silverware and the finest crystal glasses, positioned perfectly on white Damask tablecloths, offset with starched and folded napkins. An army of liveried waiting staff filled and refilled the wine glasses with the finest wines, while others bustled to and from the kitchens with endless dishes of tempting fare.

Masked and dressed in their best uniforms, the men rivalled the glamorous women in the high-fashion stakes. Many ladies of great beauty and scandalous reputation were present. Among these were two renowned beauties who were also deadly enemies. Wilhelmine, Duchess of Sagan, at 33 years of age, was ravishingly lovely, with dark blonde hair and deep brown eyes. She was also heiress to one of the largest fortunes in Europe. In her second unhappy marriage and heading for a second divorce, the duchess was involved in a torrid affair with Metternich that had become public knowledge in Vienna, providing an abundance of ammunition for the gossip-mongers.

Her rival was Princess Catherine Bagration, a 31-year-old widow, also seriously rich, beautiful and highly intelligent. She was fond of wearing extremely *risqué* low-cut evening gowns that earned her the nickname 'the beautiful naked angel'. The two had been enemies for many years and found themselves in Vienna, surrounded by admirers and competing for attention. Princess Catherine had also been seduced by Metternich, and she and the Duchess of Sagan were now attracting the attention of Russia's ostentatious tsar.

Many of the women wore elegant white or pastel-shade ballgowns with long sleeves, set off by lace edgings and matching gloves. Ribbons and flowers adorned their hair and they sparkled with an impressive display of diamonds, pearls and other precious jewels. The masks also served their purpose, maintaining the anonymity of the guests. On that evening in Vienna it would have been possible to dance with almost anyone. The food, the wine, the music, the décor, the lavish costumes of the guests and the overwhelming feeling that they were celebrating the end of a brutal war and the beginning of a new era of peace, turned the event into a fairy-tale carnival which would provide a solid and positive foundation for the weeks of difficult discussions ahead.

The leading chef for this grand feast was Paris-born Marie-Antoine Carême, often regarded as one of the first internationally renowned celebrity chefs. Carême favoured the elaborate style of cooking known as *la grande cuisine Française,* which was popular with international royalty and adored by the *nouveau riche* of Paris. He was famous for his rich sauces and for the introduction of the white, double-breasted chef's jackets and tall white caps for kitchen staff, still used to this day. He was a firm favourite of Talleyrand, often cooking exquisite dinners for him and his wealthy guests, including Napoleon himself. In fact when King Louis XVIII decided to send Talleyrand to Vienna and asked him what he required, the French foreign minister is reputed to have replied: 'Sire, I need saucepans more than instructions. Let me do my work and count on Carême.'[3] Talleyrand was convinced that Carême's cooking skills would win more diplomatic battles for France than an army of ambassadors and politicians. In fact, following his triumph in Vienna Carême was invited to London in 1815 to take up the position of head chef to the Prince of Wales, who later became George IV.

Carême was abandoned by his parents in Paris in 1794 at the height of the French Revolution. To survive, he took a job as a kitchen boy in a cheap Parisian eatery in exchange for food and lodgings. In 1798, a famous pâtissier – Sylvain Bailly – took him on as an apprentice in his shop in the fashionable Palais-Royal neighbourhood, where he quickly gained a reputation as a skilled pastry chef, making his elaborate *pièces montées,* which Bailly proudly displayed in his shop window. Soon Carême left Bailly and opened his own shop, the *Pâtisserie de la rue de la Paix,* which he ran until 1813.

His *pièces montées,* which were sometimes gigantic constructions made entirely from pastry, sugar and marzipan, rapidly became famous, and wealthy Parisians queued to purchase them. Carême spent hours studying elaborate drawings of ancient buildings, temples, pyramids and ruins in history books in the Bibliothèque Nationale, modelling his *pièces montées* on these designs. He invented *grosses meringues, gros nougats* and *croquantes* made from almonds, honey and *solilemmes.* He is also credited as the inventor of the 'cold buffet'. He soon began creating dishes for Talleyrand and other members of Parisian high society, including Napoleon.

Napoleon wasn't overly interested in food, but he knew its importance as a tool of diplomacy. In 1804 he installed Talleyrand in the Château de Valençay near Paris, which he had purchased with the specific intention of using it to forge alliances, through exploiting the exceptional culinary skills of Marie-Antoine Carême.

The sumptuous dinner prepared by Carême for the royal tables that evening in Vienna was certainly a feast fit for kings. As was common practice at the time, Carême personally supervised the laying out of the food on a series of enormous tables in the main ballroom and the smaller ballroom, the Kleiner Redoutensaal, and even the indoor arena of the Spanish Riding School, where the multitude of guests could help themselves, at least in theory, to their favourite dishes. In reality, there were so many people pushing and squeezing through the assembled throng that most had to make do with grabbing what was nearest to them. The banquet and the plan to 'grab your favourite morsel', was perhaps emblematic of the entire peace conference.

The meal opened with Russian caviar, in honour of Tsar Alexander. Caviar had been present in banquets since the fourth century BC, but it became a sought-after delicacy under the tsars. Carême served the caviar in small, decorative dishes, sitting on beds of ice and surrounded by bowls containing chopped egg yolks, chopped egg whites, lemon wedges, soured cream[4] and chopped chives, with triangles of thin buttered toast. Champagne Drappier Brut Nature, a very dry wine with no added sugar (zero dosage) allowing the true flavour of the wine to come through, accompanied the caviar. Carême knew that this wine, from a vineyard founded in 1808, opened up magnificently after exposure to the air, becoming rich, toasty and almost fruity with notes of quince and *pêche de vigne* – a perfect companion for caviar.

The caviar was followed by *pâté de foie gras de canard*, or duck liver pâté, served thinly sliced at room temperature with toasted slices of brioche. The foie gras was accompanied by a 100-year-old Royal Tokaji made from the classic blend of Furmint Hàrslevelü and Muskotály grape varieties, from the Tokaj region of Hungary. Royal Tokaji is renowned for its delicious sweetness balanced by a pronounced fresh acidity. A single bottle of this luxury aged wine would have cost more than an entire year's salary for a coachman.

Next, the royal guests were served with a rich consommé, garnished with julienne-cuts or strips of celery root, veal and leeks, accompanied by a dry Manzanilla sherry from the Andalucia region of Spain. The consommé was followed by a typical Austrian fish dish comprising freshwater carp from Styria, served on deep, warmed plates with caraway potatoes. The carp was sprinkled with horseradish and garnished with lovage, sea salt and freshly ground pepper and accompanied by a Grüner Veltliner Renner late-harvested white wine from the Cistercian-owned monastery at Schloss Gobelsburg in the Kamptal region of eastern Austria. This rich, spicy, creamy-textured wine with lively, fresh acidity, provided the perfect balance to complement the subtle flavours of the carp.

Carême was highly critical of the quality of meat he found in Vienna, but he was full of praise for the game, so the main course of his royal feast featured roasted leg of partridge with braised cabbage parcels. To complement this mouthwatering dish, the royals were served with a rich red Romanée-Conti from the Côte de Nuits region of Burgundy. One of the great aristocratic wines of Burgundy, it was even hailed in 1780 by the Archbishop of Paris as being like 'velvet and satin in bottles'.[5]

Following the French custom, Carême now served up a tempting array of cheeses, which led to a dispute at the table where Metternich, Talleyrand, Nesselrode, Castlereagh, Hardenberg and other diplomats were seated. Lord Castlereagh began to sing the praises of the English Stilton that had been served, whereupon Nesselrode spoke up for Emmenthal, the Dutch representative Falk lavished praise on Edam from the Netherlands and the Italian diplomat Alvino claimed the best cheese was Italian Strachino. Talleyrand left the table and gave instructions to one of the servants. Shortly afterwards the servant returned from Talleyrand's private kitchen storeroom with a large piece of Brie de

Meaux. As French historian Jean Orieux describes it in his book *Talleyrand – The Art of Survival*: 'The brie rendered its cream to the knife. It was a feast, and no one further argued the point. No diplomatic victory was too small for Talleyrand.' The wine served with the cheese was a sweet, velvety, 25-year-old vintage port, from the Douro Valley in Northern Portugal.

Now it was time for Carême to unveil his *pièce de résistance*. For his royal guests on 2 October, Carême and his team had prepared an amazing cake in the shape of the Hofburg imperial palace. It took four waiters to carry this vast concoction to the royal table, where it was met with gasps of praise at the detailed accuracy of the sweeping columns and arched windows of the Neue Burg wing, all rendered in carefully crafted marzipan. Carême's fantastic cake was accompanied by one of his other great specialities, a delicate orange-flower and pink champagne jelly. These desserts were washed down with glasses of the equally famous Château d'Yquem, often described as the greatest sweet wine in the world, from the village of Sauternes in the Saint-Emilion region of France.

Fresh from his diplomatic victory over the argument about which country made the best cheese, Talleyrand could now relax, eating a small slice of Carême's cake and sipping a glorious glass of golden Château d'Yquem, secure in the knowledge that bringing the legendary chef to Vienna had been a masterstroke. He was certain now that he could use the grand opening banquet and ball as the launchpad for his strategy to outwit the Big Four and win maximum concessions for his defeated motherland. The opening banquet was not without its glitches, however, with over 3,000 imperial teaspoons found to be missing the following day!

Talleyrand's influence on the proceedings of the Congress of Vienna was quickly felt. He had whipped up such anger at the attempts of the Big Four to seize total control of the negotiations that the formal opening of the conference was postponed until 1 November. In the meantime it was agreed to invite France, Spain, Portugal and Sweden, the other signatories to the Treaty of Paris, to join the ranks of the Big Four.

As the countdown to the delayed opening of the congress continued, October was filled with endless meetings, parades, hunting expeditions, shooting parties, sightseeing tours and almost nightly balls and banquets. Teams of spies employed by Francis I kept a careful watch on all the goings-on, reporting back regularly on the scandals, plots and torrid affairs that were unfolding day by day. Some of those scandals involved Metternich, who had fallen out of favour with his lover Wilhelmine, Duchess of Sagan. She had frozen out Metternich in preference for the attention and advances of the flirtatious Tsar Alexander of Russia. Metternich was dismayed and appalled. He was deeply in love with Wilhelmine and her sudden lack of interest left him wholly distracted and unable to concentrate properly on the sensitive negotiations of the congress.

His temporary preoccupation played right into the hands of Talleyrand, as did the further convulsions caused by the arrival on 7 October of Napoleon's wife, Marie-Louise, the daughter of Emperor Francis I. Marie-Louise had been married to Napoleon for only four years and had been desperately trying to join him on Elba for the past six months, following his abdication. Napoleon had even sent a cavalry escort to rescue her from her temporary home in Orléans but was beaten to it by Emperor Francis, who sent some Austrian officers to return her safely to Vienna. Francis was determined that his daughter and her three-and-a-half-year-old son, Napoleon Francis, King of Rome, should not be allowed to rejoin the defeated Bonaparte. In any case, Marie-Louise had been promised the duchies of Parma, Piacenza and Guastalla under the Treaty of Paris but had been told by both her father and Metternich that the Spanish were challenging this decision and demanding that these territories should be returned to their ownership. Francis I had warned his daughter that her presence in Vienna was vital to ensure the territories were secured by her, rather than handed back to Spain.

Another late arrival at the congress was Cardinal Consalvi, sent by the Pope to lay claim to vast territories that had been seized by Napoleon, together with countless priceless treasures Bonaparte had looted from the Vatican. Complicating matters even further, the Dutch and Italians in particular were demanding that priceless works of art looted from their territories and taken back to Paris by Napoleon should now be returned, despite the fact that the Allied powers, under the Treaty of Paris, had assured King Louis XVIII that France could keep these treasures.

These competing claims were swirling around the salons and meeting rooms of Vienna. But none were to prove as divisive or controversial as the question of Poland. Tsar Alexander had come to Vienna with one key objective: to ensure that Poland became a satellite of his expanding Russian empire. Following the Napoleonic wars, Poland had been subdivided repeatedly and was currently split between Prussia, which had seized Warsaw and Gdansk and the 'Polish corridor' that ran north to the Baltic Sea, and Austria, which had grabbed the ancient capital of Kraków and the salt mines of Tarnopol. The Russians had ended up with the lion's share of territory and were keen to consolidate their dominant position in Poland.

Tsar Alexander told Talleyrand that his troops occupied much of Poland and that he intended to 'keep what I hold'. When Talleyrand challenged him and said such inflexibility by the Russians could destroy any chance of peace, the tsar replied: 'Rather war than that I should renounce what I hold.' Alexander had formulated a plan whereby he suggested he would re-create Poland by reuniting all of the territories that had been carved up during the Napoleonic wars under an enlightened constitution. He claimed that he had the full support of Polish patriots for this enterprise. But Talleyrand was alarmed at how this plan, by vastly extending the Russian empire, could threaten the balance of power in Europe. He found a willing ally in Castlereagh. The British foreign secretary was increasingly worried about the closeness of the relationship between two of the Big Four Allied Powers, Russia and Prussia, which Britain regarded as seriously destabilising and dangerous.

A major dispute was looming and it was becoming ominously clear that the fate of Poland was increasingly intertwined with the future of the kingdom of Saxony. The two regions were connected geographically and had in fact been joined together by Napoleon who had linked Saxony to the duchy of Warsaw, placing both under the jurisdiction of the King of Saxony, who, as a long-term ally of Napoleon was now a prisoner of war in a Prussian castle. If Tsar Alexander's plans for Poland were to be realised, both Austria and Prussia would have to be compensated for their loss of territory. For Prussia, the obvious solution would be to hand them control of Saxony.

However, despite his imprisonment by the Prussians, the King of Saxony was unwilling to yield any of his lands and had even sent an ambassador to Vienna to plead his case. Talleyrand, concerned that the annexation of Saxony by Prussia would create a massive and powerful state which could later pose a threat to European peace, firmly opposed this plan. But the Russians were appalled and pointed out that as their troops were currently occupying Saxony, they could simply hand it over to their Prussian allies in exchange for their support over Poland. Metternich was equally determined to prevent Russia and Prussia combining forces to outmanoeuvre Austria and Great Britain at the congress. A dangerous impasse had been reached. The tsar was now openly ranting almost daily against Metternich, regarding him as an outright enemy, while Metternich was outraged that the tsar had stolen his beloved Wilhelmine.

Scheming against Russia, Metternich, supported by Castlereagh, offered a deal to the Prussians, stating that Austria would back their annexation of Saxony in return for a guarantee that they would oppose Tsar Alexander's plans for Poland. His idea caught the interest of the elderly and deaf Prussian chancellor, Prince Karl von Hardenberg, but news of their discussions inevitably leaked out and caused a furious confrontation at a private dinner between Emperor Francis I and Tsar Alexander. The tsar accused the emperor of betraying him in the negotiations, and when the emperor protested the tsar insisted on summoning Hardenberg, whom he then accused of defying his master by secretly plotting against the Russian proposals for Poland. It was unheard of for a ruler to address a senior minister from another power in this way, but Emperor Francis, perhaps alarmed at the tsar's increasing volatility, did nothing to defend Hardenberg and indeed ordered him to toe the line.

It soon emerged that Hardenberg was not the only minister in Vienna going against his own government's policy on Poland. News arrived from London that the British government was not against the tsar's plans for Poland and Castlereagh was acting in defiance of their position. Metternich now realised that his opposition to the tsar's plan was beginning to unravel and sensed that the only way to secure victory would be to place Poland as a key agenda item for discussion at the opening of the Congress on 1 November. He was certain that there would be such an outcry over the attempts by the tsar to extend the influence of the Russian empire right into the heart of Europe that he would be forced to back down.

Sensing an opportunity, Talleyrand floated the idea of creating a main organising committee that would deal with all the key negotiations, together with a series of sub-committees that would handle the more specialised problems. He suggested this proposal should also be endorsed on the opening day of the conference. But on the eve of the opening, Emperor Francis I, under pressure from his close ally, Tsar Alexander, ordered Metternich to postpone the conference yet again. The tsar had smelt a rat and, always keen to preserve his reputation as the conquering war hero, liberator and enlightened thinker, was unwilling to float his outrageous plan for Poland in a public forum, which would have made him look like another Bonaparte.

In the end, the formal opening of the congress was postponed for a third and final time and it never got under way at all in full plenary session. But Talleyrand's idea to set up a series of committees was agreed and it was in these meetings that all the major decisions in Vienna would finally be taken. Once again Talleyrand had prevailed, effectively breaking the power of the Big Four over the proceedings and devolving authority to the committees. But it was not all going the Frenchman's way. Returning to his quarters one evening after one of the committee meetings, he was handed a dispatch sent directly from the imprisoned King of Saxony, informing him that Russian troops had withdrawn from the kingdom and handed over control to an occupying Prussian force. Worse still, the Russians had marched straight across the border into Poland, further strengthening their position there. Tsar Alexander had carried out his threat to hand Saxony to his Prussian allies on a plate in return for their support over his plans for Poland.

Despite this setback, the congress proceeded. Eventually 10 separate committees were formed, dealing with everything from the navigation of rivers to diplomatic etiquette. But the problem of Saxony dominated the debates with many fearing that war could break out at any moment. To complicate matters, Castlereagh received strict orders from the British prime minister, Lord Liverpool, that he was to stop sidestepping government policy. Liverpool reminded him that Britain was fighting a war against the United States of America and could not afford to risk another conflict in Europe. Castlereagh was told to stop antagonising Tsar Alexander over the Polish question and to oppose the Prussian occupation of Saxony – two policies that to the British foreign minister seemed wholly incompatible. Nevertheless, obeying these instructions from London, Castlereagh broke the news to Prussian Chancellor von Hardenberg, who exploded in anger, saying that he regarded this as a stab in the back by the British.

Meanwhile, Talleyrand's star had continued to rise. Although still excluded from the Big Four inner circle, his strong defence of Saxony had earned him respect and support from a multitude of smaller states that now regarded him as their leader. Against this background he approached Metternich and Castlereagh with the controversial suggestion that France, Great Britain and Austria should form an alliance to break the deadlock in Vienna. As the New Year celebrations were being held, news arrived by dispatch rider to inform Castlereagh that the war between Britain and the USA had ended and that British and American diplomats, at a special meeting in Ghent on Christmas Eve, had signed a peace treaty. Castelreagh was jubilant; it meant that Britain could now concentrate all of her military resources in Europe and that he no longer had to countenance the increasingly aggressive threats from Prussia and Russia. Castlereagh told Metternich and Talleyrand that he would be prepared to sign the pact with Austria and France.

In strictest secrecy, a treaty was duly drawn up, committing Britain, Austria and France to support one another in the event of an attack and to contribute up to 150,000 troops for that purpose. It was a purely defensive treaty and Talleyrand, Metternich and Castlereagh signed it on 3 January 1815. Talleyrand was ecstatic. After only three and a half months in Vienna as the representative of a nation that had been regarded as a pariah state following the Napoleonic wars, he had now pulled off a diplomatic coup that would ensure his place at the top table beside the Big Four.

Rumours quickly began to circulate in the salons of Vienna that a secret pact had been signed, and they were equally quickly confirmed when, at the first meeting of the Big Four in 1815, Metternich nonchalantly proposed that Talleyrand should be allowed to join them. He was supported by Castlereagh and, to everyone's surprise, even by the Russians. Rumours of the British, French and Austrian pact and the news that Britain had ended its war with the Americans had apparently caused the tsar to have a change of heart and he was now willing to negotiate over Poland. His opinion of his former close ally Prussia had now also changed, after Metternich had shown him a letter written by the Prussian chancellor in which he stated that he only supported Russian policy regarding Poland because it would make Russia weaker. This infuriated the tsar and he decided to abandon his support for Prussia. Hardenberg rapidly found himself isolated and without friends. Talleyrand's diplomatic skills had begun to break the deadlock over Saxony and Poland.

Just at this moment of triumph, Castlereagh received the news that he was to be recalled to Britain and replaced by the widely popular Duke of Wellington, renowned for his key role in driving Napoleon out of Spain. Following Napoleon's abdication, Wellington had been appointed as British ambassador to France, where he had kept himself closely informed of the goings on in Vienna. He arrived in early February, cutting an imposing figure in his scarlet field-marshal's uniform bedecked with medals, and there was immediately great competition amongst the many diplomats and glitterati to invite this newly arrived celebrity to their balls and banquets.

But Castlereagh wished to tackle one final issue before he handed over his portfolio to his successor and departed for London. He was determined to do his utmost to abolish the pernicious slave trade, and he began a furious round of meetings and negotiations, culminating on 8 February with an announcement by the Big Four, supported by France, Spain and Portugal, condemning slavery as 'repugnant to the principles of humanity and universal morality'. A timetable was also set for the complete abolition of the slave trade. It was a considerable victory.

Three days later, on 11 February, a compromise agreement was finally reached on Poland. A new, small kingdom of Poland was to be created, largely from the former Duchy of Warsaw, with Tsar Alexander as its king. A resolution was also agreed on Saxony, with King Frederick Augustus allowed to retain his crown and two-thirds of his kingdom including, incredibly, the important cities of Leipzig and Dresden, which many, including the Prussians, had coveted. The Prussians were bought off by being given Westphalia, Pomerania, Trier and a large piece of the Rhineland, including the city of Cologne.

Castlereagh left Vienna on 15 February, convinced that he had achieved some progress in helping to resolve the Poland/Saxony question and obtaining a firm commitment on the abolition of slavery. As his coach trundled across the European continent heading back to London, neither he nor any of the others back in Vienna could have foreseen the bombshell that was about to erupt in their midst, turning the entire peace process on its head. On 26 February, Napoleon escaped from Elba and set sail for France.

When Metternich received an urgent dispatch on the morning of Tuesday 7 March informing him of Napoleon's escape, he hurried to the Hofburg Palace to inform the emperor. Francis told him to meet urgently with Tsar Alexander and the King of Prussia and to tell them that he was willing to send the Austrian army back to France and hoped that they would join forces. By mid-morning, the Allies were gathered in Metternich's study for a council of war to which Talleyrand had also been summoned. It was agreed that Napoleon had to be stopped before he could 'set the world on fire again'.

With the news that Napoleon had marched triumphantly into Paris and that Louis XVIII had fled to Ghent, it became clear that another battle against the Corsican tyrant was inevitable. In early April, Wellington departed for Brussels to take control of the Allied armies, and over the course of the next six weeks the remaining delegates made their preparations to leave Vienna. Tsar Alexander and King Frederick William departed together on 26 May. However, with war looming, Metternich, Hardenberg, Humboldt and others remained behind, rushing to complete the business of the congress. They had decided to draw up a general treaty that would contain every single decision that had been taken over the course of eight months at the congress and in due course the 121-article treaty named 'the Final Act' was prepared. It was signed at a special ceremony in the Hofburg Palace on 9 June 1815 by the Big Four, together with Spain, Portugal, France and Sweden – 'the Big Eight'.

Of all the original main players at the congress, only Metternich and Talleyrand remained to sign the Final Act. The others had all left for the field of battle and been replaced by junior ministers. Talleyrand, whose diplomatic skills had dominated the congress from the opening grand banquet on 2 October 1814, when his celebrated chef Marie-Antoine Carême had won hearts, minds and stomachs to the cause through his skilful deployment of food and wine, was one of the last to leave. Having consigned most of his voluminous papers to a large bonfire, he now prepared to rejoin exiled King Louis XVIII in Ghent. Talleyrand knew that his stunning successes in Vienna would all be lost unless Napoleon was once again defeated, this time decisively. As he set off for Ghent, he could barely have imagined the historic victory that would end Napoleon's career once and for all, at Waterloo, in less than 10 days' time.

Following Napoleon's defeat at Waterloo and his exile to St Helena, a new treaty was thrashed out that was much harsher to France than the original Treaty of Paris of May 1814. Enraged that France had once again rallied to Napoleon's side and broken Europe's peace, the Allies demanded punitive measures that would teach France a lesson. Large chunks of territory were stripped away and transferred to neighbouring states, and France was forced to pay 700 million francs' indemnity, as well as meet the full cost of a large army of occupation for the next five years.

Talleyrand was angered at these vindictive instruments in the treaty, arguing that the enemy had been Napoleon and not France, which was ruled by Louis XVIII, who was an ally. As foreign minister for France Talleyrand refused to sign the treaty, complaining that it would only make matters more difficult for the French king. On 24 September, appalled at the way France was being treated, Talleyrand offered his resignation, hoping that this gesture might shock all of the participants into reviewing the treaty. But to his surprise and shock, Louis XVIII, whom Talleyrand had deserted Napoleon to serve and whom he had loyally defended throughout the congress, accepted his resignation. Talleyrand spent the next 15 years on the sidelines, acting as an 'elder statesman'. When Louis-Phillippe claimed the French throne following the 1830 July Revolution, he appointed Talleyrand as ambassador to the United Kingdom, a post he retained from 1830 to 1834.

MENU

Russian Caviar
Pâté de Foie Gras de Canard
Consommé
Styrian Carp with Root Vegetables and Caraway Seed Potatoes

Roast Partridge with Cabbage Parcels

Fromage

Orange-Flower and Pink Champagne Jelly

Champagne Drappier Brut Nature (Zero Dosage)
100-year-old Royal Tokaji
Manzanilla sherry
Grüner Veltliner Renner late-harvested white wine
Romanée-Conti – Burgundy
25-year-old Port
Château d'Yquem

RUSSIAN CAVIAR

SERVES 6

300g Beluga Caviar (50g per guest)
500g crème fraîche
blini

Remove caviar from the refrigerator. Allow refrigerated caviar to sit (unopened) at room temperature for 5–10 minutes prior to serving. Place the caviar tin or jar in a small, decorative caviar server and sit in a larger ice-filled bowl to keep cold. Only use mother of pearl or bone or horn spoons to serve the caviar.

FOR THE BLINI

2 ½ tsp active dry yeast
250ml tepid water
2 tsp sugar
170g flour
500ml warm milk, or a little more as needed
4 tbsp unsalted butter, melted
300g plain flour
500g rye flour
2 beaten egg yolks
4 tbsp sugar
2 tsp salt
2 egg whites
oil, for frying
melted butter, for brushing

In a small bowl, stir together the yeast, warm water, sugar and first measure (170g) of flour. Cover and set aside until doubled, about one hour. Beat in all the rest of the ingredients, except for the egg whites. Then add the flour/yeast mixture and whisk until smooth and then cover. Set aside to rise until doubled in bulk, about 1 ½ hours. Stir the batter well again, recover, and let rise once more for about 45 minutes. Whisk the whites to soft peaks and fold into the batter. Don't whip the egg whites before you are ready for them, as they won't hold. Let the batter rest for another ten minutes. Heat a well-seasoned cast-iron frying pan or non-stick frying pan over medium heat. Rub the pan with oil. Spoon in about 50ml of batter, so you have an 8cm disc on the pan; cover with as many as you can. Cook until the top of the blini is bubbly and the bottom is golden brown. Carefully turn and cook the other side for about 30 seconds, brushing some melted butter on the cooked side. Repeat till it's all done. Serve warm.

WINE

Champagne Drappier Brut Nature, a very dry wine with no added sugar (zero dosage) allowing the true flavour of the wine to come through, accompanied the caviar. This wine, from a vineyard founded in 1808, opened up magnificently after exposure to the air, becoming rich, toasty and almost fruity with notes of quince and pêche de vigne; a perfect companion for caviar.

PÂTÈ DE FOIE GRAS DE CANARD

SERVES 6–12

2 lobes of foie gras de-veined and cleaned; your butcher
can do this for you
375 ml sweet white wine
60g salt
30g sugar
5g ground nutmeg
2g ground white pepper

Put the foie gras in the sweet wine, add salt and sugar, nutmeg and pepper and leave overnight. Take the foie gras out of the wine and dry in a cloth. Preheat oven to 200°C. Press into a terrine (25cm x 7.5cm x 6cm), leaving a bit of space at the top. Place terrine on 3 folded-over paper towels in the bottom of a deep oven tray and fill tray with hot water to reach halfway up sides of terrine. Cook until internal temperature of foie gras reaches 46°C on a meat thermometer, about 30 minutes. Pour off fat and reserve. Cool terrine. Cut a piece of cardboard to fit inside top of terrine and wrap it in cling-film. Gently press cardboard onto foie gras; weight with a small can for 1 hour. Remove can and cardboard, return reserved fat to terrine, cover, and refrigerate for 1–2 days. To un-mould, dip terrine in a bowl of warm water for 30 seconds, run a knife along edges and invert onto a plate. Serve thinly sliced on toasted brioche, with a side garnish of honey, Sauternes wine, jam, onion jam, fresh figs or dried fruits.

WINE

The foie gras was accompanied by a 100-year old Royal Tokaji made from the classic blend of Furmint Hàrslevelü and Muskotály grape varieties, from the Tokaj region of Hungary; Royal Tokaji is renowned for its delicious sweetness balanced by a pronounced fresh acidity.

CONSOMMÉ

SERVES 6

1 kg minced beef shin
6 litres roasted brown beef stock
50g carrots, minced
50g celery, minced
100g green of leek, minced
1 parsnip, finely chopped
8 egg whites
1 bunch parsley stems, chopped

4–5 sprigs of fresh thyme, chopped
2 bay leaves
3–4 peppercorns
bunch of fresh tarragon, chopped

In a large stockpot combine carrot, celery, leek, parsnip, minced beef shin, egg whites, herbs, and peppercorns and mix well. Stir in cold stock then set over highest heat and bring up to a boil as fast as you can, stirring all the time so it does not catch on the bottom. Drop the temperature to a very slow simmer until a raft begins to form on the surface. Simmer for 1½ to 2 hours. The raft will crack to expose some liquid; taste. Simmer longer if more flavour is desired. Add salt as necessary. Carefully ladle out consommé through the raft and pour through a fine mesh strainer. Discard raft. Serve with thinly cut herb pancakes.

FOR THE HERB PANCAKES

55g butter, melted
200g plain flour
salt and ground black pepper
1 large egg
250ml milk
20g fresh flat-leafed parsley, chopped
25g fresh chives, chopped
25g tarragon, chopped
vegetable oil for frying

Melt the butter and let it cool slightly, then place in a bowl with the sifted flour, salt, pepper, egg and half the milk. Whisk the mixture together until smooth and then mix in the remaining milk and the chopped herbs. Cover and refrigerate for at least 30 minutes.

Heat a very little oil in an 18cm crêpe pan over a high heat, pour in about 30ml batter, then swirl round to make a thin pancake. Turn heat down and cook on medium heat. Once brown, turn over to colour lightly on the other side. Repeat the process with the remaining batter.

Cover and set aside until ready to serve. Roll up each pancake like a cigar and slice into thin strips.

WINE

Manzanilla sherry from the Andalucia region of Spain.

STYRIAN CARP WITH ROOT VEGETABLES AND CARAWAY SEED POTATOES

SERVES 6

1 large carp
1 head of garlic, sliced in half
1 onion, sliced in half
1 carrot, peeled and sliced in half
10 juniper berries
bunch of thyme
salt and pepper to taste
6 bay leaves
200ml white wine
150ml white wine vinegar
2.25 litres water

Clean, wash and fillet the fish, salt the fish and let it sit for 10–15 minutes. In the meantime, boil the water, some salt, pepper and bay leaves and all the other ingredients apart from the carp. Let boil until the vegetables are tender. Then add the fish fillets. Bring to the simmer, then take off heat and cover the pot; remove from the pot and place in the middle of a platter, surrounded by vegetables and potatoes.

ALTERNATIVE METHOD

Peel the carrots and turnip, keeping the peel for the stock. Peel the potatoes and boil them in water with caraway seeds until soft. Wash the carp, pat dry and fillet them from the spine. Cut slits into the skin with a razor blade or sharp knife. Cut the fillet into 5cm wide strips and set aside.

Soak the carcass (without head) for 1 hour in about 1.5 litres of water. Bring to boil, and while the water is boiling, repeatedly skim off any foam or fat. Add the herbs, garlic, carrot and turnip peel and simmer for about 20 minutes more then add the vinegar. Drain the stock.

In another saucepan, simmer the wine until the liquid is reduced to one quarter of its original volume and mix with about 500ml of stock. Slice the peeled vegetables lengthwise with a peeler in very thin strips (or cut very finely). Halve the spring onions, cutting the green very finely. Place the fillets and vegetables into the spiced stock and simmer for about 5 minutes. Serve the carp on deep, warmed plates with the potatoes. Sprinkle the fish with horseradish and garnish with lovage, sea salt and freshly ground pepper.

FOR THE ROOT VEGETABLES

3 carrots
3 parsnips
½ celeriac, peeled and cut into 2 cm cubes
½ turnip peeled, cut into 2 cm cubes
2 tbsp rapeseed oil
clear honey, to drizzle

Heat oven to 200°C/400°F/gas 6. Toss all the veg with the oil and salt and pepper in a large roasting tin then roast for 40 minutes until starting to soften and turn golden. Remove the tin from the oven, drizzle the veg with honey and return to the oven for 10–20 minutes more until golden.

FOR THE POTATOES

100g new potatoes, peeled
4 tbsp rapeseed oil
3 tsp caraway seeds, crushed
sea salt to taste

Place the potatoes in a pan of salted water, bring to the boil and simmer for 10 minutes. Drain and leave until cool enough to handle, then halve lengthways. Heat the rapeseed oil in a large frying pan over a medium heat, add the potatoes and sauté until soft and golden brown. Stir in the caraway seeds and allow them to toast briefly. Sprinkle on some sea salt and serve.

WINE

Grüner Veltliner Renner is a late-harvested white wine from the Cistercian-owned monastery at Schloss Gobelsburg in the Kamptal region of Eastern Austria. This rich, spicy, creamy-textured wine with lively, fresh acidity, provided the perfect balance to complement the subtle flavours of the Styrian carp.

ROAST PARTRIDGE WITH CABBAGE PARCELS

SERVES 6

The trick with partridge is to make sure you don't overcook it otherwise you'll find the meat is just too tough. These birds really don't need long in the oven and are best served pink and juicy. The key is to make sure you keep checking the bird regularly when you're cooking, and it's also important to rest the bird – usually for about 5 minutes. If cooked right, you'll get a lovely rich, robust, intense flavour that just sings of winter comfort. If you're buying partridge, the best place to seek the freshest wild birds is from a local game dealer, butcher, farm shop or farmers' market. Don't be afraid to ask their advice when you're shopping. Most of them should also be able to give you guidance on how to cook it. When cooking partridge, the key is to keep it simple. This is a bird that doesn't need a lot of fuss. Young partridge is superb simply roasted or grilled and served with a lovely seasonal match of winter vegetables, or that classic combination of bacon and cabbage.

3 oven-ready partridges
3 rashers of bacon
olive oil for cooking
sea salt and ground black pepper
150g butter

Heat the oven to 180°C/350°F/gas 4. To prepare the partridges, take a small, sharp knife and cut down either side of the wishbone and remove it. Wrap the bacon rashers around the back of the partridges and tie with string (but not too tightly). Heat a non-stick ovenproof frying pan over a medium-high heat and add a drizzle of olive oil. Season the partridges all over with salt and pepper and place in the pan. Turn the birds as necessary over the heat for 3–4 minutes until they start to take on a lovely golden colour. Add half of the butter, allow it to melt and foam, then spoon over the birds to baste them. Once the birds are coloured all over, put the pan into the oven. Roast for 8–10 minutes until the partridges are just cooked. Transfer the birds to a warm plate and leave to rest for 5 minutes.

FOR THE STUFFED CABBAGE

1 Savoy cabbage
oil
150g lean pork, chopped
150g pork fat, chopped
25g chicken livers, trimmed and finely chopped
2 garlic cloves, peeled and crushed
2 tbsp mix of tarragon, chives and flat-leaf parsley, chopped
6 tsp brandy
1 small egg, beaten
salt and freshly ground black pepper

Remove twelve unblemished outer leaves from the cabbage, wash thoroughly and blanch for 1 minute in boiling water to soften. Remove with a slotted spoon and set aside. To make the stuffing, mince together the pork, pork fat, chicken livers, garlic, herbs, brandy and egg. Combine thoroughly, then season and stir to combine. Divide the stuffing into portions. Take one cabbage leaf, drizzle with oil and in the centre mound up one portion of the stuffing and put the parcel on a square of doubled cling-film. Pull the four corners in together to make a tight parcel and then twist so that the cling-film tightens around the stuffing, gathering it into a ball. Repeat with the remaining leaves to make 6 balls in total. Place the cabbage balls, in their cling-film, in a steamer over boiling water. Cover with a lid and steam for 20 minutes.

Remove the bacon from the birds. Cut off the legs, then, using a sharp knife, take the breasts off the carcasses. Remove the skin from the legs and breasts. Arrange a cabbage parcel on each plate with one leg and one breast and drizzle over the resting juices from the tray. Garnish with watercress and serve.

WINE

A rich, red Romanée-Conti from the Côte de Nuits region of Burgundy. One of the great aristocratic wines of Burgundy, it was even hailed in 1780 by the Archbishop of Paris as being like 'velvet and satin in bottles'.

FROMAGE

English Stilton, Emmenthal, Edam, Strachino, Brie de Meaux.

WINE

The wine served with the cheese was a sweet, velvety, 25-year-old vintage port, from the Douro Valley in Northern Portugal.

ORANGE-FLOWER AND PINK CHAMPAGNE JELLY

Serves 6

Carême's *pièce de résistance*: an enormous cake constructed from sugar and marzipan in the shape of the Hofburg Imperial Palace. Carême's fantastic cake was accompanied by one of his other great specialities, a delicate orange-flower and pink champagne jelly.

FOR THE ORANGE-FLOWER AND PINK CHAMPAGNE JELLY

5 leaves gelatine
750ml rosé champagne
6 tsp caster sugar
orange-flower water to taste

Place the gelatine leaves in a bowl of cold water for 5 minutes or until soft. Squeeze the leaves and discard the water. Put 200ml pink champagne into a bowl that fits snugly over a pan of boiling water; add the gelatine and sugar and heat gently until the gelatine has dissolved. Remove from the heat, add the remaining champagne and pour into a jug. Pour jelly into the glasses until each glass is almost full. Refrigerate until set.

WINE

These desserts were washed down with glasses of the equally famous Château d'Yquem, often described as the greatest sweet wine in the world, from the village of Sauternes in the St Emilion region of France.

Five

ARCHDUKE FRANZ FERDINAND'S DINNER IN SARAJEVO

27 June 1914
Hotel Bosna, Ilidža,
Sarajevo

THE GUESTS

ARCHDUKE FRANZ FERDINAND

DUCHESS SOPHIE,
his wife

*Military, civic, political and
religious leaders from Sarajevo*

Archduke Franz Ferdinand would have liked nothing better than a discreet Saturday evening dinner with his beloved wife Sophie, followed by a quiet getaway the next morning. He hated being in Sarajevo. The city was in a febrile state; there had been rowdy anti-Austrian demonstrations throughout the week. Bosnia and Herzegovina had been occupied by Austria-Hungary since 1878, and as the heir to the imperial throne, the archduke was a hated figure to nationalist Serbs. Indeed, dissident nationalists and terrorists were known to be active in the area and local officials had explicitly advised him to cancel tomorrow's planned visit to Sarajevo.

Yes, to follow their advice and his own instincts, that was what he wanted. He had completed his two-day inspection of major military exercises in the Bosnian hills – the prime reason for his visit. He had already pressed the flesh with the locals at a bazaar that afternoon, and the duchess had completed a tour of schools and orphanages. Surely his duty was fulfilled? Yet here he was, at an opulent dinner in the luxurious Hotel Bosna with dignitaries fawning on him, persuading him that he must stay a little longer, that the people loved him so much they would be disappointed if he didn't. There was also the grim, disappointed face, lurking in the back of his mind and waiting for him at home, of his uncle, the Habsburg Emperor Franz Joseph, the man who wanted to remind any troublemakers of his empire's power and its right to rule in the Balkans. It was too much. He would fight no longer. He gave in at the dinner table and agreed to go to Sarajevo. History could have been markedly different had he not changed his mind. For, unknown to him, an assassin was waiting for him in the city.

The next morning, two bullets fired by Gavrilo Princip, a skinny, 19-year-old student, would set in motion a train of events that shaped the world we live in today. The First World War, the Second World War, the partition of Europe and even the Cold War and its conclusion all trace their origins to the pistol shots that rang out that day. The assassination of the archduke and his wife, two days short of their 14th wedding anniversary, would change the course of history and catapult Europe into a catastrophic world war. The great Prussian statesman Otto von Bismarck, the man mainly responsible for the unification of Germany in 1871, was quoted as saying at the end of his life that 'One day the great European War will come out of some damned foolish thing in the Balkans'. It happened just as he predicted.

*   *   *

Before departing for the Balkans, the corpulent, 51-year-old archduke and his wife had spent their final evening together in the Austrian capital staying in the building he described as his 'Vienna apartment' – the magnificent baroque Belvedere Palace. It was Tuesday 23 June 1914. The next morning Franz Ferdinand took his leave of Sophie, who would travel separately to Sarajevo, while he boarded a train to Trieste. He was moody and concerned about the possible danger of visiting a part of the empire known for its Serbian opposition to the Austro-Hungarians. Indeed, anti-Austrian demonstrations had been held in Sarajevo only that week. But his uncle, the emperor, was adamant. It was necessary to remind the world that Bosnia and Herzegovina, which had been annexed from Turkey in 1908, were now part of the mighty Austro-Hungarian empire that stretched from Bohemia in the north as far as Lviv (in modern Ukraine) to the east, Trento (now in Italy) to the west and Sarajevo in the south. On the morning of their departure from Vienna, the couple spent a long time praying on their knees before the altar in the chapel of the Belvedere Palace.

No doubt, as his train sped towards Graz, where he had been born, the sullen Franz Ferdinand contemplated the many assassination attempts that had been carried out against his family. He may even have thought of the execution by firing squad of his uncle the Emperor Maximilian in Mexico in 1867, following the collapse of the Second Mexican Empire. The Habsburgs had lived through troubled times, but Franz Joseph had been on the imperial throne now for more than 60 years and his nephew had inherited all of the arrogance that came with his role as heir to the monarchy and access to its untrammelled wealth and power. He was intelligent, but outspoken in his views, known to loathe all Hungarians as 'infamous liars' and to regard southern Slavs as sub-humans, referring to the population of newly independent Serbia as 'those pigs'.[1]

Franz Ferdinand was a Catholic conservative who believed in the central power of the Habsburgs and had a tendency to clash with other leaders. While sympathetic to the demands of ethnic minorities in Bohemia, Croatia and Bosnia, he was openly aggressive when it came to dealing with Hungarians. In 1904 he wrote that 'The Hungarians are all rabble, regardless of whether they are minister or duke, cardinal or burgher, peasant, hussar, domestic servant, or revolutionary'. Indeed he regarded Hungarian nationalism as a revolutionary threat to the Habsburg dynasty and was furious when officers of the 9th Hussar Regiment (which he commanded) spoke Hungarian in his presence, despite the fact that it was their official regimental language. In fact the reason he had decided to take the longer scenic route to Sarajevo by train and boat, while his wife Sophie went directly by train from Vienna, was because he refused to travel through any part of the empire that was controlled from Budapest. Franz Ferdinand knew that his visit to Sarajevo would ignite strong passions and he had even stated in Vienna that 'Down there they will throw bombs at us'.

In Trieste he boarded the Austro-Hungarian flagship vessel *Viribus Unitis* (Strength in Unity) and set sail along what is now the spectacular Croatian coast. He would have enjoyed the cooling sea breezes as his ship sailed south, cutting a path through the deep azure of the Adriatic and the blistering summer heat. Arriving in the port of Ploče he transferred onto a smaller vessel, the *Dalmat*, which could navigate up the Neretva River to Metković on the border of Bosnia-Herzegovina. In Metković he boarded a train for the final leg of his journey to Ilidža.

The train stopped in Mostar, a Bosnian town which, like Sarajevo, boasted churches, synagogues and mosques side by side, where a large crowd gave him a warm and enthusiastic welcome. Encouraged by this reception, he travelled on to Ilidža where he was once again reunited with Sophie, who had arrived earlier. It was Thursday 25 June, and the couple rested in the Bosna Hotel as the archduke prepared for his military inspection on the following day.

*　　*　　*

Franz Ferdinand and Sophie were a happy couple. Theirs was a love-match that had caused great controversy in Vienna. Although a distant relative of the Habsburgs and the Hohenzollerns, Countess Sophie Chotek was deemed to be a commoner by comparison to the high and mighty Habsburg-Lorraines. In the Austro-Hungarian Empire it was forbidden for anyone to marry a member of the imperial household unless they were a part of one of the reigning or formerly reigning royal dynasties of Europe. But in 1894 Franz Ferdinand met Sophie at a ball in Prague and from that moment on he would not consider marriage to anyone else.

Emperor Franz Joseph was horrified, and it was only after the inter-vention of the Pope, Tsar Nicholas of Russia and Emperor Wilhelm II of Germany, who argued that the controversy was undermining the stability of the Austro-Hungarian Empire, that the ageing monarch relented. Nevertheless, he insisted that Sophie would not be allowed to ride in state carriages with her husband, nor would she be able to sit in royal boxes in theatres. Indeed, in most circumstances she would not normally be allowed to appear in public beside her husband. The marriage was to be morganatic, meaning none of their descendants could succeed to the imperial throne. For the rest of his life the emperor referred to the countess as 'the scullery maid' (she had previously been lady-in-waiting to the Duchess of Teschen) and he always regretted allowing the marriage. Franz Ferdinand and Sophie were married on 1 July 1900 in Bohemia, with none of the royal household in attendance.

Nonetheless, despite these difficulties, the archduke adored his wife and wrote in a touching letter in 1904: 'The most intelligent thing I've ever done in my life has been the marriage to my Soph. She is everything to me: my wife, my adviser, my doctor, my warner, in a word: my entire happiness. Now, after four years, we love each other as on our first year of marriage and our happiness has not been marred for a single second.'

By the time the ill-fated couple travelled to Sarajevo in 1914 they had three children: Princess Sophie of Hohenberg (born 1901), Maximilian, Duke of Hohenberg (born 1902) and Prince Ernst of Hohenberg (born 1904). Franz Ferdinand, who, despite his many shortcomings was a great family man, had remarked to several people that he had a foreboding of something terrible happening in Bosnia which would leave his children fatherless. But he had no choice but to obey the emperor's orders and attend the military manoeuvres in the hills above Sarajevo.

*   *   *

On the evening of Saturday 27 June, at the grand gala dinner in the Bosna Hotel in Ilidža, the warnings of the local dignitaries reignited the archduke's fears. He wondered if he should call off the next morning's proposed visit to Sarajevo. But Bosnia's Governor-General, Oskar Potiorek, frustrated at the implied criticism of his security arrangements, insisted that he must go. He said that it was only a morning visit and would involve a short speech after which the archduke could be on his way. Even Sophie argued that they would be perfectly safe in Sarajevo. In conversation over dinner with Dr Josip Sunaric, the Bosnian Croat leader, she said, 'Everywhere we have gone here, we have been treated with so much friendliness – and by every last Serb, too – with so much cordiality and warmth that we are very happy about it.'

The dinner was lavish by any standards. There were 41 guests, including Bosnia's top military, religious and civil officials. The French menu consisted of *Potage Régence*, a white soup made with ingredients including chicken, veal, herbs and celery, accompanied by a dry madeira, a fortified Portuguese wine from the Madeira islands, rather like sherry. The soup course was followed by *Soufflés délicieux*, accompanied by a rich Château Léoville claret from one of Bordeaux's greatest vineyards in Saint Julien. The fish course was locally caught trout from the Bosno River prepared as *Blanquettes de truites à la gelée*, served cold in a horseradish and samphire cream sauce. This was accompanied by a crisp, dry Forster Langenmorgen 1908, a Riesling Kabinett trocken white wine from the Pfalz (Palatinate) region of Germany.

The main course consisted of a *Pièce de boeuf et d'agneau*, cold-carved roast beef and spring lamb washed down with a Pommery Gréno sec champagne from Reims. The guests were now offered a refreshing sorbet made from sour cherries, to clear their palates, accompanied by a sweet, high-alcohol Tokaji Szamorodni 1901, from the Tokaj region of Hungary. This was followed by *Poulardes de Styrie, salade, compote* and *Asperges en branches*, a light course of fattened chickens from Styria in Austria, with salad, apple sauce and fresh asparagus, accompanied by a spectacular Chateau Margaux claret from the exceptional 1900 vintage. The dessert consisted of *Crème aux ananas en surprise*, a pineapple cream, with *fromage* and *Glaces varies* also on offer, washed down with a fabulous local Žilavka Ausbruch, Gjorgjo & Jelačić, a deliciously sweet local dessert wine from Mostar. It was certainly a banquet fit for imperial royalty.[2]

As the evening wore on, Franz Conrad von Hötzendorf, the chief of the general staff, who had presided over the military exercises, thanked the archduke and slipped off quietly at nine o'clock, following the last of the toasts. The dinner was coming to an end and many of the guests began to leave for Sarajevo. The archduke dearly would have loved to slip away as well, abandoning the next day's visit to Sarajevo. He was heard to remark, 'Thank God this Bosnian trip is over.' But his advisers warned him that if he skipped the planned visit to Sarajevo it would be seen as an insult and Austrian prestige in Bosnia would be seriously undermined. They claimed that all that remained of the Sunday programme was a brief visit to the city hall, a stop off at the museum and lunch at Konak, the governor's mansion.

Nine separate extravagant courses and six opulent wines may have helped to weaken the archduke's resolve. Famously fond of his food and wine, as his expanding waistline clearly demonstrated, Franz Ferdinand would certainly have overindulged during this lavish banquet. It was pointed out to him that 28 June was St Vitus day or 'Vidovdan', the highly charged and sensitive anniversary of the Ottoman victory over the Serbs at the 1389 Battle of Kosovo. Although the Serbs were routed at this decisive battle, they had fought bravely, so now the anniversary of this great defeat had been turned into a celebration of Serbian courage against foreign invaders. It seems that no-one had thought to tell the archduke that his visit to Sarajevo would be seen as a celebration of Habsburg rule over the Serbs, on the very day the Serbs would be feasting to honour the patriots who had fought the cruel Turkish invaders centuries before.

This was indeed a bad omen. The day also had some painful significance for the archduke and his spouse, for it was on 28 June 1900 that the Emperor Franz Joseph had forced him to sign an oath of renunciation stipulating that any offspring from his marriage to Sophie would never be able to succeed to the Habsburg throne. The archduke's visit to Sarajevo would be regarded as provocative, if not downright reckless. But the die was cast. The entreaties of his advisers, combined with the anguished plea of Governor-General Potiorek were evidently enough to overcome his fears. The archduke and his wife would visit Sarajevo the next day, where their assassin, Gavrilo Princip, was waiting.

The morning of Sunday 28 June was sunny and warm. As his chosen uniform for the day, Franz Ferdinand had selected his sky-blue cavalry general's tunic with a gold collar adorned with three silver stars. The uniform included black trousers with a red stripe. He topped this off with a black helmet adorned with green peacock feathers. The duchess wore a long, white, silk dress decorated with red and white roses. She had a blood-red sash wound around her ample waist. Her outfit was completed with an ermine stole and a white, wide-brimmed hat. The couple breakfasted then attended an early Mass in the Bosna Hotel, in a room that had been specially converted into a chapel. Franz Ferdinand then sent a telegram to his children informing them that 'Papi' and 'Mami' would be home on Tuesday and couldn't wait to see them again.

The Bosna Hotel was richly decorated with Turkish scimitars, Persian rugs and other Ottoman kitsch, but the ultra-Catholic Franz Ferdinand had grown weary of this Muslim-Oriental Ilidža glitz and was keen to get the visit to Sarajevo over and done with so that they could return home. The couple set off for the station and the train that would take them to Sarajevo a few minutes before 9.30 a.m.

*   *   *

The visit to Sarajevo had been well publicised in the press. Local newspapers even carried detailed plans of the route the motorcade would take through the city and crowds had gathered to greet the archduke and duchess. Dissidents, who passionately hated the Habsburgs, had studied newspaper information about the planned visit closely. 'Unification or Death', popularly known as 'the Black Hand', was a secret military society formed on 9 May 1911 with the aim of uniting all of the territories with a South Slavic majority not ruled by either Serbia or Montenegro. Young Serbs, many from Sarajevo, had been radicalised in the cafés of Belgrade and were actively encouraged to join the Black Hand, led by Colonel Dragutin Dimitrijević, nicknamed Apis ('The Bull') after the Egyptian god.

Apis was head of Serbia's intelligence services and one of the most powerful men in the country at the time. He was also a violent conspirator with impressive and bloodthirsty credentials, who had played a key role in Belgrade's 1903 palace coup, which saw the king and queen not merely murdered but butchered and their body parts cast onto the street below. Serbia had thus earned a reputation as a 'rogue state', and Apis was at the centre of the secret cabal that actually ran things at the top of Serbia's power structure. Dimitrijević also ran extensive agent networks inside Habsburg territory, mainly Serbs – there were more Serbs living in Austria-Hungary in 1914 than in Serbia itself – who were recruited for espionage, subversion, and sometimes terrorism. Under Apis, Belgrade was waging its own version of 'special war' in Bosnia, which Serbian nationalists hoped to liberate from Habsburg rule.

Danilo Ilić, a Sarajevo teacher, had recruited Gavrilo Princip and his two friends Trifko Grabez and Nedeljko Čabrinović to the Black Hand.

He was persuasive, and Princip and his associates agreed to join the assassination plot. They had been targeted by Ilić because they came from Sarajevo and were familiar with the city; they were also known for their opposition to the Austrians. Milan Ciganovic, the weapons instructor for the Black Hand, trained all three of them in the remote Morava Valley in Serbia. They learned how to fire guns, throw bombs, blow up bridges and much more. One month before the arrival of the archduke, the trio left Serbia and travelled by separate routes back to Sarajevo, where they melted into local society.

On the evening of Saturday 27 June, while the archduke and his wife were being wined and dined at their lavish banquet in Ilidža, Ilić invited the assassins to dinner in his home in Sarajevo. He handed out their weapons and gave each a vial of cyanide, with instructions that they must not be taken alive. He then introduced them to three other men who would also be part of the assassination attempt. They were two high-school students from Sarajevo and a Muslim man in his late twenties, Muhamed Mehmedbašić. The next morning, the six assassins met with Ilić one last time. His final words to them were, 'Be strong, be brave.' They then positioned themselves at various points along the route the archduke's motorcade would take.

Just before 10 a.m. Franz Ferdinand and Sophie arrived at the railway station in Sarajevo and were met by Governor-General Potiorek and a guard of honour that the archduke duly inspected. While Emperor Franz Joseph forbade Sophie from riding in the same car as her husband in Vienna, this ban did not apply to provincial outposts like Sarajevo and the two were ushered into an open-topped 1911 Gräf & Stift *Bois de Boulogne* phaeton limousine, built in Vienna. There were six cars in the motorcade and the archducal couple occupied the second, together with Potiorek. Next to the driver, Lojka, sat Count Franz von Harrach, head of security. The motorcade would be routed along the river to the city hall. The six assassins were strategically positioned along the route. Although there were some 60 police officers lining the streets, bizarrely Franz Ferdinand had given instructions that the military should stay out of Sarajevo that Sunday, perhaps not wishing to inflame anti-Austrian passions. It was a fatal mistake.

The motorcade drove past the first two assassins along the riverside, one of the high-school students and Mehmedbašić; both were paralysed with fear and did nothing. But around 10.12 a.m., as the cars drove along the Appel Quay, Čabrinović, who was standing by the river, primed his bomb and threw it. Lojka saw it coming and put his foot down in time. The car roared forward but the bomb bounced off the trunk and exploded beneath the car following behind. An Austrian officer in the car and several bystanders were severely injured. Čabrinović swallowed his cyanide and jumped into the shallow waters of the River Miljacka, but the poison only made him vomit and he was quickly arrested.

The motorcade raced off towards the city hall, leaving behind the smoking wreckage of the third vehicle and a deep crater in the road. The remaining assassins lost their nerve. One later told his trial: 'I didn't pull out the revolver because I saw that the Duchess was there. I felt sorry for her.'

The motorcade was now moving at such speed that Gavrilo Princip decided it was impossible to attempt an accurate shot. Dejected and convinced that the assassination plot had failed, he made his way to a shop to buy something to eat. When the motorcade arrived at the city hall several of the officials were doubtful whether the trip should proceed further. But Governor-General Potiorek had no reservations. 'What, do you think my city is full of assassins?' he said. 'We will continue,' Franz Ferdinand agreed. 'That fellow is clearly insane,' he said, referring to the assassin who had thrown the bomb. 'Let us proceed with our programme.'

The mayor of Sarajevo, Fehim Effendi Čurčić, who had been in the first car, began a nervous speech of welcome. Franz Ferdinand, still understandably flustered from the assassination attempt, interrupted, furiously: 'I come here as your guest and you people greet me with bombs!' The duchess gripped his arm and whispered into her husband's ear. He immediately calmed down and asked the mayor to continue. The archduke then read his speech from paper stained with the blood of one of the officers who had been injured in the bomb blast, saying that the cheers of the people of Sarajevo clearly signalled their relief at his survival of the attempted assassination.

The original plan was for the archduke to visit the museum following his speech at the city hall, but he decided that he wanted to see Potiorek's wounded adjutant in hospital. Sophie had not intended accompanying her husband to the museum, but now she agreed to join him in the rearranged hospital visit. So the route for the motorcade was altered. Unfortunately no-one remembered to tell Lojka, the driver of the archduke's car. As a result, when the motorcade set off from the city hall, Lojka headed for the National Museum, turning right off Appel Quay into Franz Joseph Street. Potiorek and security chief von Harrach yelled at him that he had taken a wrong turning. Flustered, Lojka stopped the car and began to reverse back out of Franz Joseph Street onto Appel Quay at the junction with the Lateiner Bridge.

Gavrilo Princip had just emerged from Moritz Schiller's cafe on the same corner of Franz Joseph Street when to his amazement he saw the open-topped limousine reversing steadily towards him. He pulled his pistol and ran forward, firing twice at point-blank range. The first shot went through the door of the car and struck the duchess in the abdomen. A second bullet struck the archduke's neck. Harrach, who had been travelling on the running board of the limousine, saw the duchess slump across her husband, her head between his knees. He heard the archduke say: 'Sopherl! Sopherl! Sterbe nicht! Bleibe am Leben für unsere Kinde!' ('Sophie, Sophie, don't die, stay alive for our children!')[3] Harrach pulled out a handkerchief and pressed it against the bloody wound on the archduke's neck, asking him if he was OK. 'It's nothing,' replied Franz Ferdinand. 'It's nothing,' he repeated five or six times, his voice becoming weaker and weaker, until blood bubbled from his mouth in a final death rattle. It was just after 11 a.m.

Gavrilo Princip was knocked to the ground by outraged bystanders, who tore his pistol and packet of cyanide from his hands. He was probably saved from lynching by his arrest. Meanwhile, the motorcade raced back to the governor's mansion, where two priests were called to perform the last rites for Franz Ferdinand and Sophie.

*　　*　　*

On 1 July 1914, the date of their 14th wedding anniversary, the bodies were transported to Trieste by the same battleship which had brought Franz Ferdinand part of the way to Sarajevo, the *Viribus Unitis*. They were then taken the rest of the way to Vienna by special train. The funeral was held in the Hofburg Palace on 3 July. Alfred, 2nd Prince of Montenuovo, Emperor Franz Joseph's chamberlain, had been given the task of organising the funeral. He hated the archduke and duchess with a passion, and with the emperor's connivance, decided to turn the funeral into a massive and vicious humiliation.

Even though most foreign royalty had planned to attend, they were now told the funeral was to be private and for members of the imperial family only, apart from Kaiser Wilhelm II, who was invited and who wanted to use the funeral as an informal peace conference to prevent the war that everyone now anticipated. However, at the last minute the Kaiser pulled out of the funeral, apprehensive for his own safety. The last chance at securing peace was thus lost. Even the dead couple's three children were only allowed to view their parents in their open coffins after the public viewing and vigils had ended. Their grief had been terrible, with 13-year-old Princess Sophie being heard to sob that God had taken their parents together as their father could never have lived without their mother.

To add to this very public snub, Montenuovo ordered the officer corps not to salute the funeral procession. He even tried, unsuccessfully, to make the children foot the bill for the funeral. The archduke and duchess were finally interred at Artstetten Castle, near the Wochau valley in Lower Austria, the traditional summer residence of the Habsburgs, because Sophie could not be buried at the imperial crypt in the Hofburg Palace, Vienna.

As the funeral bells rang out across Vienna, the assassination sent shockwaves throughout Europe. Austro-Hungarian officials quickly discovered the Serbian roots of the plot and declared war on Serbia on 28 July 1914, exactly one month after the assassination. Despite the clear animosity that existed between Emperor Franz Joseph and his nephew, he was outraged at the manner of his nephew's death and grasped at the chance to invade Serbia. War began in the Balkans. The spark that ignited the First World War had been lit. The Russians, who had been strong allies of the Serbs, now began to mobilise their troops and, fearing reprisals, the Austro-Hungarians sought to activate their alliance with Germany as a counter-balance. The Germans, in turn, sent an ultimatum to Moscow, warning them to stop their mobilisation; their warning was ignored. On 1 August 1914, Germany and Russia, declared war on each other, dragging in Britain and France, who sided with the Russians.

The Germans moved first, deciding to defeat the French before turning their attention to the Russian forces assembling in the east. But the French offered strong resistance and were soon joined by the British. The long and catastrophic bloodletting of the trenches on the Western Front had begun and soon the world would be drawn into an unprecedented slaughter that had begun with the firing of two bullets in Sarajevo, resulting in two deaths that could have been avoided but for a fateful decision taken over a lavish dinner the evening before.

*   *   *

Gavrilo Princip never lived to see the end of the world war he helped to start. Avoiding the death penalty due to his youth, he was sentenced to 20 years' imprisonment and died of tuberculosis in jail in Sarajevo on 28 April 1918. All of the assassins were eventually rounded up and several aged over 20 at the time of the assassinations were executed in 1915. Their deaths went largely unnoticed in the general carnage that had been unleashed across the European continent. But a new phenomenon had also been unleashed. By the end of the First World War, every major industrial nation had recognised the strategic and military importance of oil. The war had witnessed the rise to global prominence of the military–industrial complex with oil as its key component. The role of oil and the blood-soaked violence that its exploitation has generated continues to this day. As we shall see in the next chapter, the domination of oil resources by a handful of ruthless international conglomerates was set in concrete at a secret gathering of the world's four leading oil company executives in the summer of 1928. In the unlikely setting of a remote hunting estate in the Scottish Highlands, the 'Four Horsemen' as they came to be known, set up an illegal cartel that regulated the price of oil for years to come.

MENU

Potage Régence
Soufflés Délicieux
Blanquettes de Truites à la Gelée

Pièce de Boeuf et d'Agneau

Sour Cherry Lambic Sorbet

Poulardes de Styrie, Salade, Compote

Crème aux Ananas en Surprise

Fromage

Glaces Variés

Dry madeira
Château Léoville
1908 Forster Langenmorgen
Pommery Gréno sec Champagne
1901 Tokaji Szamorodni
1900 Chateau Margaux Pillet-Will Claret
Žilavka Ausbruch, Gjorgjo & Jelačić

POTAGE RÉGENCE (WHITE SOUP)

SERVES 6

Potage Régence or White Soup is based on a very old recipe usually involving a veal and chicken broth, egg yolks, ground almonds and cream. It originated in Scotland where it was called *soupe-a-la-reine*, a reminder of the 'Auld Alliance' between Scotland and France. A more elaborate version, Lorraine soup (possibly a corruption of La Reine) appeared frequently on fashionable dinner and supper menus. In this case it would be highly appropriate as the Archduke was a member of the Habsburg-Lorraine royal family.

1 cooked boiling chicken, meat picked off the bone and chopped
½ kg veal flank poached, left to cool and then sliced
2 litres white chicken stock
2 medium white onions, chopped
1 leek, white only, chopped
2 celery stalks, sliced
½ turnip, chopped
80g washed white rice
salt
pepper
100ml double cream
10g chopped sage, thyme, parsley, tarragon and chives

In a saucepot pop in chicken stock and all vegetables and bring to boil. Simmer for 15 minutes. Add the rice and bring to the simmer. Simmer till the rice is cooked. Take off heat and puree in blender. Put in a clean pan; season with salt pepper and herbs. Add chopped chicken meat and sliced veal and double cream, bring to boil. Take off and serve. If too thick adjust with stock.

WINE

Dry madeira, a fortified Portuguese wine from the Madeira islands.

Left. Prince Charles Edward Stuart ('Bonnie Prince Charlie'), leader of the Jacobite cause, which sought to re-establish the Stuarts as monarchs of England, Scotland and Ireland.

Below. Old Culloden House, where Bonnie Prince Charlie hosted a lavish feast for his commanders before the Battle of Culloden. His foot soldiers were to fight on empty stomachs. (© Cairns Aitken).

Above. The Battle of Culloden. Bonnie Prince Charlie's ignominious defeat signalled the end of the Jacobite dream.
(Alamy Stock Photo)

Right. Major-General Edward Braddock, Commander-in-Chief of King George II's forces in North America.
(Library of Congress)

The Battle of Monongahela, 1755: Braddock's defeat. (North Wind Picture Archives/Alamy Stock Photo)

Carlyle House, Alexandria, where General Braddock presided over a dinner during which the concept of Britain levying a tax on its American colonies was floated for the first time.

Above left. Thomas Jefferson, at whose New York residence he and James Madison sealed a bargain with Alexander Hamilton which led to the creation of Washington D.C. as US capital. An extravagant meal with five exquisite wines helped them win Hamilton over.

Above right. Alexander Hamilton, a Founding Father and the US's first treasury secretary. (Library of Congress)

Left. James Madison, 'father of the Constitution' and fourth President of the USA. (Library of Congress)

Francis I, Emperor of Austria, host of the Congress of Vienna, which met to divide up the spoils of war and re-draw the boundaries of Europe after Napoleon's defeat in 1814.

Left. Prince Charles-Maurice de Talleyrand-Périgord, who represented the defeated French republic at the Congress of Vienna.
(Pictorial Press Ltd/Alamy Stock Photo)

Below. Ministers, diplomats and statesmen locked in negotiations at the Congress of Vienna.

Archduke Franz Ferdinand and his wife, Sophie.

Franz Ferdinand and Sophie arrive in Sarajevo, June 1914. (Classic Image/Alamy Stock Photo)

The Hotel Bosna, Ilidža, the venue for a grand gala dinner at which Franz Ferdinand was warned not to go to Sarajevo the next morning. Had he heeded this advice, the course of 20th-century history could well have been very different.

Achnacarry Castle in the Scottish Highlands, where the oil cartel that was the forerunner of OPEC was born over several days of hunting, fishing, shooting and, of course, eating.
(© Cairns Aitken)

William Larimer Mellon of Gulf Oil.
(Library of Congress)

Henri Deterding of Royal Dutch Shell.
(Ullstein Bild/Getty Images)

Above left. Sir John Cadman of BP.
(Planet News Archive/SSPL/Getty Images)

Above right. Walter Teagle of Standard
Oil. (Atomic/Alamy Stock Photo)

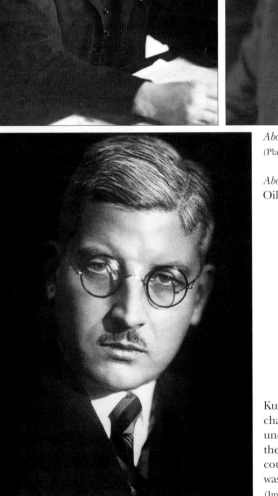

Kurt von Schuschnigg, Austrian
chancellor, who shared an
uncomfortable lunch with Hitler, at
the end of which he signed away his
country's independence and Austria
was absorbed into the Third Reich.
(Imagno/Hulton Archive/Getty Images)

Hitler's Berghof mountain retreat on the Obersalzberg near Berchtesgaden, where the Führer enjoyed light lunches of barley broth, semolina noodles, and egg and green salad. Non-vegetarian guests were offered heartier fare. (Heinrich Hoffman/Hulton Archive/Getty Images)

Hitler arrives in Vienna, March 1938, to a rapturous welcome.

(Keystone Pictures USA/Alamy Stock Photo)

Stalin, Roosevelt and Churchill at the Tehran Summit, November 1943.
(ITAR-TASS Photo Agency/Alamy Stock Photo)

Churchill presenting the Sword of Stalingrad to Stalin. A deeply emotional moment was
ruined when seconds later Marshal Voroshilov dropped the sword on his own toes.
(Hulton Deutsch/Corbis Historical/Getty Images)

Churchill's birthday banquet on 30 November 1943 at the British legation, Tehran.
(IWM/Getty Images)

President Richard Nixon meeting Mao Zedong in his residence in Zhongnanhai, Beijing.
(Keystone-France/Gamma-Keystone/Getty Images)

Nixon at the banquet in the Great Hall of the People, Beijing, admiring Chinese Premier Zhou Enlai's dexterity with chopsticks. (World History Archive/Alamy Stock Photo)

Egyptian President Anwar Sadat, US President Jimmy Carter and Israeli Prime Minister
Menachem Begin mark the signing of the Egypt–Israel Peace Treaty in Washington D.C. on
26 March 1979. The day concluded with a State banquet at the White House.

(David Rubinger/The LIFE Images Collection/Getty Images)

Sadat, Carter and Begin in more relaxed mode at Aspen Lodge, Camp David.

SOUFFLÉS DÉLICIEUX

SERVES 6

70g strong Cheddar
50g Gruyère, grated
100g unsalted butter, plus extra melted butter for greasing
handful of fresh fine white breadcrumbs
100g plain flour
1 tsp English mustard powder
good pinch of cayenne pepper
400ml milk
6 large free-range eggs, separated

Preheat the oven to 200°C/400°F/gas 6. Place a baking sheet in the oven to heat up. Brush 6 x 250ml ramekins with melted butter and sprinkle with the breadcrumbs. Melt the butter in a pan and add the flour, mustard and cayenne pepper. Cook for a couple of minutes, then gradually add the milk, stirring until the mixture comes to the boil. Boil for 2 minutes, until very thick and coming away from the sides of the pan. Take off the heat, stir in the cheese and 6 egg yolks and season well.

In a clean, grease-free bowl, whisk the egg whites until stiff. Mix a spoonful into the cheese mixture to loosen, then gently fold in the rest. Spoon into the ramekins, just up to the rim. Run your finger around the edge of the ramekins. Put on the baking sheet and bake for 8-10 minutes until risen and golden, then serve immediately.

WINE

Château Léoville claret from one of Bordeaux's greatest vineyards in Saint Julien.

BLANQUETTES DE TRUITES À LA GELÉE

SERVES 6

3 brown trout, gutted and filleted
1 litre water
20 black peppercorns
150ml champagne vinegar
salt to taste
sugar to taste
15g fennel seeds
350ml dry white wine
cucumber, peeled and sliced
4 leaves gelatine, soaked in cold water then squeezed out
2 tsp chopped dill
2 tsp chopped parsley

Wash trout. Put water with vinegar, peppercorns, salt, sugar and fennel seeds to boil for about 5 minutes. Add wine and bring to boil. Place in trout fillets and bring to just a boil, then take off heat and leave to cool down and cook in the residual heat of the liquid. Lay the cooled trout in a baking dish. Lay cucumber slices over trout fillets. Strain the cooking liquor and measure; you will only need 600ml. Warm the 600ml up and melt the gelatine in this liquid, then pour into a bowl. Set this bowl over ice in a larger bowl and gently stir till it thickens. As soon as it starts add the chopped herbs and then pour over the trout fillets, let it set in the fridge and then serve.

WINE

Crisp, dry 1908 Forster Langenmorgen, a Riesling Kabinett trocken white wine from the Pfalz (Palatinate) region of Germany.

PIÈCE DE BOEUF ET D'AGNEAU

SERVES 6–12

FOR THE BEEF

1 3-rib joint, either prime rib cut short, or wing rib cut short
salt and freshly ground black pepper
4 large onions, unpeeled but thickly sliced

Preheat the oven to 220°C/425°F/gas 7. Sprinkle the beef joint with salt and pepper. Stand on its end in a roasting tin just large enough for the joint on a bed of thick slices of unpeeled onion (the onion skin gives colour to the juices). If using a meat thermometer, insert into the meat in the thickest part. Transfer to the centre of the preheated oven for 15 minutes, then lower the temperature to 180°C/350°F/gas 4. Roast as per the chart below, basting from time to time. When the meat is done, check the thermometer. Lift out of the tin, loosely cover with foil and leave to rest in a warm place for about 20 minutes before carving. Discard the onion, squeezing any juices into the tin.

Meanwhile, make the gravy. Skim off 3 good tbsp of fat from the roasting tin and reserve. Pour juices into a bowl and put in the fridge to allow the fat to rise to the top. Return the reserved fat to the tin, measure in the flour and whisk over heat. Add the port and stock, then the Worcestershire sauce. Remove fat from the bowl in the fridge. Add juices to the tin with a little gravy browning and whisk until bubbling. Carve beef from the bone down across the grain to serve.

FOR THE GRAVY

12 tbsp fat from the beef
8 tbsp plain flour
750ml port
1 litre beef stock
a dash of Worcestershire sauce
a little gravy browning

ROASTING TIMES

Rare	180°C/350°F/gas 4	15 minutes per 450g
Medium	180°C/350°F/gas 4	20 minutes per 450g
Well done	180°C/350°F/gas 4	25 minutes per 450g

FOR THE LAMB

2kg whole shoulder of lamb
2 tbsp rosemary leaves, finely chopped
3 tbsp rapeseed oil
4 tbsp garlic, chopped
salt and pepper
2 onions, sliced
1.2 litres lamb stock or failing that chicken stock
2 tbsp plain flour
1 tbsp redcurrant jelly

Preheat the oven to 220°C/425°F/gas 7. Put the lamb on a board. Mix the rosemary, oil and garlic together and season well with salt and pepper. Rub over the lamb on both sides. Put the onions and stock into a small roasting tin, put a rack on top then place the lamb on top. Roast in the oven for 30 minutes, or until brown then reduce the temperature to 160°C/325°F/gas 3. Cover the lamb with aluminium foil and continue to roast for 3–4 hours, basting from time to time until completely tender and the meat is falling off the bone. Remove the foil and place the lamb on a plate to rest while you make the gravy. Skim off the fat into a bowl. Spoon two tablespoons of the fat into a saucepan. Sieve the roasting juices and softened onion into a measuring jug. Add boiling water to the jug to make up to 570 ml of liquid. Heat the fat in the saucepan until hot. Add the flour and stir until smooth. Still over the heat, add the roasting juices and whisk until thickened and smooth. Add redcurrant jelly and salt and pepper to taste. Serve with the lamb.

WINE

Pommery Gréno sec champagne.

SOUR CHERRY LAMBIC SORBET

SERVES 6

INGREDIENTS

500g pitted sour cherries
500g granulated sugar
250ml cherry Lambic beer

In a blender, puree the pitted cherries until smooth. Pour into a large pan, add the sugar and bring slowly to a boil making sure you stir it regularly. Once boiling turn to a simmer and simmer for 10 minutes; take off heat and pass through a fine sieve into a bowl. Stir in the cherry Lambic beer. Pour the sorbet base into an ice cream maker and freeze according to the manufacturer's instructions. Once churned, store in a tub with lid in your freezer till service.

WINE

Sweet, high-alcohol, 1901 Tokajer Szamorodner, from the Tokaj region of Hungary.

POULARDES DE STYRIE, SALADE, COMPOTE

SERVES 6

A poulard is a fattened hen, which has not reached sexual maturity, generally a French speciality – the female equivalent of a capon. In this dish served to the Archduke we find spiced chicken with apple sauce and rocket and herb salad.

1 poulard, cleaned
5 Braeburn apples, cored and quartered
8 onions, peeled and cut into large chunks
1 whole head of garlic, peeled and blanched and refreshed 3 times
2 sprigs fresh rosemary
salt and pepper
100ml apple cider
100ml Calvados
4 spring onions, thinly sliced

Preheat your oven to 180°C/gas 4. Toss the apples, onions, garlic and rosemary together in a large bowl. Split it into two roasting pans large enough to hold the chickens. Season the chicken well with salt and pepper and rest it on top of the apple mixture. Pour in the cider and calvados. Roast chicken until a meat thermometer inserted in the thickest part of one of the thighs reads 82°C/180°F, about 20 minutes per pound. As soon as the chicken is cool enough to handle, take out the apple mixture from the pan and arrange the chicken on a bed of the apple (set aside) and surround it with the apple sauce. Garnish with spring onion. This course was served with *aspèrges en branches* – stalks of asparagus served whole.

WINE

1900 Chateau Margaux Pillet-Will. Many experts hailed this luscious claret from Bordeaux as the wine of the century! 1900 Bordeaux was the product of a perfect growing season from start to finish. Margaux wines tend to be deep ruby in colour, perfumed and floral, particularly with notes of violets and lilacs, and soft, silky tannins.

CRÈME AUX ANANAS EN SURPRISE (PINEAPPLE CREAM)

SERVES 6

1 can pineapple (crushed or chunk), drained
150ml sour cream
140ml sweetened condensed milk

Take a large bowl, add the pineapple, sour cream and condensed milk. Mix together well. Refrigerate for 1 hour. Garnish with some dry fruits (optional) and serve cold!

WINE

Žilavka Ausbruch, Gjorgjo & Jelačić, a deliciously sweet dessert wine from Mostar.

FROMAGE

The cheeseboard presented to the Archduke would certainly have included Kashkaval or yellow cheese, which is a hard, sheep's milk cheese typical of the Balkans. The choice may also have included Pule cheese, which is a Serbian cheese made from the milk of Balkan donkeys. A characteristic feature of Serbian cuisine, Pule is not only extremely rare but also the most expensive cheese in the world. Zasavica donkey reserve, about 50 miles from Belgrade produces the donkey cheese by hand-milking a herd of about 100 endangered Balkan donkeys. It takes 25 litres of donkey milk to produce just one kilogram of the white and crumbly smoked cheese.

GLACES VARIÉS

SERVES 6–12

Sweets and ice cream have always been popular in Sarajevo. Traditional Turkish ice cream (*dondurma*), a popular leftover from the Ottoman Empire is made with milk, sugar, salep flour and mastic gum. Salep is a thickening agent – a flour made from the root of a type of orchid. Mastic is the resin of a type of shrub, related to the pistachio tree, with a piney scent and flavour (it is this that's at the heart of mastika liqueur). But, paradoxically, it's more the salep than the mastic that gives Turkish ice cream its famous stretchiness. Turkish ice cream is not only very creamy and super-stretchy (you can even skip with it), it takes a good long while to melt as well. *Dondurma* would almost certainly have been on offer to Franz Ferdinand and his guests.

DONDURMA

6g mastic beads
130g salep flour
1.5 litres full fat milk
500ml double cream
350g caster sugar
ground cinnamon
finely chopped pistachios

You will need to begin this recipe 1 day ahead. Freeze mastic beads for 15 minutes, then using a spice grinder or mortar and pestle, finely grind with a pinch of sugar. Whisk salep with 250ml milk until dissolved. Set aside. Heat remaining milk and cream in a large saucepan over low–medium heat. Whisk in mastic until combined, then add salep mixture. Using a ladle, scoop some of the cream mixture, then from a height, pour back into the pan in a continuous motion; this 'stretches' the mixture. Repeat, stirring constantly, to prevent the mixture burning, for 20 minutes or until thickened. (If you prefer a denser, chewier ice cream, cook for an additional 20 minutes.) Transfer to a bowl, cover the surface closely with cling-film to prevent a skin forming and cool completely.

Churn mixture in an ice cream machine according to the manufacturer's instructions until almost frozen.

Meanwhile, lightly grease 2 x 1 litre loaf tins, then line with cling-film, leaving 5cm overhanging. Pour mixture into pan, cover with overhanging wrap and freeze overnight. To serve, remove ice cream from freezer 5 minutes beforehand. Turn out onto a board and, working quickly, cut into 3cm slices and divide among plates. Dust with cinnamon and scatter with pistachios to serve.

Six

HOW PETROLEUM POLITICS WAS BORN OVER A SCOTTISH BANQUET

28 August 1928
Achnacarry Castle,
Scottish Highlands

THE GUESTS

SIR JOHN CADMAN,
Head of APOC (now BP)

HENRI DETERDING,
Head of Shell

WALTER TEAGLE,
Head of Standard Oil

WILLIAM MELLON,
Founder of Gulf Oil

*These key executives from the world's
four largest oil companies were
known as the 'Four Horsemen'*

The oil had to flow. And the oil had to flow profitably. If such mere things as governments, laws and kings were getting in the way of that, then they had to be subverted. Arrangements had to be made; and what better way of making arrangements than over dinner. A civilised meal in a quiet location – a Scottish country estate, say – where the wine and whisky would flow and where no one could possibly overhear how the diners were changing the balance of power in the world.

*   *   *

In 1927, Henry Ford watched the 15-millionth Model T automobile roll off his assembly line in Highland Park, Michigan. Over the past 19 years his mass-produced success story had put the freedom and status of the motoring dream within the hands of a burgeoning middle class. In the same period world oil production had increased by 1,000 per cent, from 20 million to 200 million TOE (Tonne of Oil Equivalent).

The breakup of the monster monopoly of Standard Oil in 1911 had created several huge powers in the US oil business, and it was said that no one could become President of the United States without guaranteeing the smooth delivery of oil to the refineries and sellers, such was the addiction to this groundbreaking new fossil fuel. Oil companies were becoming more powerful than governments.

Politicians in the major powers understood just how important this black gold was to their nations. During the First World War, Britain and France had literally drawn a line with a pencil on a map to carve up the oil-rich territories of the former Ottoman empire. In 1920, Britain gained control of further territory in the Middle East with its mandates over Palestine and Iraq. Governments were bribed by financial and military guarantees, and land with vast oil resources hidden underground was purchased from the unsuspecting landowners at knockdown prices. Soon, companies like Shell, Esso and APOC were so powerful that they could set the rules for every aspect of oil production, including its export and price.

However, the arbitrary divisions of territory and shady business dealings were causing a backlash. In 1925, Reza Shah, the former prime minister of Iran, deposed Ahmad Shah Qajar, the last shah of the Qajar dynasty, and founded the Pahlavi dynasty. He established a constitutional monarchy that lasted until his son Mohammad Reza Shah Pahlavi was overthrown in 1979 during the Iranian Revolution. Reza Shah introduced many social, economic, and political reforms during his reign, ultimately laying the foundation of the modern Iranian state. The new king was outraged at plummeting royalties from the companies exploiting his oilfields, particularly Anglo Persian (APOC). He was also angry with APOC's major shareholder – the British Government – because it had formally recognised Iraq and was actively preventing Persia from extending its sovereignty over Bahrain.

Tensions were also running high in Mexico, where a clause in the constitution stated that the subsoil belonged to the Mexican state, not to the people who owned the property above it. This posed a direct threat to the oil companies and created a deepening rift between the Mexican and American governments. As tempers flared in 1927 and the possibility of a war between the two countries loomed, 65 per cent of Mexican oil was being produced by Shell, while a further 30 per cent was being produced by a combination of Standard Oil (ESSO), Sinclair, Cities Service and Gulf. As tensions rose in Mexico, so investment in the sector fell, causing a dramatic drop in production and an equally dramatic fall in oil revenues, which the Mexican government blamed squarely on the foreign oil companies.

By 1928 political tension was seething in the oil-producing countries. There was a real fear that rising economic and political nationalism would threaten future ownership of oil resources. In such an unsettled market, competition between the big players was fierce. Cut-throat rivalries developed throughout the 1920s as executives used price cuts and buy-outs to gather crucial market share and bargaining power.

To oil executives at the very highest level there was a clear need to steady the often-savage market and to insulate the oil companies from any sort of political or governmental intervention. The only problem with creating such an arrangement was that it would be illegal in almost every way.

In this febrile atmosphere Sir John Cadman, head of APOC, rented Achnacarry Castle, a remote Scottish country house. He paid £3,000 (around £200,000 today) for two weeks' use of the estate – an extremely generous sum that would help ensure the utmost privacy. He then invited his three greatest rivals to dinner. They accepted.

*   *   *

Achnacarry Castle and its estate sit between two narrow lochs near the southwestern end of Scotland's Great Glen. A little to the south looms the bulk of Ben Nevis, Britain's highest mountain. For centuries the castle has been the home of the Camerons of Lochiel, one of the proudest clans in Scotland. Although it looks peaceful today, the castle has for most of its existence been a place where rivals clashed. From its beginnings in the middle ages, Clan Cameron fought the Mackintoshes and other rival clans for rights to land in Lochaber. Clan Cameron was loyal to the Jacobite cause, and the original Achnacarry was burned to the ground after the Rising of 1745, with the estate being forfeited to the Crown. The Camerons regained their historic seat in 1784, and around 1802, the XXIInd chief decided to build a new house.

Fifty-one years old, Sir John Cadman was a tall, slimly built academic. He had black hair, greying at the temples, heavily Brylcreemed and severely parted in the modern style. Sir John had risen through the ranks of the British civil service to become a senior adviser to the UK government. In 1908 he was appointed professor of mining and petroleum technology at Birmingham University. He resigned from the civil service in 1921 and joined the Anglo Persian Oil Company (APOC) as a director, becoming its chairman in 1927. He also chaired the Iraq Petroleum Company. His companies eventually became known as British Petroleum or BP. On the initiative of a young Winston Churchill, at that time serving as First Lord of the Admiralty, the British government had taken a stake in BP and the Royal Navy soon switched its fuel from coal to oil. With fuel-hungry ships, planes and tanks, oil became the life-blood of every war. Fabulously wealthy and a renowned connoisseur of food and wine, Sir John was particularly well known for his love of shellfish, although the lure of Scottish smoked salmon and fresh-caught trout at Achnacarry must have been attractive to him too.

Sir John's invitation to Achnacarry had been accepted by Dutchman Henri Deterding, head of Shell, who had bought oilfields in Egypt (1908), as well as the Russian Ural/Caspian oilfields (1910) and some Mexican, Venezuelan and American oilfields. Aged 62, Deterding was a robust, well-built man of medium height with thinning white hair and an imposing moustache. Known as 'the Napoleon of Oil', having exploited a find in Sumatra, he joined forces with a rich ship owner who also sold painted seashells and together the two men founded Royal Dutch Shell. Deterding had been awarded an honorary knighthood in

1920, supposedly for his service to Anglo-Dutch relations, but in reality for his work supplying the Allies with petroleum during the First World War. Achnacarry Castle was as nothing compared to the opulence of Deterding's own Norfolk pile, Kelling Hall, which he had built in 1914 in the style of a grand hunting lodge and which boasted 13 bedrooms, a trophy room and banqueting hall. Kelling Hall sat in the centre of a 1,600-acre estate.

Also attending was Walter Teagle, head of Standard Oil also known as ESSO (S.O.) (since 1972 known as Exxon). Teagle was born into a wealthy oil family in Cleveland, Ohio in 1878, and was the grandson of Maurice B. Clark, one of John D. Rockefeller's former partners in Standard Oil. He had bought a prosperous Texas Oil Company named Humble (1919) and also bought out Nobel's Russian oil interests (1920), although the new Communist regime seized the oilfields and refused to pay ESSO compensation. Tall, slim and clean-shaven, he had thick brown hair combed back to expose a large forehead.

The other American at Achnacarry was William Larimer Mellon of Gulf Oil, called 'W.L.' by his friends. Mellon was 60 years old and had been born in Pittsburgh, Pennsylvania to a wealthy banking family. Mellon Bank had invested heavily in Gulf Oil and as majority owner William Larimer Mellon founded the Gulf Oil Corporation, building it into one of the biggest oil companies in America. Mellon was a leading Republican politician in Pennsylvania. He had a shock of thick, white hair, a white moustache and neatly trimmed goatee beard.

The four oil executives had arrived at Achnacarry on the late afternoon of Friday 24 August 1928. The weather was warm and sultry, and the wealthy industrialists were charmed by the ancient baronial mansion with its huge arched windows, crenellated roof and imposing surroundings. Spruce-covered hills reared up behind the mansion, and the gardens were filled with rhododendrons, beech trees and Scots pine. The River Arkaig flowed past the mansion at the foot of a sloping field filled with newly clipped sheep. The distant mountains were clad in a glorious purple cloak from their thick covering of heather.

The men were met by Sir Donald Cameron, the XXIVth chief of the clan. Cameron of Lochiel, as the chief is known, invited the four executives to join him for a dram, while his staff carried their bags to their rooms. Sir Donald provided his guests with a quick resumé of his family's notable history and the legends of the castle. He then proposed a toast to the success of their hunting and fishing expeditions and withdrew to his own quarters. Before they got down to business, the four executives intended to enjoy all of the sporting activities that Achnacarry had to offer, to get to know each other better and see if they could find some common ground. Their hardened business resolve would be lubricated by the very best in Highland hospitality.

Over the course of the weekend, they were entertained to some spectacular country sport. The stag season runs from July to October and the gamekeeper and stalker took the four men across the hills on the Saturday, stalking red deer. The stalker knew intimately the habits of the red deer herd on the Achnacarry estate and identified the stags that could be shot. They bagged two stags that day, one with a magnificent set of antlers which were later mounted as a trophy and presented to Henri Deterding to hang in his splendid Norfolk trophy room. After each stag was shot the gamekeeper carried out the traditional 'gralloch', which involved bleeding the animal, then removing its intestines, leaving the guts on the hillside for golden eagles and carrion to feed on. The carcasses were strapped onto the back of two sturdy Highland ponies and walked back down to the castle.

On the Sunday, the oilmen were invited to fly-fish for brown trout and pike on nearby Loch Arkaig, legendary home of the mystical Scottish water horse.[1] An experienced ghillie accompanied them on what turned out to be a successful day, with over 20 brown trout caught and freshly cooked for their evening meal. Sir Donald Cameron's cook, a stout, middle-aged lady from the nearby village of Spean Bridge, prepared picnics for the party each day. Her picnic baskets were stuffed with fresh fruit, cold hams, home-baked bread, fresh-churned butter and her specialities, Scotch eggs, game pie and a tin of her homemade shortbread. She also, thoughtfully, included several bottles of Hiedsieck 1907 Diamant Bleu Cuvée champagne, would be placed carefully in a gentle burn or stream to keep cool until it was time for lunch.

These picnics were an elaborate affair with the gamekeeper and ghillie spreading tartan rugs on the damp grass and then laying out white linen tablecloths and napkins, complete with silver cutlery, special crockery and crystal glasses. The only thing that troubled the assembled executives was the inevitable cloud of midges, tiny biting flies which swarm around at this time of year in the Highlands and can be very irritating. The gamekeeper and ghillie advised the four men to smoke prodigiously, as cigarette smoke helped to keep the dreaded insects at bay. The oil executives were happy to oblige.

When evening came, the men returned to the castle, bathed and dressed for dinner, then met in the grand, wood-lined library in their dinner suits to smoke and enjoy a dram from Sir Donald's extraordinary collection of fine single malt and blended whiskies before sitting down to dine. Their favourite was the 1904 Stronachie[2] Malt Scotch Whisky Special Reserve, distilled by Alexander McDonald in his Stronachie distillery in the remote Perthshire village of Forgandenny. The luscious honey and biscuit flavour of this incredible dram, combined with its earthy heather and malty sweetness, had the oilmen smacking their lips in anticipation every evening.

Intensive discussions continued throughout the day on Monday 27 and Tuesday 28 August, when the four men were taken on a 'walked-up' grouse shoot, trekking across the open hills and moors to flush out the grouse. The Achnacarry gamekeeper had two lively black-and-white English pointer dogs and a brown-and-white springer spaniel that helped to point, flush and retrieve the shot grouse. Over the two days they bagged a total of 19 brace (38) grouse. The combination of fresh air, sporting pursuits, good company and productive discussions had set the scene for the final secret cartel agreement to be thrashed out on the evening of Tuesday 28 August.

*   *   *

As daylight dimmed on Tuesday the four gentlemen were in high spirits. Invigorated by their fine day's grouse shooting, they assembled in the library for their evening dram. Sir John Cadman had been taking careful notes of their discussions since day one and now he produced a draft agreement, which he proposed to read out to the other three. But as he was about to begin, Sir Donald Cameron's butler announced that dinner was served.

Sir John led Deterding, Teagle and Mellon into the wood-panelled dining room. The large mahogany table was set with Cameron of Lochiel's finest silver, crystal glasses and linen napkins. Sir Donald did not intend to spare any expense for his wealthy guests. The butler poured each man a glass of 1926 Riesling from the Palatinate or Pfalz region of Germany, an area renowned for its powerful, crisp and dry white wines that were then known in Germany as Rheinpfalz. Sir John raised his glass and proposed a toast to the 'As-Is' Agreement, their term for the revolutionary market-fixing agreement now known as the Achnacarry Agreement. The four oilmen sipped their wine appreciatively as the first course of Scottish smoked salmon was served; they knew instinctively that this was to be an historic dinner.

The thinly sliced smoked salmon was a luscious pinkish-red colour with a unique flavour. Purchased especially from The Old Salmon Fish House belonging to Ugie Salmon in Peterhead on the northeast Scottish coast, the actual smoking methods used by Ugie are, to this day, a closely guarded secret. The irony was perhaps not lost on the Four Horsemen, engaged as they were on their own clandestine business.

As they enjoyed their Ugie salmon and homemade coarse bread with fresh farmhouse butter, Sir John Cadman slowly worked his way through the full terms of their nascent agreement. He reminded his fellow diners how certain politicians, with the support of a portion of the press, had created the image of a greedy and extravagant petroleum industry in the public eye. Yet everyone round this table knew how false such a contention was, given the severe problems facing the oil industry. The others listened intently, with only the occasional clink of silver cutlery on plates to disturb Sir John's speech.

Sir John acknowledged the gradual depletion and final exhaustion of supplies of crude oil. The temporary shortage of supplies that existed in certain countries during the Great War had accentuated this fear and forced their companies to expend vast sums locating and developing reserves in remote parts of the world. If they were to achieve their objectives then they had to drive down costs and agree on a fair distribution of quotas. They had to share facilities and be careful not to over-supply the industry by building too many new refineries.

It was time to be blatant. They had to fix prices, markets and production, although this would be in direct breach of anti-trust laws and therefore illegal. Sir John suggested that none of the four should sign the final document. This was to remain a 'gentleman's agreement'.

The butler cleared away their white wine glasses while a youthful, liveried waiter removed their plates, and after a short pause the second course was served. This was young roast grouse, garnished with watercress and homemade redcurrant jelly and served with bread sauce, rich gravy, braised cabbage and game chips. The butler now proceeded to pour an elegant, 1923 Châteauneuf-du-Pape, marked with one of the first-ever *Appellation Contrôlée* labels, denoting the new rules recently introduced in France to prevent fraud in the wine sector.

As the men raised their glasses to examine the rich red wine, the late evening light streamed through the dining room window. They savoured the gamey flavour of their grouse as Sir John continued to read and take them ever closer to an historic agreement.

He read a detailed list of conditions that effectively set out the operational rules of the cartel that would soon govern the oil industry. When he finished reading, he laid the draft document on the table and looked questioningly at the other three executives. They all gave their assent.

Some discussion began on the intricacies of the agreement, and as they debated these points, the main course was served. This was roast haunch of venison served with a creamy celeriac purée and sautéed, locally picked field mushrooms. The butler cleared away the red wine glasses and reached for a decorative crystal decanter in which, he explained, he had decanted a 1920 Barolo, a graceful, smooth and intensely flavoured red wine made from the Nebbiolo grape from north-west Italy.

By the time the refreshingly cold Caledonian cream dessert was served and the butler had filled small crystal glasses with 1920 Climens 1er Cru Classé Barsac, the Four Horsemen had agreed to adopt the 17-page draft prepared by Sir John. As suggested, they never signed the document. Although their respective companies would be bound by the agreement, for their own legal protection they would keep the whole matter entirely secret.

When the four oilmen rose from the dinner table and returned to the library to smoke hand-rolled Cuban cigars and sip glasses of the 1904 Stronachie single malt, they had set in place a deal that would alter the world's economy for decades to come. As well as quotas, the oil companies agreed to drive down costs, share facilities and coordinate the construction of new refineries and other necessary infrastructure. Some months after the Achnacarry Agreement was adopted, the companies also agreed to control production, thus basically setting up a global cartel that could fix prices by controlling output.

Over the next five years the price of East Texas crude would be ruthlessly cut from 98 cents a barrel to just 10 cents a barrel, forcing many wildcatters and smaller oil companies out of business. Those that clung on were forced to sign up to strict production quotas that have remained in place until today.

This was possibly the most amoral agreement ever drawn up by a group of industrialists. Furthermore, the Achnacarry Agreement was so secret that it was unknown even to the governments of the key participants. News of the agreement only leaked out in the 1950s, by which time the Four Horsemen had been joined by three other major oil companies, with the new cartel nicknamed: 'the Seven Sisters', involving Standard Oil of New Jersey (Esso), Royal Dutch Shell (Anglo-Dutch), Anglo-Persian (APOC), Standard Oil Co. of New York (Sacony), Chevron, Gulf and Texaco. Together, the Seven Sisters ruled the oil world.

But as the four oil executives left Scotland, satisfied that they had pulled off a major coup, the war drums were beginning to beat once more. The fascist leader Mussolini had risen to power in Italy and in Germany, where unemployment was burgeoning, the Nazi Party, re-established after Hitler's release from Landsberg Prison, gained 12 seats in the federal elections. The next ten years would see Hitler seize control of Germany and turn his attention eastwards in his search for Lebensraum – additional territory for the German people. His first target would be Austria, the country of his birth.

MENU

*Ugie Smoked Salmon served with Homemade Coarse Bread
and Fresh Home-produced Butter*

*Young Roast Grouse with Watercress and
Homemade Redcurrant Jelly, served with Bread Sauce,
Rich Gravy and Game Chips*

*Roast Haunch of Venison served with Roast Carrots
and Roast Potatoes*

Caledonian Cream Dessert

Achnacarry Castle Picnic Food: Scotch Eggs and Game Pie

*1926 Rheinpfalz Riesling
1923 Châteauneuf-du-Pape
1920 Barolo
1920 Climens 1er Cru Classé Barsac*

UGIE SMOKED SALMON SERVED WITH HOMEMADE COARSE BREAD AND FRESH HOME-PRODUCED BUTTER

SERVES 6

500g peat-smoked salmon
2 lemons
1 onion, finely chopped

Slice the smoked salmon into thin long lengths, place onto plates with bread, butter, chopped onions and wedge of lemon

FOR THE BREAD

800g wholemeal flour
200g strong white bread flour
2 x 7g sachet dry yeast
2 tsp salt
2 tbsp soft butter
300ml tepid water

Mix the brown flour with the white, the yeast and salt in a large mixing bowl. Put in the butter and rub it into the flour. Make a dip in the centre of the flour and pour in almost 300ml (hand warm) water, with a metal spoon. Then mix in enough of the remaining water and a bit more if needed, to gather up any dry bits in the bottom of the bowl until the mixture comes together as a soft, not too sticky, dough. Gather it into a ball with your hands. Put the dough on to a very lightly floured surface and knead for 8–10 minutes until it feels smooth and elastic, only adding the minimum of extra flour if necessary to prevent the dough sticking. Place the ball of dough on a lightly floured work surface. Cover with an upturned, clean, large glass bowl and leave for 45 minutes –1 hour or until it has doubled in size and feels light and springy. Timing will depend on the warmth of the room.

Knock back the dough by lightly kneading just 3–4 times. You only want to knock out any large air bubbles, so too much handling now will lose the dough's lightness. Shape into a ball. Cover with the glass bowl and leave for 15 minutes. Now shape to make a tin loaf. Grease a 1.2-litre capacity loaf tin (about 23 x 13 x 5.5cm) and line the base with baking parchment. Using your knuckles, flatten the dough into a rectangle of about 25 x 19cm.

Fold both shorter ends into the centre like an envelope, make a quarter turn, then flatten again into the same size and roll up very tightly, starting from one of the short ends. Roll the top of the dough in extra seeds and place in the tin with the join underneath. Cover with a clean tea towel. Leave for 40–45 minutes, or until risen about 5cm above the top of the tin.

Put a roasting tin in the bottom of the oven 20 minutes before ready to bake and heat oven to 230°C/450°F/gas 8. Put the risen bread in the oven, carefully pour about 250ml cold water into the roasting tin (this will hiss and create a burst of steam to give you a crisp crust), then lower the heat to 220°C/425°F/gas 7. Bake for about 30 minutes or until golden, covering with foil for the last 5 minutes if starting to brown too quickly. Leave in the tin for 2–3 minutes, then remove and cool on a wire rack. If you tap the underneath of the baked loaf if should be firm and sound hollow.

FOR THE BUTTER

1 litre double cream
50g plain organic yoghurt
1 tsp Hebridean sea salt
1 kg ice cubes in 6 litres cold water

Culture the cream the day before you would like to make your butter, pour the cream into a bowl, add the yogurt and mix well. Cover with kitchen towel and leave in warm kitchen for 12 hours. The cream is ready when it has thickened slightly. It will smell slightly sour and tangy.

Place the cream in a mixer with whisk attachment and start it off on medium speed. While this is on, place the cheesecloth in your sieve over a bowl. When the cream is getting thick like whipped cream increase the speed so it curdles and keep it on high till you see the butter milk 'split' out of the cream and you are left with butter solids.

Strain off the buttermilk. Pour the buttermilk through the cheesecloth and strainer, holding the butter solid back. Allow the buttermilk to strain through, then plop in the butter. Gather the cloth around the butter and press it hard with your fist. Do this several times to get as much buttermilk out of the butter as possible. Keep the buttermilk to make scones or bannocks.

Wash the butter. Rinse out the bowl used for buttermilk. Remove the butter from the cloth and place it in the bowl. Add iced water to the bowl and, using a spatula, press the butter into the iced water. It will quickly become cloudy with buttermilk. Pour off the cloudy water, add more of the iced water to the bowl and keep pressing. Repeat until the water is clear. This may take up to 6 washings. The butter will firm up towards the end, so you may find it easier to use your hands. Take the butter out of the bowl and put in a dry clean bowl. Sprinkle the salt over the butter and knead in. Press into your container and pop in fridge to use when you need it.

WINE

1926 Rheinpfalz Riesling, a powerful, full-bodied, aromatic and elegant German Riesling from vineyards in the north of the region, mainly around Wachenheim, Forst, Deidesheim and Ruppertsberg.

YOUNG ROAST GROUSE WITH WATERCRESS AND HOMEMADE REDCURRANT JELLY, SERVED WITH BREAD SAUCE, RICH GRAVY AND GAME CHIPS

SERVES 6

6 young grouse
salt and pepper to taste
2 sprigs of thyme
2 bay leaves
50g unsalted butter
6 slices of streaky bacon
1 small chopped shallot
salt and pepper to taste

Remove the wing bone and the wishbone from each grouse, making sure that the skin covers all the flesh. Make a small cut into the bottom of the legs and holding the feet twist and pull until all of the sinew has come out. Season the birds inside with salt and pepper and place a sprig of thyme and a bay leaf inside each cavity. Smear the breasts with butter and lay a slice of streaky bacon cut in half on top. Preheat the oven to 220°C. Roast the grouse for about 15 minutes, turning and basting three times, remove from the oven and leave to rest for 10 minutes on a warm plate. To make the gravy (see below), put the wine and port into the roast tray and scrape up all the juices, pour in the stock and boil to a thin gravy, strain, add the whisky and keep warm.

FOR THE BREAD SAUCE

800ml milk
1 finely chopped onion
2 cloves
1 good pinch of nutmeg
4 sprigs of thyme

148

12 slices of white bread, crusts removed and made into breadcrumbs
100g butter

Put all the ingredients except the breadcrumbs and butter into a saucepan and bring to a simmer, take off the heat and leave to infuse for a while. Strain the milk into a clean pan, add the bread crumbs and stir with a whisk over a low heat until it starts to thicken, add the butter and season with salt and pepper. If it's too thick add a little more milk.

FOR THE GAME CHIPS

3 Maris Piper potatoes
vegetable oil for deep-frying

Slice the potatoes as thinly as possible on a mandolin as for crisps and place in a container under running water for half an hour to remove the starch. Drain and dry well and deep-fry in hot oil until golden brown, drain on kitchen paper and season with salt.

FOR THE GRAVY

175ml of red wine
175ml port
50ml of whisky
800ml game stock

FOR THE GAME STOCK

2kg of game bones (venison, pheasant, grouse, pigeon etc),
cut into pieces if they are big
2 medium onions, unpeeled
2 carrots, washed and cut into big chunks
2 sticks celery, each cut into 4 pieces
1 leek, split, and carefully washed
1 400g tin of chopped tomatoes and juice
25g tomato purée
1 bouquet garni
2 extra bay leaves
1 tsp whole black peppercorns

1 head of garlic
1 bottle 750ml red wine
1 bottle 750ml madeira
6 litres water

Heat the oven to 230°C/450°F/gas 8. Put the bones in the roasting tray and roast them for about 40 minutes, stirring occasionally, until they start to brown. Add the onions, carrots, celery and leek, and cook for a further 30 minutes.

Remove the roasting tin from the oven carefully, and allow it to cool for a few minutes. Deglaze the roasting tray with half the wine, by stirring vigorously the base of the roasting tin to remove as much caramel as possible – the liquid should turn a pleasant brown.

Transfer the ingredients and their liquid into a stock pot large enough for all the ingredients, then add all the other ingredients. Bring this mixture slowly to the boil on top of the stove, skimming off any froth if necessary. Simmer the mixture for about 5 hours, then strain the liquid into a clean fresh pan, discarding the solids, but squeezing as much juice as possible from the vegetables as you go. Simmer this stock down to 800ml and use.

WINE

1923 Châteauneuf-du-Pape is the most prestigious southern Rhône red wine. It was here that the *Appellation Contrôlée* system began in 1923, when a group of local winemakers, led by Baron Le Roy, drew up a charter of six stipulations, which have remained largely unchanged to this day, to regulate and safeguard the quality of their wines.

ROAST HAUNCH OF VENISON SERVED WITH ROAST CARROTS AND ROAST POTATOES

SERVES 12

FOR THE VENISON

2kg small haunch of venison
100g bacon lardons plus 8 rashers
salt
black pepper
6 sprigs of thyme
500g chopped carrots, leeks and parsnips
12 garlic cloves, sliced
750ml red wine
150ml port
250ml stock
50g butter
50g plain flour

Preheat the oven to 180°C/350°F/gas 4. Trim the joint, rinse and pat dry, make deep little incisions all over the meat and push a bacon lardon into each one. Brown the joint all over. Season well and lay the remaining bacon over the top with some thyme. Put the vegetables, garlic and more thyme into a large roasting tray. Place the venison on top and pour in all the liquids. Cover with a piece of baking parchment and then a double layer of tin foil and slow roast for about 4 hours. Open the tin foil and transfer venison to a serving dish, cover with foil and rest for 20 minutes. Strain the contents of the roasting tray into a jug and skim off the fat. Melt the butter in a saucepan, add the flour and cook for a couple of minutes; add the juices then boil hard for 10 minutes to reduce by half. This will make quite a concentrated sauce. Taste and season, strain into a warm sauceboat and serve with the venison. Carve the rested meat and serve with the strained gravy.

FOR THE ROAST CARROTS

500g young bunched carrots, washed and scrubbed
100ml rapeseed oil
sea salt
freshly ground black pepper
a few sprigs of fresh thyme
2 tsp crushed coriander seeds
150g butter
chopped parsley

Preheat oven to 200°C/400°F/gas 6. Toss carrots with oil, salt and pepper, the thyme sprigs and the coriander. Place in a roasting tray or earthenware dish, cover tightly with tin-foil and cook for 30–40 minutes until just tender. Remove the foil, add butter and cook for a further 10 minutes until the carrots have browned and caramelised; take out, mix with parsley and serve.

FOR THE ROAST POTATOES

1kg Maris Piper potatoes
200g beef dripping
2 tsp plain flour
sea salt to taste when you serve the roast potatoes

Put a roasting tin in the oven (one big enough to take the potatoes in a single layer) and heat oven to 200°C/400°F/gas 6. Peel the potatoes and cut each into 4 even-sized pieces if they are medium sized, 2–3 if smaller (5cm pieces). Drop the potatoes into a large pan and pour in enough water to barely cover them. Add salt then wait for the water to boil. As soon as the water reaches a full rolling boil, lower the heat, put your timer on and simmer the potatoes uncovered, reasonably vigorously, for 2 minutes. Meanwhile, put the beef dripping into the hot roasting tin and heat it in the oven for a few minutes, so it's really hot.

Drain the potatoes in a colander. Now it's time to rough them up a bit – shake the colander back and forth a few times to fluff up the outsides. Sprinkle with the flour and give another shake or two so they are evenly and thinly coated. Carefully put the potatoes into the hot fat – they will sizzle as they go in – then turn and roll them around so they are coated all over. Spread them in a single layer making sure they have plenty of room.

Roast the potatoes for 15 minutes, then take them out of the oven and turn them over. Roast for another 15 minutes and turn them over again. Put them back in the oven for another 10–20 minutes, or however long it takes to get them really golden and crisp. The colouring will be uneven, which is what you want. Scatter with salt and serve straight away.

WINE

1920 Giacomo Conterno Barolo Riserva. A graceful, smooth and intensely flavoured red wine made from the Nebbiolo grape from the village of Monforte d'Alba in northwest Italy.

CALEDONIAN CREAM DESSERT

SERVES 6

150g good quality Dundee marmalade
500g cottage cheese
100ml whisky (or more to taste)
50g Muscovado sugar
2 tbsp lemon juice
120ml whipped double cream
6 sweet table oranges, peeled and segmented

Put all the ingredients together in a liquidiser or food processor and blend. When the mixture is smooth, fold in the double cream. Place segmented oranges into 6 martini glasses. Take cream mixture and pour into the glasses; place in fridge for 4 hours. Take out 1 hour before serving. Serve with shortbread.

WINE

1920 Climens 1er Cru Classé Barsac. Château Climens Barsac is probably one of the finest sweet wines in the world. This exceptional French dessert wine combines the richness and power of a Sauterne with the fineness and vivacity of a Barsac.

ACHNACARRY CASTLE PICNIC FOOD: SCOTCH EGGS AND GAME PIE

SERVES 6

FOR THE SCOTCH EGGS

6 large free-range eggs
600g sausage meat
3 tsp fresh chopped tarragon leaves
6 cloves of garlic, finely chopped
½ tsp ground cumin
50g fresh curly parsley, chopped
6 shallots, finely chopped
salt
pepper
500g plain flour, seasoned with salt and freshly ground black pepper
4 eggs, beaten with 150ml of milk
500g panko breadcrumbs
vegetable oil, for deep frying

Place the eggs, still in their shells, in a pan of cold salted water. Place over a high heat and bring to the boil, then reduce the heat to simmer for exactly 9 minutes. Drain and cool the eggs under cold running water, then peel. Mix the sausage meat with the tarragon, garlic, cumin, parsley and shallots in a bowl and season well with salt and freshly ground black pepper. Divide the sausage meat mixture into 6 equal balls and flatten each out on a clean surface into ovals about 12.5cm long and 7.5cm at the widest point.

Place the seasoned flour onto a plate then drench each boiled egg in the flour. Place each onto a sausage meat oval then wrap the sausage meat around each egg. Make sure the coating is smooth and completely covers each egg. Dip each sausage meat-coated egg in the beaten egg, rolling to coat completely, then dip and roll into the breadcrumbs to completely cover.

Heat the oil in a deep heavy-bottomed pan, until a breadcrumb sizzles and turns brown when dropped into it. (CAUTION: hot oil can be dangerous; do not leave unattended.) Carefully place each Scotch egg into the hot oil and deep fry for 8–10 minutes, until golden and crisp and the sausage meat is completely cooked.

FOR THE GAME PIE

HOT WATER PASTRY

340g plain flour, plus extra for flouring
¾ tsp salt
90ml water
90ml milk
150g lard, chopped into cubes
1 beaten egg yolk, for brushing

Put the flour and salt in a large bowl and make a well in the centre. Put the water, milk and lard in a saucepan and heat gently. Once the lard has melted, bring to the boil. Pour the boiling liquid into the flour. Use a wooden spoon to combine the mixture until cool enough to handle. Bring together into a ball.

Dust your work surface generously with flour and knead the dough briefly – it will be soft and moist. Work quickly as the warmth keeps the dough pliable. Set aside a third of the pastry and roll the rest of the pastry out on a well-floured surface. Line the terrine with the pastry using your fingers to press it right up the sides.

FOR THE GAME PIE FILLING

500g venison loin, cut into strips about 4cm long
200ml cognac
6 cloves, crushed
1 tbsp fresh herbs, chopped thyme and rosemary mixed equally
600g minced mixed game meat (whatever your butcher can give you; they
usually have a game pie mix that they can mince for you)
10 chicken livers
180g unsmoked bacon, diced for each 140g of minced meat
60ml red wine
1 tsp olive oil
½ tsp nutmeg
salt and freshly ground black pepper
250g pork back fat
a little fresh egg yolk for brushing
250ml jellied game stock, warmed until melted

Combine the venison loin with the cognac, crushed cloves and half the mixed herbs and use this mixture to marinade the venison for 12 hours (cover and place in the refrigerator).

When ready to assemble the terrine, drain the venison and pat dry and keep to one side. Combine the game mince, chicken livers and the bacon and mince finely. Combine the mixture with the chopped herbs and mince. Turn this mixture into a food processor; add the red wine, olive oil, nutmeg, salt and black pepper then process until you have a smooth paste. Set aside.

Remove the pastry-lined terrine from the refrigerator. Cut the pork fat into thin strips and use just over half to line the base of the pastry. Arrange the venison meat strips and creamed savoury mixture in layers in the dish, finishing with the remainder of the mixed herbs and the remainder of the fat.

Place a pie vent or pie chimney in the centre of the pie, then roll out the remaining pastry and use to cover the pie, crimping the edges together to seal. Set aside to stand for 60 minutes. Brush the top with egg then transfer to an oven pre-heated to 180°C and bake for about 120 minutes, or until the meat has cooked through (if the pastry is browning too quickly turn the heat down a little and cover the pie with foil). Remove from the oven and set the pie aside to cool. When the pie is almost cold, remove the chimney and pour in the melted jelly. Allow to stand for 12 hours in a cool place, so that the jelly has time to set, then turn out of the mould, slice and serve.

WINE

1907 Hiedsieck Diamant Bleu Cuvée champagne. This sumptuous champagne was originally the wine for the imperial court of Tsar Nicholas II of Russia.

Seven

AUSTRIAN ANSCHLUSS

12 February 1938
The Berghof,
Bavaria

THE GUESTS

KURT VON SCHUSCHNIGG,
Austrian Chancellor

GUIDO SCHMIDT,
Austrian Foreign Minister

ADOLF HITLER,
Führer

GENERAL WALTHER VON REICHENAU

LUFTWAFFE GENERAL HUGO SPERRLE

GENERAL WILHELM KEITEL

MARTIN BORMANN,
Hitler's private secretary

JOACHIM VON RIBBENTROP,
Reich Foreign Minister

FRANZ VON PAPEN,
German Ambassador to Austria

Adolf Hitler was pacing up and down the wide terrace of the Berghof – his mountain retreat near Berchtesgaden in the Bavarian alps. The spectacular background of snow-covered peaks provided an almost magical scene, but did little to lighten the Führer's dark mood. It was a freezing afternoon in early February 1938 and as his shoes clacked on the flagstones he looked across the valley to the craggy massif of the Untersberg. According to ancient legend, King Frederick Barbarossa lay sleeping within the mountain, waiting for the call to reawaken at Germany's hour of need. On the other side of the Untersberg lay Austria: Hitler's homeland, his next challenge and, currently, his greatest problem.

It was not by chance that Hitler had his favourite retreat in this mountainous borderland. One of his prime ambitions was for Anschluss – the union of Germany and Austria as the foundation of a massive and powerful thousand-year Reich. He was now in the perfect position to make this happen. He was the supreme leader. He was supreme commander of the resurgent armed forces. He had achieved greatness and was convinced of his historic role as Germany's man of destiny. Austria was so close, literally and politically; now he had to reach out and take it.

Hitler's problem was that Austria was not playing along. The Austrian chancellor, Kurt von Schuschnigg, who had been cooperating with Hitler, was now standing his ground. Schuschnigg had signed an agreement in 1936 that aligned Austria's foreign policy with Germany's and allowed Nazis to hold official posts in Austria. Now, in January 1938, he had emphatically refused to have any Nazis in his cabinet. Hitler knew he could simply mobilise his forces and take control of Austria. But Austria was the land of his birth; could this not be done without bloodshed? Would it not be better if Austria *wanted* him to come? Yet how could Hitler persuade the Schuschnigg – a proud, vain man – to just lay down his country? It would have to be a most remarkable act of persuasion and coercion; an exceptional conversation. Perhaps over an extended lunch? Here, at his home in the mountains? Yes, that would be perfect.

*　　*　　*

Four years earlier, Hitler had sealed his inexorable rise to power, ruthlessly crushing the leadership of the Sturmabteilung (the paramilitary wing of the Nazi party known as the Brownshirts) in the Night of the Long Knives, as the murderous night of 30 June 1934 had come to be known.

Ernst Röhm and the SA had become a seriously destabilising force in the regime and had even begun to threaten Hitler's own position. Hitler knew that the army had viewed the SA as a rival and had celebrated their demise, now pledging their total loyalty to their Führer.

By early 1938, Hitler's struggle to achieve total power in Germany was complete. The Nazi Party was in full control. Following the death of President von Hindenburg in the summer of 1934, Hitler had combined the role of President and Chancellor, or as he preferred to be known – Führer und Reichskanzler. This move was approved by a massive 90 per cent majority of the German people in a plebiscite, effectively propelling him one step closer to the dictatorship he craved. On 7 March 1936 German troops marched into the Rhineland in direct violation of the Treaty of Versailles. This was the first illegal action in foreign affairs that Hitler had undertaken since coming to power in 1933, and it caused great confusion and consternation among France, Britain and their allies. They were frozen with fear like rabbits in the headlights, watching and waiting nervously for Hitler's next move. They did not have to wait long.

In 1937 Hitler abolished cabinet government altogether and assumed the role of absolute dictator. He had in the meantime rearmed Germany, introduced conscription and entered into a pact with Mussolini's Italy and he now began actively planning German expansion in his quest for new Lebensraum. He longed for Anschluss, a vision outlined in his book *Mein Kampf*.

But Hitler was deeply troubled by Austria. The unauthorised actions of the Austrian Nazis had become a serious embarrassment to the Führer. In Vienna on 25 July 1934, 150 Nazis dressed as Austrian soldiers and police officers had overwhelmed the unarmed guards at the Chancellery building and seized it as part of a plot to install a Nazi government. Their objective was to kidnap all of the ministers, including the chancellor, and force them to appoint a Nazi as the head of a new pro-German government. They also briefly occupied Austria's national radio network and tried to kidnap the Austrian president.

During the course of this uprising, Austrian Chancellor Engelbert Dollfuss was shot twice at close range as the Chancellery was being occupied; one of the bullets paralysed him below the waist. The other bullet caused extensive bleeding around his throat, but the Nazi plotters refused to allow a doctor to treat him or a priest to visit him, and he slowly bled to death in his office. The attempted coup by the Nazis was quickly put down, but not before considerable international damage had been caused. Mussolini, a supporter of Dollfuss, was outraged by the assassination, and rather than alienate the Italians, Hitler moved quickly to distance himself from any involvement in the affair.

The pompous and strutting Kurt von Schuschnigg, who thought himself an equal match for Hitler, was appointed chancellor to replace Dollfuss. He ordered a crackdown on the Nazis, who now appealed to Hitler for assistance, fearing that the Germans had left them in the lurch. But Hitler was nervous. The damage to Germany's relations with Italy was significant. For a time it even looked like Mussolini might intervene in Austria, and Hitler was furious that the hare-brained schemes of the Austrian Nazis had caused him so much humiliation. He decided to bide his time, determined to seize the first opportunity for Anschluss that presented itself.

Schuschnigg had long attempted to counter threats from Germany by seeking the support of Austria's neighbours to the south and east – Italy and Hungary. But Mussolini had now formed an alliance with Hitler over the second Italo-Ethiopian war and was no longer prepared to antagonise the massively rearmed and militaristic Germany. The Hungarians were likewise afraid to raise their heads against the Third Reich, forcing Schuschnigg to adopt a new policy of appeasement and sign an Austro-German agreement in July 1936. This led to the release of the jailed 1934 Putsch Nazis, as well as the appointment of so-called 'moderate' pro-Nazi sympathisers Edmund Glaise-Horstenau and Guido Schmidt to the Austrian cabinet. Nevertheless, the ban on the Austrian Nazi Party remained in place, causing relations with Germany to plunge further. When Hitler publicly threatened to take control of Austria's internal politics, Schuschnigg boasted in January 1938 that 'There is no question of ever accepting Nazi representatives in the Austrian cabinet. An absolute abyss separates Austria from Nazism'.

As the New Year dawned in 1938, Europe held its collective breath. Would Hitler's expansionist policies lead to war? Could Nazi Germany be contained? The Nazi Party was on the rise in Austria, secretly funded by Germany, but many sympathisers and party activists had been arrested and interned by Schuschnigg, and Hitler was angry and frustrated. He had sent Franz von Papen, the former German chancellor under President Hindenburg, as ambassador to Vienna to calm things down and to reassure Schuschnigg of the good intentions of the Nazis. Clearly Papen had failed.

In early February 1938 Hitler ordered Hans Lammers, chief of the Reich Chancellery, to telephone Papen and inform him that he was being dismissed. 'Your mission in Vienna has ended. I wanted to inform you before you read it in the newspapers,'[1] Lammers told Papen. The aristocratic Papen, who regarded Hitler with contempt, was outraged. To find out what was behind his sudden sacking, he decided to go straight to Berchtesgaden to confront Hitler personally. He found the Führer exhausted and disturbed and unable to concentrate on their conversation. 'His eyes seemed unable to focus on anything and his thoughts seemed elsewhere. He sought to explain my dismissal with empty excuses,' Papen later recalled.[2]

Papen suggested that the only way to resolve the many differences between Austria and Germany was to invite Chancellor von Schuschnigg to Berchtesgaden for a face-to-face meeting. Hitler agreed with this idea and despatched Papen straight back to Vienna to make the invitation, which Schuschnigg accepted nervously and with some hesitation. Schuschnigg had heard a rumour that one of the leaders of the Viennese Nazis had told Britain's fascist leader, Sir Oswald Mosley, that the Austrian Nazis were preparing for an armed uprising in the spring which would be supported by the German Reich.

Schuschnigg told his pro-Nazi foreign minister Guido Schmidt that he would accept the invitation to Hitler's Berghof 'to forestall a coup and to gain time until the international situation should improve in Austria's favour',[3] and joked that he only wished his place at the dinner table with Hitler could be filled by a psychiatrist. Few could have foreseen that over the course of a lengthy luncheon on Saturday 12 February 1938, Austria's fate would be sealed and its independence lost.

On the evening of 11 February the Austrian chancellor and his foreign minister set off on the night train to Salzburg. The next morning they drove through the city of Mozart's birth and across the Salzach River into southern Germany where Papen was waiting at the border. Papen snapped his heels together and cried 'Heil Hitler', giving Schuschnigg the Hitler salute. The smartly uniformed German customs officials did likewise, quickly followed by their Austrian counterparts, for whom the Hitler salute was a violation of the law. It was an ominous portent of what lay ahead.

With Papen leading the way, the party took their seats in a specially adapted half-track military vehicle that could negotiate the icy roads leading up to the Berghof. As their convoy climbed slowly up the mountain, Schuschnigg was amazed to see the roadsides lined with a guard of honour from Hitler's so-called Austrian Legion, which outnumbered his own Austrian army by two to one. Hitler had prepared for Schuschnigg's arrival like the director of a Wagner opera. The chancellor considered himself to be Hitler's equal, but he had only a fraction of Hitler's authoritarian stature, debating ability and cunning, and as he was about to discover, he was sure to come off worse in any encounter with the Führer.

On arrival at the Berghof around noon, Hitler greeted Schuschnigg attired in his Nazi Party uniform of black trousers, brown jacket and red swastika armband. Nervously, Schuschnigg complimented Hitler on the fabulous view from the picture windows of his mountain retreat. 'We did not come here to discuss the view,'[4] snapped Hitler, leading the way to his first-floor study, where the two began an intense two-hour discussion. Hitler later recalled how his Austrian counterpart had 'shrivelled' when he accused him of laying mines along the border with Germany, which Hitler assured him, 'will not even delay me for half an hour'. Hitler shouted at him to 'get rid of those silly little barricades facing our frontier, otherwise I will send in a couple of engineer battalions to clear them up for you'.

Hitler blasted Schuschnigg for Austria's anti-German and anti-democratic policies and said that he had decided to solve the Austrian problem '*so oder so*' (one way or another). Hitler went on to say that he had even decided to launch an invasion of Austria on the following Saturday but had been persuaded against this course of action by his generals. Schuschnigg was becoming increasingly unnerved.

Hitler continued threateningly: 'The history of Austria is just one uninterrupted act of high treason. That was so in the past and is no better today. This historical paradox must now reach its overdue end. And I can tell you right now, Herr Schuschnigg, that I am absolutely determined to make an end to all of this. The German Reich is one of the great powers and nobody will raise his voice if it settles its border problems. I have a historical mission and this mission I will fulfil because Providence has destined me to do so. Who is not with me will be crushed.'

Schuschnigg protested that if Hitler invaded Austria, the Allies would rise up in protest and come to his country's defence. But Hitler retorted that Austria was isolated and Italy would do nothing: 'I see eye to eye with Mussolini. England will not move one finger for Austria. And France could have stopped Germany with ease over the Rhineland. Now it is too late for France. I will give you once more, and for the last time, the opportunity to come to terms, Herr Schuschnigg.'[5] Having accused his guest of being a traitor to Austria, Hitler added 'Schuschnigg, you now have the chance to put your name alongside the names of other famous German leaders, such as Goering, Hess, Frick, Epp, Goebbels and others.'[6]

This lengthy tirade was interrupted only when Hitler abruptly rang a bell on his desk and the doors of his study were silently opened. Two uniformed SS men escorted the two chancellors downstairs to the ground-floor dining room. What followed was perhaps one of the most decisive meals in European history, during the course of which the independence of a sovereign nation was lost.

*   *   *

The Berghof was a thick-walled building, decorated with heavy wooden panelling and hung with Gobelin tapestries and costly works of art by painters admired by Hitler, such as Tintoretto, Tiepolo and Schwind. His favourite painting was a depiction of the Berghof's construction by the artist Erich Mercker. Hitler would point to this painting and explain how his Alpine residence had been massively extended to meet his requirements as an alternative headquarters and place to entertain foreign dignitaries. Hitler's mistress, Eva Braun, lived anonymously upstairs with her two Scots terriers and never joined the dictator when foreign guests were present. Downstairs, uniformed orderlies watched over the comings and goings of the leaders of Nazi Germany.

Meals at the Berghof were not usually lavish affairs. Hitler and his secretary, Christa Schroeder, were both vegetarians. Indeed Hitler often boasted that he was the only vegetarian, teetotaller and non-smoker in his entire household, although he did in fact enjoy an occasional cognac or Schnapps. Light lunches of *Graupensuppe* (barley broth) followed by *Griesnudeln* (semolina noodles), *Ei und Grunem Salat* (egg and green salad) would be the normal vegetarian fare served up for the Führer and his secretary. Other guests would be offered a choice of *Schweinswurste* (pork sausages), *Sauerkraut und Kartoffeln* (sauerkraut and potatoes), followed by *Kase und Obst dessert* (cheese and fruit pudding) and a selection of local cheeses. Guests at mealtimes would be forced to listen to Hitler's rambling monologues, or to his incessant ribbing of Martin Bormann who had grandiose agricultural ambitions and had built an extravagant, and extremely smelly, model dairy only a few hundred yards from the Berghof.

Lunch on Saturday 12 February 1938 followed a similar pattern, although the table had been prepared with meticulous precision. For this meal, Hitler had ordered his table to be set with the best crockery and silver service. The tablecloth was of finest white linen, with oak-leaf sprays embroidered in golden thread around its edges and a large embroidered golden swastika inside a circle in the centre. The Bavarian chef Arthur Kannenberg, a corpulent and jovial restaurant owner who, together with his wife, had been appointed to oversee Hitler's household in 1933, carefully prepared the menu. The Kannenbergs organised state dinners in Berlin and the Obersalzberg and Arthur Kannenberg had selected dishes for the Schuschnigg luncheon, which had been approved by Hitler. His menu included the usual fare as well as platters of cold meats, salads, fried potatoes with eggs and meat or noodles with tomato sauce and cheese. Fresh vegetables and fruit from Martin Bormann's greenhouses in his model nursery garden were also available.

The finest German and French wines were selected to complement the range of appetising dishes on offer. A 1934 St Emilion and a young Alsatian Riesling were presented. Hitler was determined to dazzle Schuschnigg with the trappings of his power before drawing him relentlessly into the snare he had meticulously set.

Following a carefully arranged theatrical plan, the Führer had invited General Walther von Reichenau and Luftwaffe General Hugo Sperrle – 'my two most brutal-looking generals' – and General Wilhelm Keitel, to attend the luncheon dressed in full military uniform including, in Keitel's case, ceremonial dagger, sword and spurs. Thus adorned like gods of war, the three generals were positioned around the table opposite the Austrian chancellor and his foreign minister in a way that was designed to be as intimidating as possible. Schuschnigg was wearing his customary dark, thick, three-piece business suit, placing him at an immediate disadvantage to the uniformed military warlords. Hitler had also invited his sinister private secretary Martin Bormann and foreign minister, Joachim von Ribbentrop. Also present was Franz von Papen, the German ambassador to Austria.

Hitler, a stickler for cleanliness, disdainfully recalled later that Schuschnigg had not shaved and his fingernails were dirty. He mockingly imitated how the Austrian chancellor bowed stiffly and murmured 'Schuschnigg,

Schuschnigg' like a provincial schoolteacher when he was introduced to the generals, and he made fun of the Austrian visitor's nicotine addiction, joking that his cigarette habit had cost Austria its independence.

Deploying all of his skills as a negotiator, Hitler now completely switched tactics. Over lunch he stopped playing the bully and became the charming and genial host, discussing his plans for grand architectural projects including skyscrapers that would outdo anything in America. He made sure to mention the vast strength of the Luftwaffe and its new, deadly bombs and he spoke at length about how his Panzer armies would smash the Reich's enemies. Schuschnigg picked at his food nervously. He frequently sipped his Riesling and an SS waiter was on hand to refill his glass after every mouthful. Hitler and his generals drank only water.

Hitler drew a sketch of a gigantic bridge that he and his chief engineer Fritz Todt intended to construct across the River Elbe. It was to be the longest bridge in the world, Hitler said, explaining that it would in fact be cheaper to build a tunnel, but he wanted to have something so outstanding it would impress the Americans when they visited Germany. He added that it was his intention to invite Schuschnigg to the opening ceremony when the bridge was completed.

Coffee and schnapps were served to Schuschnigg in the adjoining living room by handsome young SS men in crisp white jackets over black trousers. Schuschnigg, a chain-smoker, was by now sweating profusely and desperate for a cigarette, but he had to wait for the Führer to leave the room before he could go outside onto the dark, freezing terrace to light up. Hitler, as a non-smoker, forbade anyone to smoke in his presence and the Austrian visitor had been forewarned not to do so. But the minute the Führer left the dining room Schuschnigg rushed outside onto the terrace and began smoking and chatting to the two generals, neither of whom was quite sure why they had been summoned to the Berghof.

Schuschnigg said later that, although he had met neither of them before, he regarded General von Reichenau as an enemy of Austria because of his well-known hostile public statements; General Sperrle he viewed as 'indifferent'. He also reported that he held a fairly perfunctory conversation with the generals and that Sperrle had mentioned his role in charge of the Condor Legion during the Spanish Civil War. This conversation was perhaps not accidental, as during his fiery encounter with Hitler later that afternoon, the enraged Führer shouted: 'Do you want Austria to become another Spain?'[7]

It wasn't until after 7 p.m. that Ribbentrop, the newly appointed Reich foreign minister, entered the room and placed Hitler's typewritten demands for Austria on the coffee table, stating that this was the document that Schuschnigg must sign and that its contents were non-negotiable. The document was essentially an ultimatum. It stated that the Austrian Nazi Party must be legalised. Artur Seyss-Inquart, a pro-Nazi Viennese lawyer currently serving in the Austrian cabinet, was to be promoted to the post of interior minister, and to take control of all internal security matters. The key cabinet posts of Defence and Finance were also to be given to leading Austrian Nazis. Finally, all interned or imprisoned Nazis were to be immediately released and reinstated and Austria was to accept full integration into a new economic and financial union with the German Reich. The document was to be signed at once, Ribbentrop reminded Schuschnigg.

The Austrian chancellor and his foreign minister baulked at this and Schuschnigg demanded a further meeting with Hitler. He was escorted once again up to the Führer's second-floor study. 'There is nothing to be discussed,' snarled Hitler. 'I will not change a single iota. You will either sign it as it is and fulfil my demands within three days, or I will order my army to march into Austria.'[8] Trying hard not to lose his temper, Schuschnigg began to dissect the document point by point in lawyerly fashion, but Hitler yelled: 'You will either sign it as it stands or else our meeting has been useless. In that case I shall decide during the night what will be done next.'[9]

After more than one hour of heated disagreement, Schuschnigg still refused to sign. He argued that it was pointless for him to do so as the Austrian constitution only provided for Federal President Miklas to appoint cabinet ministers and grant legal amnesties to prisoners. Hitler was furious. He rushed to the door of his study and screamed for General Keitel to come. 'I shall have you called later,' Hitler shouted at Schuschnigg, ushering him out of the room. As the trembling Austrian chancellor made his way downstairs he passed a breathless Keitel on the way up, answering his master's command. When Keitel asked Hitler what he wanted, the Führer answered: 'I don't want anything. Just sit there.' Hitler had sized up Schuschnigg perfectly. He knew his game of bluff and bluster was having an impact.

Schuschnigg hurried back to his cabinet colleague Guido Schmidt, bitterly complaining that the document Hitler wanted him to sign would mean an end to Austrian independence. He related excitedly how the Führer had lost his temper and said, 'I wouldn't be surprised if he had us arrested within the next five minutes.' An embarrassed Papen assured Schuschnigg and Schmidt that he had no idea Hitler had intended to issue this ultimatum, but nevertheless he advised the Austrian chancellor that it would be best if he signed it.

Time passed slowly. Schuschnigg waited in a nervous sweat before Hitler sent for him again and said to him: 'For the first time in my life, I have changed my mind. You must sign the demands that I have made upon you, then report them to the Federal President Miklas, and within three days from now Austria must fulfil the Agreement, otherwise things will take their natural course.'

It was 11 p.m. and the exhausted and completely shaken Austrian chancellor, in the presence of Ribbentrop, Guido Schmidt, Papen and Hitler, signed the demands and retaining a copy for the Austrian government. Hitler, in an entirely changed mood, turned to Papen and said, 'Herr von Papen, through your assistance I was appointed Chancellor of Germany and thus the Reich was saved from the abyss of communism. I will never forget that.' Papen replied: '*Ja wohl, Mein Führer.*'

It was pitch-dark outside and approaching midnight. Hitler, ignoring the late hour, invited Schuschnigg to stay for dinner, but the Austrian leader was desperate to leave and knew that he had a lot to do if he was to meet the Führer's three-day deadline, failing which he was convinced Hitler would launch an all-out assault on Austria. As a shattered Schuschnigg and Schmidt made their way back down the mountainside to Salzburg, Hitler gave orders to his generals to begin sham invasion manoeuvres near the Austrian border for the next few days, to heap pressure on Schuschnigg and Miklas and ensure that they did not renege on the deal.

Once Schuschnigg returned to Austria, he immediately met with President Miklas, who reluctantly agreed to all of the demands except the appointment of Seyss-Inquart as interior minister. The president said there was no way in which he could countenance a Nazi in charge of the police and the army. Schuschnigg next called an emergency meeting of his cabinet and gave them a detailed outline of the meeting in Berchtesgaden. The ministers were appalled, but constant news was being brought to the cabinet room of German military formations massing on the Austrian border and, one by one, the ministers lost their nerve.

Desperate to avoid the Anschluss at all costs, Schuschnigg once again tried to plead with Mussolini for help. The Italian dictator remained strangely silent, having been warned by Hitler that his intervention was unwelcome.

With only 24 hours to go before Hitler's deadline expired, Schuschnigg called an emergency meeting in the office of the president, where he and Miklas were joined by the mayor of Vienna, the president of the National Bank and a former chancellor. Schuschnigg said that he was convinced Hitler would invade Austria if even a single one of his demands was not fulfilled. Finally President Miklas capitulated. He agreed to accept the Berchtesgaden ultimatum.

When this news was made public, there was uproar. Hundreds of Jews withdrew all of their money from Austria's banks and sought to leave the country. Austrian securities nosedived in Switzerland and London. Meanwhile Hitler addressed the Reichstag, telling the assembled parliamentarians that he and Schuschnigg had 'made a contribution towards European peace'.

In desperation, Schuschnigg decided to call for a plebiscite in which the citizens of his country would be asked whether they were in favour of a free and independent Austria. In London, Churchill penned an article for the *Evening Standard* in which he claimed that at least two-thirds of Schuschnigg's countrymen were prepared to defend their independence. The following day he received a letter from his wife's cousin, Unity Mitford, a renowned Nazi sympathiser and personal friend of Hitler. Addressing Churchill as 'Dear Cousin Winston', she proceeded to accuse him of being ill-informed about Austrian affairs and, having just returned from Vienna, she wrote:

> The jubilation which broke out among all classes must have been one of the most tremendous demonstrations of belief the world has ever seen … Everyone looked happy & full of hope for the future … in Graz, Linz and Vienna I witnessed demonstrations in which the people went mad with joy and one could not move in the streets for people shouting "Heil Hitler! Anschluss!" & waving Swastika flags. By night, the hills around Vienna were ablaze with bonfires in the shape of Swastikas.[10]

She predicted that 80 per cent of Austrians would vote for the Nazis in a plebiscite.

Churchill passed Mitford's letter to the Austrian ambassador in London, Georg Franckenstein, seeking his advice and promising that their communications would remain entirely confidential. Franckenstein told Churchill that the Austrian Nazis were being deliberately noisy and highly visible in an attempt to provoke a violent reaction, which would trigger immediate German intervention. However, he added that his countrymen were remaining 'quiet and orderly', on the strict advice of Schuschnigg, to avoid any bloodshed. Franckenstein reckoned that only around 25–35 per cent of Austrians favoured any form of union with Germany.

Inevitably, news of the plebiscite infuriated Hitler, who imagined a majority 'Yes' vote scuppering his plans for Anschluss. Hitler sent an envoy to Vienna armed with a whole new set of demands, including the appointment of a Nazi economics minister. Schuschnigg was incredulous. His concessions to the Nazis had caused massive street protests. Supporters of Austrian sovereignty were daily confronting bands of swastika-waving Nazis. The country was rapidly descending towards civil war.

Enraged by Schuschnigg's defiance, at 2 a.m. on 11 March Hitler ordered plans for the imminent invasion of Austria to be readied, with himself in full control. The ringing of Schuschnigg's bedside telephone woke him up at 5.30. It was his Austrian police chief informing him that the border at Salzburg had just been closed and all railway traffic halted. Soon news came that German divisions in Munich had been mobilised.

At 10 a.m., Schuschnigg received a new ultimatum signed by both Hitler and Goering, demanding his immediate resignation and postponement of the plebiscite. The message ended ominously that if Goering did not receive an answer by noon he would 'act accordingly'. After hurried consultations with President Miklas and his cabinet, the Austrian chancellor agreed to call off the plebiscite. A desperate call to London for help fell on deaf ears, and at 4 p.m. Schuschnigg resigned. Still President Miklas refused to replace him with the Nazi Seyss-Inquart, and as the minutes ticked by Goering screamed down the phone from Berlin that unless Seyss-Inquart was appointed he would give the orders for the invasion of Austria to begin.

Finally, Schuschnigg decided to make an emotional appeal for calm to his countrymen over the radio. From a microphone in the Chancellery, he said: 'President Miklas asks me to tell the people of Austria that we have yielded to force. Because, under no circumstances, not even in this supreme hour, do we intend that German blood shall be spilt, we have instructed our army to retreat without offering any resistance in the event of an invasion and to await further decisions.'[11]

The German 8th Army marched into Austria as dawn broke on 12 March. Schuschnigg was immediately arrested and Seyss-Inquart was appointed as both chancellor and president, despite the fact that President Wilhelm Miklas had refused to stand down. Hitler entered Austria later that day, welcomed by huge, cheering crowds, some of whom were genuine, although many of the displays of enthusiasm were clearly staged. He returned to his birthplace in the village of Brunnau, visiting his former home and school, where it was said he became quite emotional. His Berghof lunch had paid off. Austria was now his. His dream of Anschluss had come true.

But the Führer's ambitions did not stop there. The German invasion of Poland in September 1939 triggered the onset of the Second World War and by late 1943, as the tide began to turn against the Axis powers, the three most powerful leaders of the Allied forces agreed to meet for the first time to work out a combined strategy for defeating Hitler. Churchill, Roosevelt and Stalin met in Tehran, and over the course of four tempestuous days, worked out a plan for driving the Nazis from power and carving up post-war Europe.

MENU

Graupensuppe

Griesnudeln & Ei und grünem Salat

Schweinswürste, Sauerkraut und Kartoffeln

Käse und Obst Dessert

Käse

1934 Chateau Cheval Blanc, Saint-Emilion Grand Cru Classé
1936 Vin d'Alsace Frey-Sohler Riesling
Johann Guggenbichler apple schnapps

GRAUPENSUPPE
(BARLEY BROTH)

SERVES 6

250g Katenspeck (German cured ham), cut into lardons
150g unsalted butter
2 small white onions, finely chopped
100g pearl barley, well washed and drained
2 litres light pork or roast chicken stock
100g peeled russet potato, finely chopped
100g carrot, finely chopped
100g celery, finely chopped
100g leek, finely chopped
15g fresh sage
10g fresh thyme leaves
120g Mettwurst (German sausage), chopped
freshly grated nutmeg, to taste
salt and freshly ground black pepper, to taste
chopped parsley to garnish.

In a large heavy-bottomed pot melt the butter on a medium-high heat. Sauté the Katenspeck till it releases its aroma and fat, add the onion and cook, stirring until soft, for about 5 minutes. Add barley and cook, stirring until lightly toasted, for about 5 minutes. Add stock and bring to boil then simmer till the barley is cooked. Then add potato, carrot, celery, leek, and the Mettwurst, stirring occasionally until sausage is cooked. Season soup with nutmeg, salt, pepper and herbs. To serve, ladle soup into 6 serving bowls.

WINE

1934 Chateau Cheval Blanc, Saint-Emilion Grand Cru Classé. Château Cheval Blanc is a wine producer in Saint-Émilion in the Bordeaux wine region of France.

GRIESNUDELN & EI UND GRÜNEM SALAT
(SEMOLINA NOODLES WITH EGG AND GREEN SALAD)

SERVES 6

FOR THE GRIESNUDELN (SEMOLINA NOODLES)

340g flour
160g semolina flour
large pinch of salt
3 large eggs and 3 egg yolks, at room temperature, lightly beaten

Mix the flour and the salt and shape into a volcano on the work surface, or a wooden board. Make a well in the middle and pour in two thirds of the eggs. Using your fingertips in a circular motion, gradually stir in the flour until you have a dough you can bring together in a ball, adding more egg if necessary. Knead for about 10 minutes until it is smooth and springs back when poked, wetting your hands with cold water if necessary. Divide the dough in two and wrap in a damp cloth. Allow to rest for about an hour in a cool place.

Roll out the first ball of dough on a lightly floured surface until it is about 1cm thick and will go through the widest setting of your pasta machine comfortably. Put it through each setting twice, then fold it back in on itself and repeat the process, cutting it in half when it becomes too long to handle. Store the other half under a damp cloth until you're ready to continue working on it. If you don't have a pasta machine, divide the dough into 3 pieces, then roll each piece into a thin circular sheet on a lightly floured surface.

When the dough has a good sheen to it and is thin enough for your liking, cut it by rolling up the sheets of pasta one at a time like a swiss roll, then slice them and shake out the rolled-up strands. Alternatively, use the cutter on a pasta machine. Curl into portion-sized nests and leave on a floured surface, under a damp cloth, while you repeat with the rest of the dough.

Bring a large pan of well-salted water to the boil, add the noodles, in batches if necessary, and cook for a couple of minutes, stirring occasionally to keep it moving. Drain the noodles in a colander then spread out on trays, sprinkle with oil and allow to cool.

For this dish only pure durum wheat semolina is used. Durum wheat semolina distinguishes itself against the cheaper soft wheat semolina mainly through its substantially higher amount of protein. The protein which is included in the durum wheat semolina, also called 'glue', is, contrary to its misleading name, responsible for the fact that the noodles do not remain glued to each other during the cooking procedure but can be brought to the table *al dente*. In addition, the amber-coloured durum wheat semolina is responsible for the beautiful yellow colour of the noodles.

FOR THE EI & GRÜNEM SALAT (EGG AND GREEN SALAD)

6 hard-boiled eggs
120ml mayonnaise
90ml crème fraiche
20ml cider vinegar
3 dill pickles, diced into 1 cm dice
2 small apples, peeled cored and quartered, then sliced thinly
3 tomatoes, blanched, quartered, de-seeded and sliced
1 white onion, finely chopped
100g petits pois
100g fine beans, blanched and cut into 2 cm pieces
40ml olive oil
pepper
salt

Mix together mayo, crème fraiche, oil and vinegar, season to taste. Mix in all the other ingredients. Refrigerate for one hour. To serve nest up noodles on 6 plates and spoon in veggie mix.

WINE

1936 Vin d'Alsace Frey-Sohler Riesling. The Frey-Sohler estate is located near the village of Scherwiller, 50 km south of Strasbourg, 20 km from the border with Germany.

SCHWEINSWÜRSTE, SAUERKRAUT UND KARTOFFELN (PORK SAUSAGES, SAUERKRAUT AND POTATOES)

SERVES 6

1 kg Bockwurst sausage, cut into 1 cm pieces
4 medium-sized Maris Piper potatoes, peeled and cubed
800g sauerkraut, rinsed and well drained
2 small onions, thinly sliced
200ml chicken stock
200ml wheat beer
1 tsp caraway seeds
salt
pepper
chopped parsley
2 tbsp vegetable oil

Cover the base of a heavy-based casserole pot with vegetable oil then mix together the potatoes, sauerkraut, onion, stock, beer, caraway seeds and sausage and season with salt and pepper. Bring to boil on the top of the stove then cover and cook until the potatoes are tender, on low heat in the oven – 100°C for about 40 minutes. Sprinkle with parsley and serve.

KÄSE UND OBST DESSERT
(CHEESE AND FRUIT PUDDING)

SERVES 6

200g quark
250g thick Greek-style yogurt
1 vanilla pod
190g caster sugar
300ml double cream, whipped to ribbon stage
1 tin of peaches, drained and chopped into 2cm pieces
6 ginger nut biscuits, crushed

Blend the quark cheese in a blender or food processor until smooth with yogurt, vanilla seeds scraped out of vanilla pods and sugar till smooth. Let mixture stand for 10 minutes. Fold in the double cream and chopped peaches; pour into bowls and top with crushed ginger nut biscuits then serve.

KÄSE (CHEESE)

Germany is one of the world's leading cheese producers. Seventy-five per cent of Germany's cheeses (more than 400 different varieties) are produced in Bavaria, with Allgäu (the Alpine region of Southern Germany) being the largest cheese-producing region. Here, raw milk cheeses, such as Allgäuer mountain cheese or Emmentaler, are made from the milk of brown-and-white Simmental cows grazing in natural pastures. These would be the customary cheeses served by Hitler's Bavarian chef Arthur Kannenberg at the Berghof.

DIGESTIF

Johann Guggenbichler apple schnapps. The Johann Guggenbichler distillery is surrounded by orchards of fruit trees in the picturesque foothills of the Chiemgau and the Bavarian Alps.

Eight

CHURCHILL'S BIRTHDAY BANQUET IN TEHRAN

30 November 1943
The British Legation,
Tehran

THE GUESTS

WINSTON CHURCHILL,
British Prime Minister

FRANKLIN D. ROOSEVELT,
US President

JOSEPH STALIN,
Soviet Premier

*… and 30 other diplomats,
relatives and soldiers*

Agreement was essential. The Second World War was at a tipping point. The Russians had won the Battle of Stalingrad, but at a terrible cost, and they were still engaged on the Eastern Front in the largest military confrontation in history. Russian soldiers and civilians were dying by the tens of thousands and they badly needed a diversion – a new front in Western Europe to draw German forces away. The British needed guarantees over their risky plans in the Mediterranean. America wanted Russian help in dealing with Japan. And all of them knew they had to form a plan for the future, should this war be won, to prevent conflict breaking out yet again. If they couldn't reach a consensus now, perhaps they never would. Millions more might die unnecessarily; Hitler could unleash some devastating new strategy and win the war after all. It was time to talk.

So Churchill, Roosevelt and Stalin – the three most powerful figures of the major Allies – gathered for a four-day conference in Tehran in November 1943. Even getting these men in the same room had been a challenge: Stalin didn't want to leave Moscow and hated flying, while Roosevelt was physically disabled and found any sort of travel difficult. Now that they were here, time and diplomacy were of the essence.

There was one final and apparently insurmountable stumbling block: after two days it was clear they weren't getting on. Not personally, not professionally. The air fizzed with arguments and outright insults. Then, on 30 November, it was Winston Churchill's 69th birthday and he was to host a dinner. This was the last throw of the dice. Could he pull off a remarkable piece of diplomacy and get these powerful statesmen to thrash out a strategy for defeating Hitler?

*   *   *

The conference was scheduled to run from 28 November to 1 December 1943. Stalin had at first been unenthusiastic about meeting Roosevelt and Churchill at all and Roosevelt had to make various concessions to get him to attend the conference, including agreeing to a venue that would be acceptable to the Soviet dictator. Stalin had argued for the summit meeting to be held in the USSR. He had suggested Astrakhan or Archangel. But Roosevelt and Churchill demanded a neutral location and suggested Tehran, where US, British and Soviet troops were already ensconced, having deposed the pro-Nazi shah and replaced him with his son. Stalin reluctantly agreed and arrived a few days ahead of the others, determined to play the role of host and dominate the conference.

Bizarrely, claiming there was a high risk of assassination, he persuaded Roosevelt that the safest place for him to stay was inside the Soviet legation, where the three leaders had agreed to hold the conference. Inevitably, Roosevelt's accommodation was bugged and NKVD agents were able to watch his every move and listen to every word, providing Stalin with daily reports on what was being discussed by the US President and his team. The conversations were so detailed that Stalin wondered if Roosevelt suspected he was being bugged and was deliberately planting misinformation.

But as the days passed it became clear that the Americans were naively unaware of the eavesdropping. Stalin couldn't believe his luck. Churchill had issued an invitation for Roosevelt to stay at the British legation, which was next door to the Soviet compound in the centre of Tehran and had even ordered ramps to be constructed to facilitate the wheelchair-bound president, but his invitation remained unanswered. Roosevelt was determined to make friends with Stalin, whom he had never previously met, and readily accepted the offer of a villa in the grounds of the Soviet legation.

According to Robert Payne, the author of *The Rise and Fall of Stalin*, 'Stalin was in the position of an emperor dealing with kings. He spoke always briefly and often rudely. Once when the President asked him a question while he was looking at a document, he said, without looking up, "For God's sake allow me to finish my work!"'[1] But despite his overbearing feeling of superiority, he nevertheless was usually guardedly deferential to Roosevelt, instead concentrating his efforts on irritating Churchill, whom he regarded with contempt. In this, he found a willing collaborator in the American president. Roosevelt too disliked Churchill, while Churchill mistrusted Roosevelt and abhorred Stalin and communism. According to Alan Bullock, the author of the authoritative *Hitler and Stalin – Parallel Lives*, Stalin's attitude showed that he clearly distinguished between Roosevelt and Churchill, the former the representative of the rising power of the USA, the latter of the declining power of the British Empire.[2] Stalin was certain he could out-manoeuvre both to the Soviet Union's advantage.

Stalin perplexed Roosevelt; he couldn't figure him out, but quickly realised that making a fool of Churchill was the best way to endear himself to the Soviet leader. So began a series of disagreeable skirmishes, with Roosevelt often firing insults at Churchill while Stalin smirked and chuckled. Roosevelt later told Frances Perkins, his secretary of labor from 1933 to 1945, that he found he could please Stalin by making a laughing-stock of Churchill. Roosevelt said that this helped to break the ice so that he and Stalin could talk like men and brothers.

In her memoirs entitled *The Roosevelt I Knew*, Perkins recounted an incident that took place in the later stages of the Tehran Conference as described to her by the president, when Roosevelt 'began to tease Churchill about his Britishness, about John Bull, about his cigars, about his habits. It began to register with Stalin. Winston got red and scowled and the more he did so, the more Stalin smiled. Finally Stalin broke out into a deep, hearty guffaw.'[3] Roosevelt whispered to Stalin on one occasion, 'Winston is cranky this morning, he got up on the wrong side of the bed.' These stage whispers, of course, had to be interpreted, adding to the British prime minister's evident discomfort and embarrassment.

*   *   *

Churchill had arrived in Tehran with a bad sore throat and made his apologies to Roosevelt, who had organised a steak and baked-potato dinner for the three leaders' first get-together on the opening evening of the conference. It was planned for each of the leaders to host a dinner, but a disgruntled Churchill ate his meal alone, in his bed in the British legation. Stalin hosted a dinner on the second night, when the taunts and barbs were aimed at Churchill by the US President, aided and abetted by the Soviet dictator. Once again it was not a good night for the British prime minister.

In fact, it was on this occasion that Churchill's temper snapped completely, when Stalin suggested that after the end of the war 50,000 German officers should be summarily executed. This was a pet project of Stalin's, which he was undoubtedly capable of carrying out, as had been proved in the 1940 Katyn Forest massacre by the NKVD of around 22,000 Polish military officers, carried out on orders signed by the Soviet leader. Churchill was appalled. He reminded Stalin that 'The British Parliament and public will never tolerate mass executions. Even if in war passion they allowed them to begin, they would turn violently against those responsible after the first butchery had taken place. The Soviets must be under no delusion on this point.' He said that this would amount to cold-blooded murder, whereupon Stalin accused him of being a secret admirer of the Germans. Churchill denied any affection for the Germans, replying, 'I would rather be taken out into the garden here and now and be shot myself than sully my own and my country's honour by such infamy.'[4]

Seeing his chance to rile the British prime minister further, Roosevelt chipped in with the suggestion that perhaps 50,000 executions was a bit excessive and maybe 49,000 would suffice. By now Churchill was reaching boiling point, and when Roosevelt's son, Lieutenant Colonel Elliott Roosevelt, who was also in attendance, claimed that Marshal Stalin was absolutely correct and that the US Army would almost certainly support this proposal, Churchill rose to his feet in a fury and stomped out of the dining room. He sat glowering in an armchair in an adjoining study until Stalin and his foreign minister, Vyacheslav Molotov, came to explain that they had only been joking and finally persuading him to return to the dinner table.

The first two days of the conference did not go well. As was customary, the mornings were reserved for staff and military meetings so that papers could be prepared for the three statesmen to consider when they met in plenary sessions each evening. The key players in the morning meetings became known as 'the Little Three' in contrast to 'the Big Three' who met in the evenings. The Little Three consisted of Harry Hopkins, who was Roosevelt's closest adviser (some said he was the second most powerful man in America), Molotov, the Soviet foreign minister and Anthony Eden, the British foreign secretary. The key focus of the conference was how to win the war against fascism, and Stalin repeatedly emphasized the need for the Allies to launch Operation OVERLORD in early May to take the pressure off his troops in the east. He quickly won the support of Roosevelt, who was convinced an all-out invasion of northern France in early May 1944 was the Allies' top priority.

But Churchill would not be moved. He had worked out a strategy that would devote the main part of the Allied forces to OVERLORD while smaller forces would be retained in Italy, Turkey, the Aegean and Adriatic. Stalin became angry and frustrated at this, shouting at one point, 'What do you gain by getting Rhodes?' Churchill growled, 'There is a great deal to be gained by getting Turkey.'

So the arguments continued, with Churchill convinced that an Allied landing in Italy and securing a line north of Rome, from Pisa to Rimini, was of paramount importance. This would require troops and landing craft that could not therefore be spared for the invasion of northern France. Churchill argued that he could not commit to any deadline for OVERLORD and certainly not for 1 May 1944, the date favoured by Roosevelt and the US Army Chief of Staff General George Marshall. The first day broke up after Roosevelt's dinner in his villa in the Soviet legation without any conclusive result.

The second day of the conference, 29 November, began as usual with a meeting of the British, American and Soviet general staffs, although once again there was no sign of an agreement. The three leaders met for the second time that same evening, but the day ended with no commitment from Churchill to OVERLORD. It looked as if the conference was heading for disaster, until a strangely touching and emotional ceremony took place which had the effect of bringing Churchill and Stalin closer together.

King George VI had given Churchill a ceremonial sword inscribed with the words 'To the steel-hearted citizens of Stalingrad, a gift from King George VI as a token of homage of the British people'. Churchill had been instructed to present the fabulously wrought weapon to the Soviet leader and when he did so, he made a brief but stirring speech. Standing between Foreign Minister Molotov and his personal envoy and former military commander Kliment Voroshilov, Stalin solemnly accepted the sword, and tears in his eyes, raised it to his lips and kissed the scabbard. It was a deeply emotional moment, spoiled only slightly when the Soviet leader handed the sword to Voroshilov, who promptly managed to drop it on his own toes.

But when the talks resumed again on the next day – Churchill's birthday – tempers flared. The American and British chiefs of staff had met again that morning, with the British suggesting that they could only agree to the invasion of northern France if the date was pushed back to June 1944 (it subsequently was). The Americans insisted on May, arguing that any cross-Channel invasion could only be successfully contemplated in weather conditions in the English Channel that typically occur in May.

The arguments raged all morning until at last the US and British chiefs of staff thrashed out an agreement that the Italian offensive should continue until the Pisa–Rimini line was reached and that the Allies would conduct amphibious landings in southern France concurrently with the mounting of OVERLORD. Roosevelt and Churchill agreed that the invasion of northern France could be undertaken in May subject to these conditions and they duly set off to inform Marshal Stalin of the good news at a special luncheon organised by Roosevelt.

Stalin's interpreter, Valentin Berezhkov, recorded the talks that then took place between the leaders. He noted that the American president had a twinkle in his eye when he informed Stalin that he had 'pleasant news' to impart. He then read out the decision of the British and American chiefs of staff. According to Berezhkov, Stalin became visibly excited at this news but restricted himself to the curt comment: 'I am satisfied with this decision.' Churchill quickly pointed out that the precise date of the invasion would depend on the phase of the moon, as the Allied forces would have to rely on a moonless, dark night to ensure the success of the Normandy landings. Stalin replied that he did not need to know a precise date and that he understood that in any case, one or two weeks in May would be necessary to complete the operation. He agreed that he would launch a major offensive on the Eastern Front to divert German troops away from France.

*   *   *

So, after three days of gigantic personality clashes, psychological manoeuvring and stormy meetings, Churchill's 69th birthday dinner took place. Although the groundbreaking agreement on a May invasion of northern France had raised everyone's spirits, there was still vital business to conclude. Roosevelt and Stalin had held talks in the margins of the summit about the US president's ambition to set up a postwar organisation that could ensure worldwide peace and conflict resolution. The two statesmen needed Churchill's approval for this plan. In addition, Stalin was keen to thrash out the postwar dismemberment of Europe, which would later define the boundaries of the Iron Curtain and the opposing sides in the Cold War. Churchill was determined to patch up his differences with Roosevelt and Stalin, and he prepared the birthday banquet at the British legation meticulously, fretting over every detail with his staff.

Before the dinner began, officers and men from the Royal East Kent Regiment ('The Buffs'), together with men from the Indian Cavalry, presented Churchill with Persian works of art and decorative plates to commemorate his birthday, following which he was given an elaborate gift by the Shah of Iran. Wearing the uniform of an Honorary Air Commodore and puffing happily on a huge cigar, Churchill posed for press photographs while a Pathé News film crew shot some historic footage. However, for security reasons, news of the Tehran Conference, codenamed EUREKA, was not released until three days later and details of the key decisions taken were not revealed until after the end of the war.

Churchill's momentous birthday dinner was an altogether more good-humoured affair, although it started awkwardly with Stalin refusing to shake Churchill's hand, but he redeemed himself rapidly by agreeing to have his photo taken standing beneath the royal coat of arms at the entrance to the legation. Churchill used dinner parties to achieve what could not always be accomplished in the more formal setting of a conference room. Where better could he get to know an ally or opponent, or display his charm and breadth of knowledge, than at a dinner table? Where better to rally political supporters and plan strategy and tactics?[5]

The dinner was scheduled to start at 8.30 p.m. A page from Roosevelt's White House diary for 30 November 1943, lists the following guests:

Attended a dinner at the nearby British Legation in honor of Prime Min. Winston S. Churchill on the occasion of his 69th birthday. Present were: Winston S. Churchill, FDR, Joseph V. Stalin, Anthony Eden, Harry L. Hopkins, Sgt. Robert Hopkins, Elliott Roosevelt, Adm. William D. Leahy, Comdr. Thompson, Charles E. Bohlen, Fleet Adm. Cunningham, Mrs. Oliver, Adm. Ernest J. King, Sir Alexander Cadogan, Maj. Birse, Field Marshal Sir John Dill, W. Averell Harriman, Lord Moran, Gen. Henry H. Arnold, Lt. Gen. Ismay, Maj. John Boettiger, Mr. Holman, John M. Martin, Lt. Gen. Somervell, Gen. Brooke, Mr. Berezhkov, Marshal Voroshilov, Sir Reader Bullard, Commissar Molotov, Sir Archibald Clark Kerr, John G. Winant, Air Chief Marshal Portal, Gen. George C. Marshall, Capt. Randolph Churchill.

Churchill had changed into a dinner jacket and black bow tie, while Stalin stuck to his familiar military tunic. Roosevelt arrived in his wheelchair and was helped up specially erected ramps to the first-floor dining suite. The US president was also dressed formally in his tuxedo and bow tie and the evening began with champagne, Johnny Walker Black Label whisky and Bloody Mary cocktails. There was a feeling that the official part of the conference was over and that the time had come to relax. Churchill later wrote in his memoirs that everyone seemed to be in a good mood. Roosevelt's son Elliott recounted how everyone wished 'Happy birthday' to Churchill, who was

> absolutely in his element, jovial, beaming with good cheer, wreathed in smiles and cigar smoke . . . Cocktail glasses clinked and the air buzzed with friendly talk. Presently Stalin entered, together with Molotov and Voroshilov, and followed by his interpreter, Berezhkov; he was in time to sip two cocktails before we all moved in to dinner – thirty marshals, generals, admirals, ambassadors, ministers, diplomats, and lesser officials following the Prime Minister, the President, and the Marshal – and the one lady of the party, Sarah Oliver.[6]

In fact 34 people had been invited to the dinner, including both Churchill's children – Captain Randolph Churchill and his sister Sarah – and two long tables had been laid with sparkling silver cutlery, candelabra, linen napkins and three crystal glasses per person, two for wine and a smaller one for port. Stalin, still in rumbustious form, criticised the profusion of silverware at each table setting, claiming that this was a typical sign of British bourgeois decadence, although he then asked Churchill's interpreter, Major Birse, to point out which knives and forks he should use for which course.

Churchill ignored this jibe and took his seat in the middle with Stalin on his left and Roosevelt on his right. A birthday cake with 69 candles in the shape of a 'V' for victory was carried in and set down in front of the three leaders. Summoning up as much breath as he could, Churchill, after several attempts, blew out all the candles to thunderous applause from the assembled guests. Stalin then rose to his feet and proposed the first toast of the evening 'to my fighting friend Churchill!' He turned to Churchill, clinked glasses, hugged him and drained his glass in a single gulp. There was a cacophony of clinking glasses around the room as all of the guests, who had risen to their feet, followed suit. Next, Stalin turned to Roosevelt and announced a toast 'to my fighting friend Roosevelt!' Again the same procedure was followed with the Soviet leader bending to hug the American President in his wheelchair, then gulping down his glass of wine, as once again everyone followed suit.

Getting into the spirit of the occasion, Churchill stood again and proposed a toast 'to my friend Marshal Stalin', stating that the Soviet leader had become 'a great figure in the history of Russia and richly deserved the title "Stalin the Great"'. In similar vein, Churchill toasted Roosevelt with the words: 'You have devoted your life to great ideas, to the defence of the weak and poor and to the service of the principles of the civilised world.' Adopting the Russian way, the prime minister then walked around the room clinking glasses with all and sundry before returning to his place. Toast after toast followed, with embassy staff racing to refill the constantly drained glasses and most of the guests spending a large part of the evening on their feet. As the night wore on, the heat and the noise levels steadily rose.

*　　*　　*

The elaborate menu included a starter of a Persian soup made with chicken stock, pearl barley and lime juice. This was followed by boiled salmon trout from the Caspian Sea garnished with Caspian Beluga caviar. The fish was followed by roast turkey, with boiled potatoes and vegetables. The meal was washed down with copious glasses of French Chablis and Persian Shiraz wines. The *pièce de résistance*, prepared specially by the senior British legation chef, was a pudding, which he had named the 'Persian Lantern Ice'. This was an extravagant affair consisting of a large block of ice, four inches thick, which formed the base, into the centre of which had been drilled a three-inch diameter hole. A perforated steel tube had been placed precariously in this hole, concealing a huge candle, the light from which glittered through the perforations. On top of the steel tube the chef had placed a circular plate dusted with icing sugar on which sat an enormous mound of Persian ice cream.

White-gloved waiters ceremoniously carried two of these sumptuous concoctions around the room to great applause. However, as one of the waiters headed back to serve Stalin, it became apparent that the heat from the candle had begun to melt the block of ice, and the steel tower and plate of ice cream was now starting to lurch sideways like the Leaning Tower of Pisa. At this point Valentin Berezhkov, who was standing behind the Soviet leader doing his best to make sense of a toast from one of the military chiefs, when the entire pudding collapsed, splattering down his front and covering his shoes as he tried gamely to continue with his task, while waiters rushed to dab at his clothes with cloths and towels. This crisis provoked guffaws of laughter around the room and Air Chief Marshal Sir Charles Portal was heard to mutter audibly, 'Missed the target,' no doubt referring to Stalin. The final course of the birthday banquet was a cheese soufflé, after which the port was served along with tea and coffee.

An exhausted Roosevelt retired to his quarters around 11 p.m. But Stalin showed no inclination to do likewise. Used to heavy drinking well into the small hours, the now jovial Soviet leader was in party mood and keen for Churchill to join him. No slouch himself when it came to alcohol, Churchill didn't need much encouragement and soon the pair were clinking their glasses for the umpteenth time, toasting each other in increasingly extravagant terms. At one point Churchill was heard to say to Stalin, 'Call me Winston; I call you Joe behind your back.' 'No,' Stalin replied, 'I want to call you my friend. I'd like to be allowed to call you my good friend.' This led to yet another toast with Churchill raising his glass 'to the proletarian masses' and Stalin proposing a toast to 'the Conservative Party'!

At 1 a.m., Sir Alexander Cadogan, permanent under-secretary at the Foreign Office, went to check on Churchill only to find him sitting with Stalin and Molotov, surrounded by 'innumerable bottles' and complaining of a slight headache, although he was 'wisely confining himself to a comparatively innocuous effervescent Caucasian red wine'.[7] Cadogan noted that Stalin and Churchill did not engage in much military talk during the course of the evening, which continued until three a.m., but that Churchill did probe the Soviet dictator about his domestic policies, asking him what had happened to the Kulaks, the relatively rich farming class that Stalin had vowed to liquidate. Cadogan reported that Stalin responded 'with great frankness', stating that the Kulaks had been given land in Siberia but that they were 'very unpopular with the rest of the people'. The final toasts of the evening, made with only a few stragglers left in the room, was proposed by Stalin. Spotting Churchill's valet, Frank Sawyers, lurking in a corner, no doubt concerned for his master's well-being, Stalin proposed not one, but two toasts to the bemused Sawyers.

Few of the dinner guests stirred until late morning on 1 December. The Little Three and the military chiefs of staff were the exception, meeting for their usual morning session, this time confident that the previous evening's excesses had cemented better relations between the three leaders and that now almost anything was possible. When Stalin, Roosevelt and a slightly jaded Churchill met for their final plenary session, Stalin agreed in principle that the USSR would immediately declare war on Japan once an Allied victory had been secured over Germany.

Now came the sensitive discussions about the dismemberment of postwar Europe, with Stalin demanding that vast swathes of Polish territory should be ceded to the Soviet Union. In a deal that later caused outrage amongst Poles, Churchill and Roosevelt agreed, with the proviso that having lost huge tracts of land in the east, postwar Poland should be compensated by being given large chunks of German territory in the west. This decision was agreed provisionally in Tehran and was eventually ratified at the Potsdam Conference attended by the Big Three in 1945. The three leaders also agreed that after the defeat of the Nazis, Germany would be split into Allied occupied zones, although it was decided that a European Advisory Commission should be set up to look at the proposed boundaries for the zones.

Roosevelt once again outlined his plans for a global organisation that could resolve conflict and secure peace for the future. He had in mind a 'United Nations' run, effectively, by the four great powers of America, Britain, China and the Soviet Union acting as global policemen. The three statesmen were in broad agreement. As a final gesture of thanks to Iran for hosting the conference, the three leaders pledged to provide economic assistance both during and after the war.

All three leaders departed from Tehran believing that they were the winners. Roosevelt had secured agreement from Churchill on an invasion of northern France in early May and, of equal importance, Stalin had agreed to launch a new onslaught on the Eastern front to draw German troops away from OVERLORD. Roosevelt was also delighted that Stalin had agreed to declare war on Japan and had signed up to his vision of a United Nations organisation to police future conflicts.

For his part, Stalin was overjoyed that at last the Americans and the British had signed up to opening a second front in France that would relieve pressure on his tired and beleaguered forces in the east. He was also rubbing his hands together in glee at the gigantic territorial gains implied by the tentative agreement on the dismemberment of postwar Europe.

Churchill, having arrived in Tehran with a sore throat and having withstood a constant barrage of insults and affronts from Stalin and Roosevelt, was satisfied that his 'dinner diplomacy' had paved the way to a solid agreement. Although committed to OVERLORD he had not undermined his Mediterranean military campaign. In addition, Stalin's agreement to join the war against Japan represented a significant breakthrough. Churchill also believed that he had advanced his argument that Turkey must enter the war against Hitler, although Stalin and Roosevelt remained deeply sceptical. (Turkey did not, in fact, declare war on Germany until 23 February 1945, just weeks from the end of the conflict.)

Following lunch on 1 December, the three leaders signed a final agreement which set out all of the points on which they had reached an accord. So ended the first major conference of the Big Three during the Second World War. The decisions taken in Tehran opened a new chapter that influenced the political and strategic realities for months and years ahead. There was no doubt that the climax of the Tehran Conference had been Churchill's birthday banquet, which had brought the three leaders closer together and cemented agreements that shaped the world for years to come.

The Allied victory over Germany and Japan in 1945 set the stage for the emergence of a new world order. America, which had accelerated the Japanese surrender by exploding atomic bombs on Hiroshima and Nagasaki, had become a global nuclear power. Its closest ally was the United Kingdom, now engaged in a massive rebuilding programme as it tried to crawl from under the shattered ruins of the war. Confronting the West from behind what Churchill termed the Iron Curtain were the communist nations of the Soviet Union and the vast and mysterious People's Republic of China. Both were racing to develop their own nuclear weapons. As we shall discover in the next chapter, it was in an effort to re-establish dialogue with the Chinese and their despotic leader Mao Zedong that US President Richard Nixon set out on a visit to Beijing in February 1972 that surprised the world.

MENU

Aperitifs

Bloody Mary Cocktails
Pol Roger Champagne
Johnny Walker Black Label Whisky

Ash-e-Jow (Persian Barley Soup)

Poached Salmon Trout with Beluga Caviar Garnish
Roast Turkey with Roast Potatoes and Seasonal Vegetables

Persian Saffron Ice Cream

Cheese Soufflé

1936 Maison Louis Jadot Chablis
1934 Domaine Laurent Combier Crozes-Hermitage
Graham's Vintage Character Port

ASH-E-JOW (PERSIAN BARLEY SOUP)

SERVES 6

3 litres chicken stock
50ml olive oil
100g red onion, finely diced
90g uncooked pearl barley
½ level tsp turmeric
juice of 2 limes
6 ripe or overripe tomatoes blended to a purée in food processor
salt
black pepper
150g pumpkin, peeled and diced
a good handful chopped fresh parsley
6 lime wedges

Bring stock to a gentle simmer in a pot. Heat the oil in a large pot over medium heat and sauté the onion until translucent. Add the pearl barley to the pot and stir for 1 minute. Stir in the hot chicken stock, turmeric, lime juice, tomato, salt and pepper. Bring the mixture to the boil, reduce heat to low, and simmer for 1 hour. Mix in the pumpkin and continue simmering for 30 minutes or until the soup has thickened and the pumpkin and barley are tender. If the soup is too thick, add hot water or more stock if you have to, one tablespoon at a time. Stir in the fresh parsley. Serve with fresh lime wedges. This soup can be served with crème fraiche if desired, although Churchill disliked creamy soups!

POACHED SALMON TROUT WITH BELUGA CAVIAR GARNISH

SERVES 6

Salmon trout, named for its pretty pink hue, is not salmon at all; it is a brown trout that swims from lakes and streams to the sea and is sometimes referred to as steelhead. Brook trout and rainbow trout are also good poached, a technique that is restrained enough to preserve the delicate flavour of any of these fish.

6 rainbow trout, gutted and filleted
120g Beluga caviar
1 litre water
150ml champagne vinegar
20 black peppercorns
salt to taste
2 tsp chopped dill
2 tsp chopped parsley
3 leeks, white only, sliced on the angle into 5cm pieces
4 carrots, peeled, channelled and sliced on the angle ½ cm thick
350ml dry white wine

Wash the trout. Bring the water with vinegar, peppercorns, salt, herbs and vegetables to the boil for about 5 minutes. Add more water and wine and bring to the boil. Place in the trout fillets and bring to just a boil; take off the heat and leave to cool down and cook in the residual heat of the liquid for 5 minutes. Arrange the fish, carrots and leeks on a platter and garnish with Beluga caviar. Add lemon wedges and serve.

WINE

1936 Maison Louis Jadot Chablis. The Chablis region is the northernmost wine district of Burgundy in France. The grapevines around the town of Chablis are almost all Chardonnay, making a dry white wine renowned for the purity of its aroma and taste. The cool climate of this region produces wines with more acidity and flavours less fruity than Chardonnay wines grown in warmer climates. The wines often have a 'flinty' note, sometimes described as 'goût de pierre à fusil' ('tasting of gunflint'), and sometimes as 'steely'. In comparison with the white wines from the rest of Burgundy, Chablis has on average much less influence of oak, although many Grand Cru and Premier Cru wines receive some maturation in oak barrels, but typically the time in barrel and the proportion of new barrels is much smaller than for white wines of Côte de Beaune. Since it was founded in 1859, Maison Louis Jadot has been one of the most venerable and revered wine houses in Burgundy.

ROAST TURKEY WITH ROAST POTATOES AND SEASONAL VEGETABLES

SERVES 6

7kg fresh bronze turkey
3 onions, halved
2 lemons, cut into quarters
salt
pepper
175g salted butter, softened
4 tbsp fresh sage, finely chopped
3 tbsp plain flour
375ml port
150ml red wine
1 litre chicken stock
100g tbsp cranberry jelly

Heat oven to 170°C/325°F/gas 3 and place the turkey in a large roasting tin. Tuck 4 of the onion halves and the lemon quarters into the cavity and season with salt and pepper. Cover with foil, make sure there's plenty of space between the turkey and foil for the air to circulate and seal the edges tightly so that no steam escapes. Roast for 4 hours.

Meanwhile, finely chop the remaining onion and mix with the butter and sage. Take the turkey out of the oven and raise the heat to 200°C/400°F/gas 6. Brush the sage and onion butter all over the turkey and return to the oven, uncovered, for 45 minutes until crisp and dark golden. Transfer the turkey to a warm serving plate, cover loosely with foil and leave to rest for 30 minutes.

Tip the juices out of the pan into a bowl, leave for a moment to settle, then scoop the buttery oil from the surface into a separate bowl. Spoon 4 tbsp of this oil back into the tin and return to the heat. Stir the flour into the tin using a wooden spoon, scraping the residue off the bottom of the tin as you go. Cook for 2 minutes, then stir in port and wine and bring to the boil. Take the reserved turkey juices and hot chicken stock and pour into the tin. Bring to the boil and simmer for a few minutes, then add cranberry jelly. Keep warm until ready to serve. Serve with roast potatoes and seasonal vegetables.

WINE

1934 Domaine Laurent Combier Crozes-Hermitage: Hermitage is a French wine *Appellation d'Origine Contrôlée* (AOC) in the northern Rhône wine region of France, south of Lyon. The appellation was created in 1937, so this wine served at Churchill's birthday banquet pre-dates the AOC designation. The region produces mostly red wine from the Syrah or Shiraz grape, which originated in Persia.

PERSIAN SAFFRON ICE CREAM

SERVES 6–12

12 yolks from large free-range eggs
250g caster sugar
1 tsp Iranian saffron
500ml milk
500ml double cream
200g shelled and peeled Iranian pistachios

Beat the egg yolks and sugar together until smooth and creamy. Grind most of the saffron in a mortar and pestle, and put half of the powder into the milk and heat until boiling point. Pour the boiling milk into the beaten yolk/sugar mixture while continuously beating and then return to the pan. Continue to warm on low heat until thickened, carefully stirring all the time. When thickened take off the heat, pour in the cream and mix it briefly. Add the rest of the saffron powder. Let it sit until it's cool enough to put in an ice cream machine. Put it in the ice cream machine according to the instructions; when nearly frozen pour in 90 per cent of the nuts and finish churning. Serve with a few strands of the remaining whole saffron threads and pistachio slivers on top.

CHEESE SOUFFLÉ

SERVES 6

100g strong Cheddar cheese, grated
70g Gruyère cheese, grated
150g unsalted butter, plus extra melted butter for greasing
100g panko breadcrumbs
80g plain flour
1 tsp English mustard powder
5 drops Tabasco sauce
600ml milk
7 large free-range eggs, separated

Preheat the oven to 200°C/400°F/gas 6. Place a baking sheet in the oven to heat up. Brush a 12 x 250ml ramekin with melted butter; chill and then repeat and sprinkle with the breadcrumbs. Melt the butter in a pan and add the flour, mustard and Tabasco. Cook for a couple of minutes, then gradually add the milk, stirring, until the mixture comes to the boil. Boil for 2 minutes, until very thick and coming away from the sides of the pan.

Turn off the heat, stir in the cheese and egg yolks and season well. Whisk the egg whites until stiff. Mix a spoonful into the cheese mixture to loosen, then gently fold in the rest. Spoon into the ramekins, just up to the rim. Run your finger around the edge of the ramekins. Put on the baking sheet and bake for 8–10 minutes until risen and golden, then serve immediately

WINE

Graham's Vintage Character Port was a personal favourite of Sir Winston Churchill with invoices from his wine merchant, Hatch, Mansfield and Co., indicating it was the only brand of port the politician had ordered throughout his lifetime. Made from the very oldest vines on Graham's Douro vineyards, the Special Edition, known as 'Six Grapes' was produced from the oldest vines from across Graham's five Quintas, many of which were over 50 years old.

Nine

NIXON
IN
CHINA

21 February 1972
The Great Hall
of the People,
Beijing

THE GUESTS

ZHOU ENLAI,
*Premier of the People's
Republic of China*

RICHARD NIXON,
US President

PAT NIXON,
First Lady

HENRY KISSINGER,
National Security Advisor

WINSTON LORD,
his assistant

WILLIAM ROGERS,
US Secretary of State

In 1972, at the height of the Cold War, an event occurred that shocked the Western powers to the core and left Chinese jaws dropping in disbelief. After decades of naked hostility between the USA and China it was announced that US President Richard Nixon was to visit Beijing. Political pundits in the West were incredulous. Would the ageing despotic leader of a revolutionary communist state of 800 million people really meet and discuss global peace with the leader of the world's largest military force and capitalist powerhouse? President Nixon's visit to China and his historic meeting with Chairman Mao and the shrewd, calculating Chinese Premier Zhou Enlai, astounded the world. Discussions over a lavish banquet in Beijing's Great Hall of the People would take superpower diplomacy – and modern history – in a bold new direction. To understand why this meal was such a radical idea and how it changed political perceptions at a stroke, it is necessary to look back a few years to the ruthless manoeuvrings of Chairman Mao.

In 1966 Mao was determined to regain total control after the abject failure of his Great Leap Forward plan to turn China into a global economic powerhouse. His utopian schemes, involving the mobilisation of peasant farmers to build blast furnaces in every village, from which steel could be produced, together with the collectivisation of China's farms, caused the near-collapse of the Chinese economy and the death from starvation of tens of millions. By 1966, Mao's reputation and leadership were being questioned and he resolved to reassert his authority by unleashing a new bout of Marxist fervour aimed at reinforcing communism through the imposition of Maoist orthodoxy. The Cultural Revolution was launched.

Over the next decade, millions were persecuted and hundreds of thousands were killed as China's youth, inspired, goaded and encouraged by Chairman Mao, went on the rampage. Bands of young revolutionary Red Guards hunted down, tortured and killed imaginary bourgeois capitalist infiltrators within the Communist Party's ranks. Teachers, doctors, writers, artists, poets and indeed virtually all intellectuals were publicly humiliated and often brutally murdered by frenzied mobs of students clutching copies of Mao's *Little Red Book*. Ancient Confucian temples, priceless stone carvings and historic buildings and artefacts were smashed and destroyed in an orgy of zeal, to rid China of the 'Four Olds' – Old Customs, Old Culture, Old Habits and Old Ideas.

Mao emerged from this chaotic tumult with his authority once again restored and his personality cult soaring to new heights. For a while he enjoyed almost godlike status in China, with millions of peasants uttering thanks to him before every meal in a devotional, almost religious passion. To reinforce his position, Mao set about purging those in the highest echelons of the Communist Party and People's Liberation Army (PLA), removing anyone whom he regarded as a threat, including some of his oldest and most loyal comrades.

To the horrified shock of the entire nation, two of Mao's longest-serving and closest colleagues were exposed as traitors. Liu Shaoqi, who had been chairman of the National People's Congress Standing Committee from 1954 to 1959 and then President of the People's Republic of China from 1959 to 1968, was denounced by Mao as a 'scab and renegade'.[1] Mao regarded Liu as a threat and he was arrested in 1967 and regularly trotted out and savagely beaten in front of mass party rallies to symbolise Mao's determination to rid China of 'capitalist roaders'. At the Ninth Party Congress in 1969, Liu was described by Premier Zhou Enlai as 'a criminal traitor, enemy agent and scab in the service of the imperialists, modern revisionists and the Kuomintang reactionaries'.[2] Denied medical treatment for his diabetes and for pneumonia, which he developed as a result of his constant mistreatment, he died soon afterwards.

Another major scalp quickly followed. From 1966 to 1969 Chen Boda was head of the Cultural Revolution Group set up by Mao to oversee and determine the course of the Cultural Revolution. It became one of the most important political bodies in the country, surpassing even the Politburo Standing Committee. The importance of his role inevitably gave rise to concerns in Mao that he could pose a threat to his leadership. The Cultural Revolution Group was dissolved by the Chinese Communist Party's Ninth Congress in the Spring of 1969 and Chen Boda was denounced as a 'sham Marxist and a revisionist secret agent'.[3]

Mao had cleverly engineered the downfall of his two former senior colleagues, but the attempted defection of Marshal Lin Biao and evidence that he had been contemplating a military coup, came as a complete shock to the Party chairman. Lin Biao was a military genius; he had been at Mao's side for decades, rising to the position of leader of the People's Liberation Army (PLA) and Vice Premier of China. He played a central role in the Cultural Revolution, laying the foundations for the fanatical personality cult that was built around Chairman Mao. He was rewarded for his endeavours by being nominated by Mao as his chosen successor. Lin Biao died together with members of his family in a plane crash in Mongolia in September 1971, fleeing from what appeared to have been a failed military coup aimed at ousting Mao. He was, in turn, denounced as a 'counter-revolutionary careerist'.[4]

This extraordinary chain of events had begun to stretch the credulity even of the long-suffering Chinese people. How could so many of Mao's closest colleagues and senior Party leaders have been devious traitors all along? Could Mao's judgement have been flawed? Was 'The Great Helmsman' perhaps not so great after all?

By late 1971, Mao was tired, ill and depressed. China had few allies. Under Mao's oppressive rule it had been virtually a closed society for decades. China and Russia were the two biggest communist states in the world and until the death of Stalin in 1953 had been mutually supportive. But disagreements between the two super-states erupted when the new Soviet leader, Nikita Khruschev, denounced Stalin and his policies in a keynote speech in 1956 and began to implement major economic reforms.

Mao regarded Khruschev as a dangerous revisionist who would undermine the goal of worldwide Marxism, and relations between Beijing and Moscow soured. The USSR had reneged on a previous promise to provide China with a nuclear bomb and the Cold War was now at its height, with the Soviets and the West pointing countless nuclear weapons at each other in pursuit of their policy of Mutual Assured Destruction. It was into this tense and politically charged atmosphere that the idea for a most unlikely dinner was floated.

*   *   *

The Americans feared that the border clashes between China and Russia, which had escalated with the ambush and killing of 59 Soviet troops by the Chinese army in the disputed Zhenbao island on the Ussuri River in March 1969, could spiral into full-scale war. Although a meeting between the Soviet Premier Alexei Kosygin and his Chinese counterpart Zhou Enlai had taken place at Beijing Airport on 11 September 1969, while Kosygin was on his way home from the funeral of Ho Chi Minh, deep tensions still remained. US President Nixon and other senior Americans were convinced that these tensions between the two giant communist neighbours could be exploited to the advantage of the US. Nixon was certain that the way to do this was to wean China from its 'angry isolation', a phrase that he used in his inaugural address in 1969.[5]

Meanwhile, determined to build his own nuclear arsenal, Mao was increasingly looking to the West to supply China with the necessary technology. Thus began an intricate 'fan dance' involving private messages delivered through third countries, proposed prisoner exchanges, the withdrawal of US naval destroyers from the Straits of Taiwan and ultimately what became known as 'ping-pong diplomacy'.

Mao was reluctant to be seen openly wooing the American president, so he asked Zhou Enlai to send a message inviting Nixon to Beijing via the Romanians, who enjoyed a good relationship with both the US and China. Nixon did not wish to appear overly eager to accept and told his National Security Advisor Henry Kissinger to make no reference to the invitation in his regular communications with Beijing.

But Mao was not to be put off so easily. On 21 March 1971, the ideal opportunity presented itself in the unlikely shape of a world championship table tennis tournament in Japan. Mao had personally approved the participation of a Chinese ping-pong team, one of the first sports teams to be given permission to travel outside China since the beginning of the Cultural Revolution. The team had been ferociously briefed on how to behave and although they were exempted from waving their *Little Red Books* before every match, they had been instructed not to shake hands with the Americans or to initiate conversations with them.

But on 4 April, the US table tennis player Glenn Cowan climbed onto the Chinese bus and started to chat to the Chinese men's champion Zhuang Zedong.[6] Next day the Japanese newspapers were filled with pictures of the two shaking hands. When Mao was shown the photos he was delighted and called Zhuang 'a good diplomat'. Later that evening he instructed his foreign ministry to invite the American table tennis players to China. Inviting a group of Americans to China would be a sensational breakthrough in diplomatic relations between the two great nations and Zhou Enlai set about preparing an elaborate welcome for the visiting players, ensuring the event leapt from the sports pages to the front pages of global newspapers.

In one fell swoop, Mao had greased the slipway for Nixon to undertake a visit and sure enough, by the end of May, secret arrangements for the proposed trip had been settled. In July 1971 Henry Kissinger made the first of several clandestine trips to Beijing to finalise details for the presidential visit, bringing many extravagant gifts for the ageing despot and even suggesting that the US might abandon Taiwan and restore full diplomatic relations between Beijing and Washington.

Nixon regarded his intended visit to China as a key political asset in the run-up to the 1972 presidential elections, and sacrificing Taiwan to its fate at the hands of a belligerent China seemed to him an acceptable price to pay for re-election. Kissinger even offered to divulge every detail of America's Strategic Arms Limitation Talks (SALT) with the Soviets, making clear to the Chinese: 'We will tell you about our conversations with the Soviets; we do not tell the Soviets about our conversations with you.'[7]

Kissinger further promised that US forces would withdraw unilaterally from Vietnam and would not return. For Mao, this was more than he had anticipated and it was being handed to him on a plate. He was ecstatic, telling senior Chinese diplomats that Nixon was like a common prostitute, 'tarting herself up and offering herself at the door'.[8] Mao concluded that Nixon was going to be a walkover and that he could get what he wanted from the US president without making any major concessions.

On 15 July 1971, immediately following Kissinger's secret visit, it was publicly announced that Nixon had been invited to Beijing. This sensational news was followed by an equally sensational vote in the UN, when Taiwan was ousted from its UN Security Council seat, seeing it transferred to China. Studying the UN vote Mao declared that 'Britain, France, Holland, Belgium, Canada and Italy had all become Red Guards'. But there was little doubt that it was American support that had swung this breakthrough for China. Mao and Zhou Enlai began actively planning a programme for the anticipated visit of President Nixon, including a lavish dinner in the Great Hall of the People that would change the course of history.

*   *   *

By late 1971, Richard Nixon was experiencing major problems at home and abroad. America was deeply divided over the Vietnam war and although Nixon had pledged to end the conflict and to aim for 'peace with honor' in Indochina, in fact the war had escalated with the invasion of Cambodia in 1970 and Laos in 1971. Around 300 American soldiers a day were being killed in Vietnam and there was increasing unrest in cities across the US with students and anti-war protesters demanding the complete withdrawal of US forces.

Richard Milhous Nixon had made his name politically as a fierce anti-communist, but he was sincere in his belief that he could negotiate a peaceful accord with the North Vietnamese. In his inaugural address he said: 'The greatest honor history can bestow is that of a peacemaker,' a statement that was later carved on his gravestone as an epitaph. He knew that his re-election in 1972 depended on fulfilling his 'peace with honor' pledge and he was desperately seeking ways of achieving it.

At the same time, Nixon was struggling to handle a severe economic recession. He had introduced harsh wage and price controls, causing turbulence in many towns and cities across America. The racial crisis was also at its height and deep divisions were evident in the southern states where Nixon was determined to bring in new de-segregation legislation.

So it was that Nixon and Mao, two leaders of vast nations with diametrically opposed political systems, both facing major challenges at home and abroad, moved inexorably towards an historic encounter that would boost their respective reputations internationally. Both calculated that such a meeting would deflect attention from chronic domestic problems, potentially help to resolve the conflict in Indochina, while also reducing Cold War tensions between America, China and the Soviet Union.

As the date for Nixon's impending visit grew nearer, Mao suddenly became seriously ill with heart disease and a chronic bronchial lung infection, no doubt exacerbated by decades of heavy smoking. He lost consciousness and apparently came close to death. His body had become terribly swollen from a build-up of fluids, and new clothes and shoes had to be made for him prior to Nixon's visit. However, the prospect of Nixon's imminent arrival in Beijing, together with large doses of antibiotics, helped to revive him.

The study in Mao's house in Zhongnanhai, west of the Forbidden City, was converted into a partial medical facility with a large bed and copious bits and pieces of medical kit. Screens had been erected to hide the medical equipment and a team of doctors and nurses began an intensive course of physiotherapy to ensure that Mao would be physically able to greet his important visitors. He was made to stand up, sit down and walk around, to exercise his muscles after the many weeks he had spent confined to bed.

On 21 February, the day Nixon, his wife Pat, Henry Kissinger and a vast army of over 100 mostly TV journalists (Nixon despised newspapers, particularly *The Washington Post*, which despised him and eventually brought him down over the Watergate affair) were due to arrive at Beijing airport, Mao was visibly excited and sat by his telephone waiting for news. Zhou Enlai had been sent to the airport to meet the president and his entourage and thousands of police had been deployed to stop all traffic and clear a path for the presidential motorcade through the Beijing streets, which would normally be congested with great swarms of bicycles and rickshaws.

When Air Force One touched down at Beijing airport, Nixon was rather bemused and disappointed to find that instead of cheering crowds, there was only a small group of officials led by Zhou and a military guard of honour. Nevertheless, Nixon strode down the aircraft steps into the shivering cold of the Chinese winter and shook the premier's hand enthusiastically. The photograph of this first encounter made the front page of newspapers around the world.

No meeting had been scheduled with Mao on the first day of the visit, but as soon as the procession of black limousines, bedecked with fluttering red communist flags, arrived at the Diaoyutai State Guesthouse, Mao telephoned Zhou and demanded that Nixon be brought immediately to see him. Zhou insisted that the visitors must be given a little time to rest and have some lunch, but in the early afternoon Nixon's motorcade again swept off through the empty Beijing streets, taking President Nixon to Zhongnanhai for his first historic encounter with Chairman Mao.

In his memoirs, Henry Kissinger describes what happened next:

> In Mao's study, manuscripts lined bookshelves along every wall; books covered the table and the floor; it looked more like the retreat of a scholar rather than the audience room of the all-powerful leader of the world's most populous nation ... Except for the suddenness of the summons, there was no ceremony. Mao just stood there ... I have met no-one, with the possible exception of Charles de Gaulle, who so distilled raw, concentrated will power. He was planted there with a female attendant close by to steady him ... he dominated the room, not by the pomp that in most states confers a degree of majesty on their leaders, but by exuding in almost tangible form the overwhelming drive to prevail.[9]

In fact, the frail and still visibly ill Mao had two nurses on hand to look after him. Armchairs had been positioned in a horseshoe shape to accommodate Mao, who sat next to Nixon in the centre, and Nancy Tang, the interpreter, to Mao's right, with Zhou sitting to her right. Henry Kissinger and Winston Lord, Kissinger's assistant, sat on Nixon's left. Green tea was served and topped up by glamorous girls in long, traditional silk Chinese cheongsam, while spittoons had been strategically positioned between each armchair to accommodate the Chinese aptitude for spitting, even in polite company.

Despite his great excitement, Mao was determined to discuss philosophy at this first meeting rather than politics. At one point he even chided Nixon to do a little less briefing, clearly finding the president's long explanation about US relations with India tedious. He insisted on giving the floor to Kissinger, reminding Nixon that the two leaders should not monopolise the conversation. At one point he said, 'People like me sound like a lot of big cannons. For example, we say things like "the whole world should unite and defeat imperialism."'At this, both Mao and Zhou roared with laughter.[10] But the only statement of real importance to emerge from the meeting was when Nixon affirmed that the biggest threat America and China faced came not from each other, but from the Soviet Union. Mao did not demur.

Winston Lord attended the meeting to take notes, and his recollection of the encounter is illuminating: 'Mao went from topic to topic in rather a casual way. It seemed that sometimes he did not quite know what he was talking about.'[11] Lord did however acknowledge as highly significant the fact that Mao had summoned Nixon to a meeting within two hours of his arrival in Beijing, sending out a powerful message to the world. Nevertheless the actual content of the meeting had been a disappointment. Lord stated in his account that it was clear Mao had considerable presence and radiated power and ruthlessness, but it was equally clear he came from rough, peasant stock, while Zhou Enlai, by contrast, exuded the elegant qualities of a mandarin. The meeting lasted just over one hour with Zhou fearing that Mao might become over-tired and constantly looking at his watch.

It was clear from the outset that although Mao sat on the throne, real political influence was wielded by the power behind the throne – Zhou Enlai. If Nixon's visit to China was to be a success, then negotiations with China's premier would be of paramount importance. The opportunity quickly arose. Zhou informed the Americans that they were to attend a welcome banquet that evening in the Great Hall of the People in Tiananmen Square. A meal that would change the world was about to take place.

Somewhat jet-lagged and tired out by the 13-hour time difference, Nixon and his wife Pat, Kissinger, Lord and US Secretary of State William Rogers, were whisked to the Great Hall of the People by motorcade, where a lavish state banquet had been prepared. Zhou sat between Richard and Pat Nixon at a massive round table beneath enormous floodlit flags of the United States and the People's Republic of China. Each place setting had chopsticks as well as a knife and fork. Most of the Americans gamely tried to use the chopsticks with varying degrees of success. Occasionally Zhou would pick delicacies from the multitude of plates with his own chopsticks, which he was using to stuff food in his own mouth, and place them demurely on the president's and First Lady's plates, to their obvious bemusement. The US president and his wife had spent weeks in the White House practising using chopsticks and learning some basic greetings in Chinese like *nǐ hǎo* (hello) and *xiè xiè*, (thanks), but their prowess was being sorely tested.

The top table had 20 guests around it while all the other tables had 10. The table decorations consisted of an explosion of ornamental grasses with strategically positioned kumquats. A small orchestra from the People's Liberation Army mingled American favourites like 'America the Beautiful' and 'Home on the Range' with Chinese folk songs. The entire affair was televised and broadcast live around the world, including, thanks to the time difference, on the US morning news.

Course after course was followed by an endless round of toasts, washed down with crystal-clear, 30-year-old Maotai, the sorghum-based Chinese liquor that to the uninitiated can be seriously unforgiving. Max Frankel, who covered the trip for *The New York Times*, described it as 'pure gasoline'. Another American journalist said it was 'like Japanese *sake* times ten!' Indeed, prior to the visit an aide to Dr Kissinger had tasted Maotai and, gravely concerned about its effect on Nixon, cabled back a warning: 'Under no, repeat no, circumstances should the president actually drink from his glass in response to banquet toasts.' But undeterred by such warnings, Nixon matched Zhou glass for glass, visibly wincing each time he drained a shot of the powerful liquor, while a battalion of white-jacketed waiters hovered behind the guests, refilling the Maotai and fruit juice every time a sip was taken or a toast was concluded.

In a toast offered by Nixon, he said that he had been warned about Maotai and had been told that it was over 50 per cent alcohol. He then told a joke about a man who had been drinking Maotai and tried to light a cigarette, exploding in the process. The assembled guests roared with laughter and Zhou grabbed a match, lit his goblet of Maotai and with a blue flame licking from the glass, held it aloft for Nixon to see, provoking more roars of laughter.

But the American president did not intend to drink only Maotai with his dinner. He had brought 13 cases of Schramsberg 1969 Blanc de Blanc sparkling wine with him on Air Force One. When TV images of Nixon's historic dinner in the Great Hall of the People were broadcast back to the US, Americans could see their president proposing a 'toast to peace' and raising a glass with Premier Zhou of sparkling Schramsberg, from the Napa Valley, in his home state of California.

The official menu for the banquet listed hors d'oeuvres, hundred-year-old eggs, bacon and small carp in vinegar sauce, spongy bamboo shoots and egg white consommé. Also on the menu were cucumber slices, tomato slices, sliced roast duck with pineapple, duck liver spring rolls and bread and butter. Guests were also served with sharks' fin soup, fried and stewed prawns, mushroom and mustard greens, steamed chicken with coconut, almond junket, pastries and finally a selection of fruit including, Zhou proudly pointed out, tangerines from northern China. There was a constant rotation of traditional blue-and-white Chinese willow-pattern dishes from which the guests could choose a dazzling array of unusual (for the Americans) titbits.

The hundred-year-old or 'century' eggs must have intrigued the US president and his team. These duck, chicken or quail eggs are preserved in a mixture of clay, ash, salt, quicklime and rice hulls for several weeks or months, causing the yolk to turn a dark green or grey colour with a creamy consistency and a taste like sulphur or ammonia. The white turns into a dark brown translucent jelly and the shell sometimes produces a strange pattern like the branches of pine trees. This Chinese delicacy is certainly an acquired taste and was probably gently pushed to the side of their plates by most of the American guests.

For the most part, these were classic Chinese dishes, elegantly served, with the main courses focusing on food that the Chinese thought the Americans might be familiar with, which is why there was a preponderance of duck and prawns. But with few exceptions, most of the dishes contained exotic ingredients that the Nixons would never have come across in America. The emphasis was on purity and elegance of taste, typified perhaps by the sharks' fin soup and the almond junket, both basically bland foods which, like the hundred-year-old eggs, delighted the ultra-refined Chinese palate in the upper ranks of the ruling Communist Party.

As was common at the time, the Chinese furiously smoked pungent cigarettes throughout the dinner, often holding their chopsticks in one hand and a cigarette in the other, Nixon, as an avid pipe-smoker often consuming up to eight bowls a day, didn't object. Indeed packs of cigarettes from Air Force One were distributed around the tables by the Americans and later it was noticed that several of the Chinese guests were studying the packets and discussing excitedly what was written on the labels. It was their first encounter with the ubiquitous health warning: 'The Surgeon General states that smoking these cigarettes can be harmful to your health.'

The friendly atmosphere at the dinner and the lengthy and productive discussions that took place between Zhou and Nixon culminated in a toast from Zhou in which he said: 'The social systems of China and the US are fundamentally different and there are great differences between the US government and the Chinese government. However, these differences should not hinder China and the US from establishing normal state relations. We hope, through a frank exchange of views between our two sides, to gain a clearer notion of our differences and make efforts to gain common ground. A new start can be made between our two countries.'

Zhou finished by proposing a toast to the health of President Nixon and his wife, and to friendship between the two countries. Nixon responded by stating: 'The Chinese people are a great people. The American people are a great people. We have at times in the past been enemies. We have great differences today. What brings us together is that we have common interests, which transcend those differences. And so let us in these next five days start a long march together, not in lock-step, but on different roads leading to the same goal; the goal of building a world structure of peace and justice in which all may stand together with equal dignity and in which each nation, large or small, has a right to determine its own form of government, free of outside interference or domination.'

Nixon concluded his speech by proposing a toast to Mao, Premier

Zhou and to the friendship of the Chinese and American people 'which can lead to friendship and peace for all people in the world'.

Thus began the historic visit that was later hailed by the international media as 'the week that changed the world'. Mao in his brief one-hour meeting with Nixon on day one of the visit had perhaps set the scene by chatting warmly to the American president and acquiescing in his view that their shared problem was the Soviet Union. But there is no doubt that it was the state banquet hosted by Zhou that forged the new alliance between these two former warring nations. The Chinese bent over backwards to be hospitable and friendly to their former arch-enemies, plying the Americans with food and drink. The Americans duly reciprocated with lavish pledges of peace and reconciliation.

Throughout the week, when not in meetings with Zhou and senior members of the Chinese government, Nixon attended cultural and athletic performances, toured the Forbidden City and the Ming tombs, and climbed the Great Wall of China, about which he commented: 'I think that you would have to conclude that this is a great wall and it had to be built by a great people.' The First Lady, meanwhile, was followed by an army of American and Chinese journalists and photographers, who had been shut out of the official meetings, as she toured communes, schools, factories and hospitals.

For their part, the Chinese media devoted unprecedented attention to the Nixon visit. While few Chinese owned TV sets, they listened avidly to official radio broadcasts, and rushed to buy copies of newspapers like the *People's Daily*, which featured front-page stories and photographs of the Nixon–Mao summit. The extraordinary publicity given to the visit by the government-controlled Chinese media was in itself newsworthy, and widely featured in American television and newspaper reports.

The week culminated with a brief visit to Hangzhou in the Yangtse River Delta in eastern China and Shanghai, where the final outcome of the summit was announced. The document, called the Shanghai Communiqué, pledged that the US and China would work towards a normalisation of relations and that neither they nor any other power would seek hegemony in the Asia–Pacific region. This was of key importance to China due to their shared, heavily militarised border with the Soviet Union. The communiqué controversially also acknowledged the One China policy and agreed to cut back military installations on Taiwan.

Nixon and his party returned to Washington on 28 February. There was an immediate outcry over his apparent sellout of Taiwan, but this was quickly forgotten in the surge of positive press comments on the historic importance of the visit, which ushered in a new era of Sino–American relations. Kissinger subsequently wrote in his memoirs:

> For once a White House public relations strategy succeeded and performed a diplomatic function as well. Pictures overrode the printed word; the public simply was not interested in the complex analyses of the document after having watched the spectacle of an American President welcomed in the capital of an erstwhile enemy.

Nixon's success in China, which helped him achieve re-election in 1972, was quickly overwhelmed by the Watergate scandal. Congress began the process of impeachment and Nixon resigned, leading to the lacklustre Gerald Ford assuming the presidency in 1974. The Democratic Governor of Georgia, Jimmy Carter, narrowly defeated Ford in 1976. It was Carter's firm belief that he had been chosen by God to broker a peace deal in the Middle East and in the next chapter we will see how he brought together two arch-enemies, President Anwar Sadat of Egypt and Prime Minister Menachem Begin of Israel, to thrash out a peace accord over 13 tortuous days at Camp David in September 1978.

MENU

Sticky Chicken Wings
Spare Ribs
Spring Rolls
Salt and Pepper Prawns
Hundred-Year-Old Eggs
Bacon and Small Carp in Vinegar Sauce
Spongy Bamboo Shoots with Egg White Consommé
Chinese Roast Duck, Smashed Cucumber Salad
Mustard Greens and Dried Shrimp
Steamed Chicken Dim Sum
Almond Junket

1969 Schramsberg Blanc de Blanc
Maotai

STICKY CHICKEN WINGS

SERVES 6

1 kg chicken wings, separated at the joints, wingtips removed
5g Maldon salt
1 tsp ground white pepper
250ml pineapple juice
150g sugar
150ml light soy sauce
150ml Mirin (rice wine)
zest and juice from 2 oranges
100g chopped garlic
150g chopped fresh ginger
200g chopped onions
2 tbsp toasted sesame oil
1 tsp crushed red chilli flakes
30g sesame seeds
½ bunch diagonally sliced spring onions, for garnish

Preheat the oven to 200°C and line a baking sheet with 2cm sides with tin-foil. In a large bowl, season the chicken wings with the salt and pepper, tossing to coat well. Spread the seasoned wings in the prepared roasting pan evenly and bake until browned for about 35 minutes. While the wings are baking, in a large pan, combine the remaining ingredients, except the sesame seeds and spring onions, set over medium-high heat. Bring to a boil, stirring occasionally, until the sugar is dissolved and the liquid has reduced to a syrup – 7 to 8 minutes. Remove from the heat and cover to keep warm until ready to use. Remove the wings from the oven and reduce the oven temperature to 170°C.

Place the wings in a large, heat-proof bowl. Drizzle half the prepared sauce over the wings, reserving the other half, tossing to coat well. Sprinkle the sesame seeds over the wings and toss again. Place a wire cooling rack inside a large baking sheet lined with tin-foil and arrange the coated wings on top of the rack. Return the pan to the oven and bake for an additional 20 to 25 minutes, or until cooked through and crispy. Arrange the wings on a large serving platter and top with sliced spring onions. Serve immediately with the remaining sauce passed on the side for dipping.

SPARE RIBS

3kg rack pork spare ribs, trimmed of excess fat
150g Chinese five-spice powder
Maldon sea salt
black pepper, freshly ground
250ml dark soy sauce
100ml hoisin sauce
200ml ketchup
70ml rice vinegar
150g honey
3 bird's eye red chillies, chopped seeds and all
10 garlic cloves, smashed
150g fresh ginger, whacked open with the flat side of a knife
150ml water

Preheat the oven to 150°C. Rub the ribs all over with the five-spice powder, then season generously with salt and pepper. Put the ribs in a single layer in a roasting pan and slow-roast until they are almost tender, about 2 hours.

Meanwhile make the glaze. In a large bowl, combine the water, soy sauce, hoisin sauce, ketchup, vinegar, honey, chilli, garlic and ginger. In a saucepan bring the sauce to a simmer over medium heat. Cook until the sauce reduces and thickens then remove from the heat. Strain the sauce and reserve. When the ribs are about 30 minutes away from being done, baste them with the sauce. Cook until the meat pulls easily from the bone (about 1cm of bone will show). Just before serving, preheat the grill. Baste the ribs again with the sauce and brown them under the grill for 5 to 8 minutes. Separate the ribs with a cleaver or sharp knife, pile them on a platter, and pour on the remaining sauce. Sprinkle with sesame seeds and serve.

SPRING ROLLS

6 spring roll sheets
1 egg, beaten
vegetable oil, for deep-frying

FOR THE SAUCE

50ml peanut oil
14 shallots, diced
2 small red chilli peppers, finely chopped
200g honey
70ml red wine vinegar
70ml balsamic vinegar
350ml duck stock

FOR THE FILLING

2 duck breasts, skin still on, thinly sliced
3 tsp sesame oil
1 carrot, finely sliced
2 small red chili peppers, finely chopped
2 tsp root ginger, peeled and chopped
150g peppers, mixed, de-seeded and finely sliced
6 tsp dark soy sauce
3 garlic cloves, chopped
20g sesame seeds

Start with the sauce. Heat the oil in a wok and add shallots and chillies. Cover and sweat over a medium heat for 5 minutes. Next, add the honey, red wine vinegar, balsamic and stock and bring to the boil. Gently simmer until reduced by half and remove from heat. Transfer to a jug and keep warm.

Start the filling by cleaning and drying the wok. Place on a medium to high heat and add the duck. When the fat starts to render, remove the duck from the wok with a slotted spoon and wipe the wok clean. Heat the sesame oil in the wok and add the carrot, chillies, peppers, grated ginger and soy sauce. Stir-fry for 2–3 minutes. Next, add the garlic, sesame seeds and heat until the duck is cooked through. Combine well and transfer into a bowl. Heat the deep fryer or large pot of oil to 180°C. Lightly brush the spring roll wrappers with the beaten egg. Spoon the stir-fried mixture into the centre of each one and roll up, tucking in the ends before you make the final layer. Deep-fry the spring rolls until golden brown, remove with a slotted spoon and drain on kitchen roll. Serve immediately with the sauce.

SALT AND PEPPER PRAWNS

---

24 large sized prawns, cleaned but with shell and head left on
peanut oil for frying
2 tbsp Maldon salt for rubbing the prawns before cooking
24 cloves garlic, finely chopped
12 spring onions, sliced
12 bird's eye chilli peppers, sliced with seeds
2 tsps salt to taste

First, butterfly the prawns for easier cleaning then rub them with the salt and leave to marinate for at least 1 hour in the fridge. Prepare a wok for deep-frying the prawns. Once oil is hot, turn heat to medium. Fry the prawns in batches, as you have to make sure you don't overcrowd your wok. Fry for about 3–4 minutes depending on the size of the prawns.

Continue with the rest of the prawns until all have been completed.

Clean your wok. Heat wok until almost smoking. Add about 2 tbsp cooking oil and turn heat to low. Swirl to coat. Add the garlic, onions and chilli slices into the wok. Stir-fry till aromatic. Add another 2 tsp of salt. Add in the prawns from earlier and stir well to coat. Turn heat to high again and stir briskly for another 30 seconds. Serve hot.

HUNDRED-YEAR-OLD EGGS

Hundred-year-old eggs are a Chinese delicacy dating back centuries to the Ming Dynasty. They may resemble (and smell like) eggs of that vintage, but in fact they only take four to five weeks to prepare.

Traditionally hundred-year-old eggs were made by preserving chicken or duck eggs in a mixture of salt, lime and ash, then wrapping them in rice husks for several weeks. During this time the pH of the egg rises, transforming the egg; the chemical process breaks down some of the proteins and fats into smaller, more complex flavours. After curing, the yolk of the egg turns a dark green and has a creamy consistency, while the white turns amber and is gelatinous.

6 fresh duck eggs
475 ml very strong black tea
100g salt
120g each ashes of pine wood, ashes of
charcoal and ashes from fireplace
150g lime

Combine tea, salt, ashes and lime. Using about ½ cup per egg, thickly coat each egg completely with this clay-like mixture. Line a large crock with garden soil and carefully lay coated eggs on top. Cover with more soil and place crock in a cool dark place. Allow to cure for 4–5 weeks. To remove coating, scrape eggs and rinse under running water to clean thoroughly. Crack lightly and remove shells. To serve, cut into wedges and serve with sweet pickled scallions (green onions) or any sweet pickled vegetable.

Serve with sauce of 2 tbsp each vinegar, soy sauce and rice wine and 1 tbsp minced ginger root.

BACON AND SMALL CARP IN VINEGAR SAUCE

SERVES 6

*1 3kg carp washed, gutted, rubbed with salt and left for
24 hours then washed well under cold water
100g sliced fresh ginger
1 bunch of spring onions, washed and sliced
1 tsp toasted and ground star anise
4 bay leaves
200ml rice vinegar
200ml rice wine
12 slices lap yuk (pork belly)*

Preheat oven to 175°C. Pat the carp dry. Mix the ginger and spring onions together, split and stuff in the carp, place the stuffed carp on a pine board (green, not seasoned, rough sawed just bigger than the carp). Place in a large roast pan. Mix the rest of the ingredients well and pour over the carp. Cover the roast pan with foil, cone-shaped to hold in the heat and juices. Bake at 175°C for 1 hour 45 minutes. Drain juices from pan and keep to serve with the carp. Cut the lap yuk and fry to crispy texture and serve as garnish with each portion of fish.

SPONGY BAMBOO SHOOTS WITH EGG WHITE CONSOMMÉ

SERVES 6

1 1kg boiling hen
1kg pork shoulder, chopped
3kg pork bones
250g lap yuk (pork belly)
½ kg chicken feet
100g dried scallops
10 litres water
100g ginger
25g white peppercorns
50g dried longan fruit
100g rock sugar
young bamboo shoots and spring onions
(for the garnish)

Chop the hen, pork, lap yuk and pork bones into big pieces. Place all the meat ingredients into a big pot, add enough room-temperature water to cover and parboil for about 10 minutes. Remove them and clean thoroughly. Place them and the dried scallops into a very large stock pot, add the water, ginger and white peppercorns. Bring to a boil and lower to medium heat. Cook for 6 hours on slow simmer so it does not cloud. After 6 hours, add the dried longans and rock sugar. Cook for another 2 hours on slow simmer. Strain the stock through double muslin. Serve with young bamboo shoots and spring onions.

CHINESE ROAST DUCK, SMASHED CUCUMBER SALAD

SERVES 6

1 roast Peking duck from an Asian supermarket,
re-heated and sliced served with salad (see below)
2 cucumbers
½ tsp salt
½ clove garlic, finely chopped
1 ½ tbsp soy sauce
1 tbsp black rice vinegar
1 tbsp caster sugar
1 tsp toasted sesame oil

Wash your cucumber thoroughly. Cut off the tips. Holding one end, carefully bang on the cucumber with the flat of your cleaver until it splits and flattens out. It will be a little mushed up, which is what you want. Once the whole cucumber is flattened, chop into bite-sized pieces. Do the same to each cucumber. Add ½ tsp salt, mix and place into colander. Let cucumber drip juices out for 15–20 minutes in the fridge. Squeeze cucumber lightly to remove most of the juice. Mix together the chopped cucumber, garlic, soy sauce, vinegar, sugar and sesame oil. Taste. It should be equal parts salty, sour and sweet. Adjust seasonings to taste. Let it marinate in refrigerator for at least half an hour, stirring once or twice, before serving. The longer it is marinated the tastier it will be.

MUSTARD GREENS AND DRIED SHRIMP

SERVES 6

½ kg mustard greens washed, drained and
cut into 2 cm lengths
4 tbsp small dried shrimp (soak in warm water for about
10 minutes), drained; but save water
2 tbsp dried belacan paste (hardened shrimp paste)
100ml peanut oil
8 cloves garlic, finely chopped
10 shallots, finely chopped
4 red Thai bird's eye chillies, sliced

With mortar and pestle mix shrimp and dried belacan paste together, breaking up the softened shrimp into small pieces. Heat a large wok or pan on high, add oil and when oil is hot (i.e. when it smokes), add garlic, shallots and belacan paste mixture. Stir for a minute or so and you will really smell the belacan becoming more fragrant. Add the mustard greens and quickly stir-fry until just wilted. Toss in the chilli and add a tablespoon or two of the shrimp water if desired for a bit of moisture to the sauce. Do not overcook; immediately take off heat and serve.

STEAMED CHICKEN DIM SUM

SERVES 6

150g minced chicken breast
100g pork belly, minced twice
7 shallots, finely chopped
1 tbsp dark soy sauce
2 tbsp hoisin sauce
4 garlic cloves, chopped
18 square wonton wrappers
peanut oil

FOR THE DIPPING SAUCE

100ml light soy sauce
200ml hoisin sauce
50ml chilli garlic sauce
30g Chinese-style mustard (or a hot English mustard)

Mix all the ingredients for the dipping sauce together.

In a bowl, combine the meats, shallots, soy sauce, hoisin sauce and garlic. Place 8 wonton wrappers on a clean surface and brush edges with water. Place 1 tablespoon of the mixture in the centre of each wrapper. Gather edges of the wrapper together over the filling. Press the edges of the wrapper together, enclosing the filling completely. Repeat with remaining wrappers and filling.

Place a collapsible metal steamer rack in a large wide pot. Fill the pot with 1cm water. Rub steamer rack with peanut oil. Bring water to a simmer. Working in batches, arrange dumplings on rack 2cm apart. Cover the pot with lid and steam dumplings until cooked thoroughly (about 8 minutes). Watch the water level and add more as needed. Transfer dumplings to a platter and serve with dipping sauce.

ALMOND JUNKET

500ml water
24g agar-agar
150g icing sugar
750ml milk
2 tsp almond extract
3 mangoes, peeled and diced into 2cm cubes

Pour 500ml cold water into a large pan, break in the agar-agar and set the pan over a very gentle heat until the agar-agar has completely dissolved – this will take at least 10 minutes. Add the sugar, milk and almond extract and mix well, but do not boil. Pour the mixture into a large dish. Let it cool, then chill it in the refrigerator for at least 3–4 hours, or overnight. When the junket is set, cut it into small cubes about the size of sugar lumps and spoon it into individual bowls. Top with diced mango and serve.

WINES AND SPIRITS

1969 Schramsberg Blanc de Blanc vintage sparkling wine. Schramsberg Vineyards is a winery located in Calistoga, California in the Napa Valley region. The vineyard, which was originally founded in 1862, produces a series of sparkling wines using the same method as champagne.

Maotai is a Chinese spirit distilled from fermented sorghum. It comes in different versions ranging in alcohol content from the standard 53% by volume down to 35%. It is produced in the town of Maotai near the city of Renhuai in southwestern China's Guizhou province, which possesses a unique climate and vegetation that contributes to the taste of the drink.

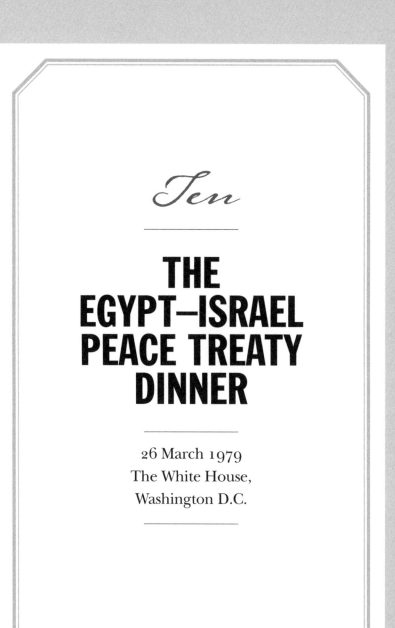

Ten

THE EGYPT–ISRAEL PEACE TREATY DINNER

26 March 1979
The White House,
Washington D.C.

THE GUESTS

Menachem Begin,
Prime Minister of Israel

Anwar Sadat,
President of Egypt

Jimmy Carter,
US President and host

In early 1978 Palestinian terrorists murdered one of Egyptian President Anwar Sadat's close personal friends in the Hilton Hotel in Nicosia, Cyprus. They then hijacked a plane and in the bungled rescue operation 15 Egyptian soldiers were killed. Weeks later, 11 more Palestinian terrorists landed on the Israeli coast and in a killing spree murdered 38 men, women and children in cold blood. The violent reprisals launched by Israeli Prime Minister Menachem Begin saw Israeli forces sweep into Lebanon, ostensibly in a bid to punish Palestinian units in that country. However, over 1,000 Lebanese civilians were killed in the operation and tens of thousands were left homeless. The savage bloodshed in this troubled corner of the world looked set only to escalate and endure.

Yet just a year later, in late March 1979, US President Jimmy Carter hosted a sumptuous State dinner for Begin and Sadat in a specially erected tent in the south grounds of the White House. The three leaders feasted on Columbia River salmon and roast sirloin of beef as they fêted the success of their talks, which had culminated in an historic peace accord. Toasting the triumph of their negotiations, President Carter said: 'When others could not or would not move to end the seemingly endless tragedy of the Middle East, two men – President Anwar Sadat and Prime Minister Menachem Begin – dared to think the unthinkable, dared to do what others feared could not be done, dared to seize history in their hands and to turn history toward peace.' It was, in Carter's own words, a 'miraculous' outcome. The three men, from different nations, different cultures and different religions, had brokered a deal that would bring peace between the warring nations of Egypt and Israel for decades to come, but which would cost President Sadat his life at the hands of fanatics. The peace agreement between Egypt and Israel, brokered after 13 tortuous days of negotiations at Camp David in September 1978, stunned the world. Never had any agreement seemed less likely; never had any three world leaders seemed less compatible. The State dinner on 26 March 1979 and the momentous agreement that it celebrated truly shaped the world for years to come.

*   *   *

Jimmy Carter, the peanut farmer from Plains, Georgia, who served a single term as US President from 1977 to 1981, was a devout Christian. Reared in the rural south at a time when racial segregation was the norm and the Ku Klux Klan was rampant, Carter, a Democrat and a liberal, nevertheless succeeded in becoming the Governor of Georgia from 1971 to 1975 before narrowly defeating Gerald Ford to become president in the 1976 presidential elections. As a devout Southern Baptist, Carter regarded the Bible with great seriousness. He believed it to be God's divinely inspired revelation to mankind and as a youngster he learned whole passages of the Old and New Testaments by heart.[1]

Carter had only limited experience of foreign affairs before he became the Governor of Georgia. As a young man he had dreamed of joining the navy and he was finally admitted to the Naval Academy at Annapolis, Maryland in 1943, graduating 60th out of 820 midshipmen in the class of 1946. He went on to serve as an officer in America's fledgling nuclear submarine fleet, but on the death of his father in 1953 he resigned his commission and returned to Georgia with his wife Rosalynn to take over the family peanut farm.

For 10 years he and Rosalynn grew their agribusiness into a successful enterprise, then in 1963 he ran for the state senate, winning a controversial election only after he exposed voting fraud and the courts ordered a re-run. He served two terms as a state senator before running for governor against the demagogic segregationist Lester Maddox in 1966. Maddox's victory came as a severe blow to Carter. He later recounted how his faith had been tested at this time, as he could not understand why God and the voters of Georgia would allow such a person to beat him. Nevertheless he persevered and stood again, winning the election and being sworn in as the 76th Governor of Georgia on 12 January 1971.

As a biblical scholar, Carter had always cherished the idea of visiting the Holy Land to follow in the footsteps of Jesus. In 1973 he and Rosalynn travelled to Israel, visiting many of the holy sites and meeting with Israeli Prime Minister Golda Meir. From his biblical studies, Carter knew the geography of ancient Palestine almost better than he knew the geography of the United States, and the experience of visiting the occupied West Bank and Jewish settlements that had been taken over by the Israelis following the Six Day War in 1967 convinced him that he had a God-given mission to broker peace in the Middle East. Israel had seized vast tracts of territory during the Six Day War, including the Golan Heights in Syria, the Sinai Peninsula in Egypt, the West Bank of Jordan, the Gaza Strip and even the Old City of Jerusalem. Tensions across the region had been at boiling point ever since.

Soon after entering the White House, Carter turned his attention to the Middle East, marking out peace in the zone as a key priority for his presidency. Even Henry Kissinger, a veteran of Middle East negotiations under Nixon and Ford, warned him that he was embarking on an almost impossible task. Undeterred, Carter began a series of meetings with Arab leaders, most of which were 'beset with overheated rhetoric and impractical demands'.[2] This all changed when Anwar Sadat came to the White House for the first time. Carter said he found him to be 'a shining light'.[3] He was convinced that he had discovered somebody with whom he could negotiate a meaningful peace treaty.

In many ways, Sadat's upbringing mirrored that of Jimmy Carter. Born into poor farming stock in the Nile Delta of Egypt, Sadat had inherited the dark skin of his maternal grandfather, an African slave. Like Carter, Sadat, a Sunni Muslim, was a devout believer, and had learned to recite the Koran as a boy. And like Carter he too had become obsessed with the belief that he was a man of destiny. Sadat loathed the British occupiers of Egypt and during the Second World War was imprisoned by them for colluding with the Axis powers. But, ironically, it was through the influence of a British doctor who was a friend of his father that he secured a place in the prestigious Royal Military Academy in Cairo, graduating as an officer in 1938. Following his posting to Sudan, Sadat set up the revolutionary Free Officers Movement together with Gamal Abdel Nasser. They pledged to end British domination of Egypt and Sudan and to overthrow the corrupt Egyptian monarchy.

The Free Officers launched the Egyptian revolution of 1952 and overthrew King Farouk in a military coup. But following an attempt on his life by the Muslim Brotherhood, Nasser cracked down hard on the movement, placing Muhammad Naguib, Egypt's first president, under house arrest, effectively assuming executive control of Egypt. Nasser was sworn in as president in 1956. Nasser appointed Sadat as minister of state and he steadily rose in status until he became vice president to Nasser in 1964, a position he held until he became president in 1970, following Nasser's sudden death from heart failure. In this role, Sadat's popularity soared. He quickly ordered the arrest of the pro-soviet vice-president Ali Sabri and the deeply unpopular Sahrawi Gomaa, head of the detested secret police. He followed this by expelling the Soviet military from Egypt and reforming the Egyptian army in preparation for a new confrontation with Israel.

Around this time Menachem Begin had also become something of a revolutionary legend, determined to end the British mandate in Palestine. As a founding member and leader of Irgun, the Zionist paramilitary organisation, he believed that it was the fundamental right of every Jew to enter Palestine and that a Jewish state could only be achieved by armed force. Irgun had broken away from the more moderate Haganah, led by David Ben Gurion, and was soon listed by the US, UK and UN as a terrorist organisation.

Begin played a leading role in the bombing of the King David Hotel in the heart of Jerusalem, where the British had set up their administrative HQ. On Monday 22 July 1946, seven milk churns filled with explosives were hidden in the hotel basement directly beneath the busy restaurant, and although a telephone warning was sent, the subsequent explosion demolished much of the hotel and led to the deaths of 91 people, including many Arabs, British and even Jews. The attack caused outrage and ultimately led to Britain's withdrawal from Palestine. Begin was a wanted man and spent many months on the run from the police and the British military, on one occasion spending four days hiding in a cupboard without food or water and on another disguising himself as a rabbi. Later, as leader of Irgun, he led their campaign against the Arabs during the 1947–48 civil war in Mandatory Palestine.

Born in Brest-Litovsk in 1913, which was then part of the Russian Empire and is now in Belarus, Begin studied law at Warsaw University and became a militant Zionist, even founding a Jewish student self-defence society to counter anti-Semitism. When the German invasion of Poland was launched in 1939, the Nazis murdered Begin's father, mother and elder brother. Begin escaped to Vilnius in Lithuania, where, as a prominent Zionist, he was arrested by the NKVD and tortured before being sentenced to eight years in the Soviet gulags. In 1941, following the German invasion of Russia, Begin was released and joined the Polish Free Army as an officer cadet. In this role he was sent to Palestine in 1942, where he faced the choice of returning to Europe to fight the Nazis or joining Irgun to fight for a Jewish state. He decided to join Irgun and quickly rose through its ranks, recognised for his leadership qualities and for his harsh criticism of Haganah, which he regarded as appeasers of the British.

In August 1948 Begin founded a right-wing political party called Herut. He was elected to the Knesset (Israeli parliament) where he gained a reputation as an impassioned speaker. Begin was seen by many people as being too inflammatory and demagogic, and as a result Herut spent many years languishing in opposition. But he finally took office in June 1967, at the start of the Six Day War, when Prime Minister Levi Eshkol appointed him as minister without portfolio in a coalition cabinet that his party had joined. In 1973 Begin agreed to a plan drawn up by Ariel Sharon to bring together a number of smaller parties, forming a new political bloc called Likud (Consolidation) which in the elections that year, two months after the Yom Kippur War, won 39 seats in the Knesset, although they still remained in opposition. Likud, led by Begin, won a landslide election victory on 17 May 1977. Begin was sworn in as prime minister on 20 June 1977. His emergence as Israel's new leader sent shockwaves around the world; he was regarded by many as an extremist, and the prospects for peace in the Middle East now seemed more distant than ever.

Bringing together these two characters – the former Jewish terrorist Menachem Begin and the revolutionary Arabist Anwar Sadat – in a bid to secure peace seemed like an impossible dream, but Carter was determined. The first sign of a potential thawing of relations between the two warring nations of Egypt and Israel came with the wholly unexpected visit of Sadat to Tel Aviv and Jerusalem. On 19 November 1977, Sadat's plane landed at Ben Gurion Airport in Tel Aviv. He had concluded that after losing two wars against the Israelis in 1967 and 1973, peaceful co-existence between Egypt and Israel was the only viable prospect. Eleven days earlier he had stated in a speech in Cairo that he was 'willing to go to the ends of the earth' to obtain peace, but his visit to Israel provoked outrage in the Arab world and he was widely condemned by many Middle East leaders who believed it was immoral even to speak to the Israelis.

In a speech to a packed Knesset in Jerusalem Sadat said: 'Let us put an end to wars, let us reshape life on the solid basis of equity and truth.' Having broken Egypt's ties with the Soviet Union, Sadat was also keen to cement a better relationship with the US and he knew that his visit to Israel would jump-start that process. But he was not about to capitulate to Israeli aggression. He told the Knesset that the price of peace was Israel's complete withdrawal from the occupied Arab territories including Jerusalem. He even hectored Israel for setting up a home on land that did not belong to it and demanded the creation of a Palestinian state. The euphoric mood in the Knesset was quickly subdued, as parliamentarians realised they were listening to the same old familiar Arab demands.

Sadat's speech provoked a belligerent response from Begin, who avoided any mention of peace and instead defended Israel's right to exist. 'No sir, we took no foreign land,' he said. 'We returned to our homeland.'[4] The prospect for a breakthrough in the Middle East, which had risen so dramatically with Sadat's visit, departed with him on his flight back to Cairo. The Palestinians, nevertheless, felt that he had betrayed them and there were widespread protests throughout the Arab world, with the offices of Egypt Air bombed in Beirut and Damascus and attacks on Egyptian embassies. However, Carter regarded Sadat's visit to Israel as a potential platform for peace. He was also encouraged by Sadat's earlier overtures to the Christian community. Sadat had invited the American evangelist Billy Graham to Egypt in 1975 and then visited Pope Paul VI in the Vatican in April 1976. But these were straws in the wind. In early 1978 came the terrorist bloodshed in Cyprus and Lebanon. This was the situation confronting Jimmy Carter as he issued invitations to Sadat and Begin to come to the US for a peace summit in the autumn of 1978. He had decided that the ideal location for the peace talks would be Camp David, the 140-acre presidential retreat in Maryland, 60 miles from Washington. Carter brought with him a formidable team of foreign policy advisers led by Secretary of State Cyrus Vance and National Security Advisor Zbigniew Brzezinski.

The Camp David summit began on 5 September 1978. Sadat was the first to arrive, emerging from a US helicopter to hug Jimmy Carter and kiss Carter's wife Rosalynn on both cheeks. Sadat had been to Camp David before; he knew the Carters well and the US President hoped that the informal setting would help to stimulate agreement between the Egyptian and Israeli leaders. Sadat was accompanied by Mohamed Ibrahim Kamel, his foreign minister and Boutros Boutros-Ghali, minister of state for foreign affairs. He had also brought along Deputy Prime Minister Hassan el-Tohamy who also acted as the Egyptian president's private astrologer and mystic. Every member of Sadat's team was opposed to a peace deal with Israel.

Next to arrive was Menachem Begin. The Israeli prime minister was dressed formally in a smart suit and tie and throughout the 13-day summit refused to accept Jimmy Carter's blandishments to wear casual clothes, insisting that as a prime minister in the presence of two presidents, he felt obliged to dress formally. Begin's team included Moshe Dayan, the legendary Israeli military leader with the sinister black eye-patch, who was now the Israeli foreign minister. Begin had also brought along Ezer

Weizman, his defence minister. Weizman had been the mastermind behind the invasion of Lebanon earlier that year, which had led to such widespread death and destruction. He was also responsible for the creation of the impressive Israeli air force, which had played such a devastating role in the 1967 Six Day War, wiping out the Egyptian air force in less than three hours.

Politicians and the press in America and around the world were fascinated that Carter had managed to bring such a diverse group of enemies together at Camp David. A vast international press corps had gathered and daily press conferences were organised in the American Legion Hall in the nearby town of Thurmont, Maryland. Almost every hotel and bed-and-breakfast establishment in the area had been booked up by journalists. Few held out any hope of a successful outcome to the negotiations, and Carter did not want any unwarranted distractions from the media, so kept them at arm's length, telling them very little.

On the first evening in Camp David, Begin went to Carter's cabin for preliminary discussions. Carter's popularity as president had been plummeting and he knew that his entire future was at stake. If these talks failed, his reputation would be ruined. Carter set out his vision for the talks, explaining that he would act as the honest broker, simply trying to arbitrate a deal between the two warring parties. If a deal could not be achieved, an opportunity for peace might never arise again, he argued. Carter knew that Begin would do nothing that might undermine Israel's security. He was well acquainted with Begin's unshakable views, but he was also aware of the fact that the Israeli prime minister was a pragmatist and recognised the importance of maintaining strong links with America.

But if Carter had thought a peace deal could be achieved in a matter of days, his dreams were quickly shattered by Begin, who pointed out that whatever might be agreed, there could be no compromise over Israeli settlements in Sinai. These would remain, he insisted. Carter knew that for Sadat this was a red-line issue and he tried to convince Begin that Israel's occupation of the West Bank, Gaza and Sinai was a direct violation of international law. But Begin dug in his heels. These territories had been won by Israel during the Six Day War after she had been forced to defend itself against an aggressive attack by the Egyptians, and there could be no question of handing them back, he argued. Indeed, while Israel might contemplate stopping building any new settlements in Sinai, it was determined to continue expanding its settlements in the West

Bank, Begin exclaimed. Carter was dismayed. Faced with such intransigence he told Rosalynn that night that he felt the Camp David Summit was doomed from the outset.

Next morning, Sadat met with Carter at 10 a.m. and handed him a document entitled *The Framework for a Comprehensive Peaceful Settlement of the Middle East Problem*. It was a lengthy document, which set out the Egyptian position in stark and uncompromising detail. Once again Egypt demanded total Israeli withdrawal from all of the occupied territories and the dismantling of all Israeli settlements. The proposal even demanded that Israel should pay Egypt reparations for the damage it had caused during successive wars. In a final flourish the document noted that within five years a Palestinian state would be created. Carter realised that none of this would be acceptable to Begin and his sense of doom deepened. When Sadat stated that it was his intention to read aloud the entire document at the first scheduled meeting with Begin that afternoon, Carter told him that it would be a grave error, which could pull up the drawbridge on the entire summit. But Sadat refused to heed Carter's advice and, sure enough, when the three leaders met at 3 p.m. that afternoon, after exchanging a few pleasantries, Sadat put on his glasses and proceeded to read all eleven pages of his 'peace proposal'. He droned on for more than an hour while Begin sat, stony faced.

When Begin returned to his quarters that evening he was fuming. He told his team that he felt as if Sadat had set out to humiliate Israel. He was still raging the next morning when he met Carter who, sensing that the peace summit was on the verge of collapse, pled with the Israeli prime minister to offer some concessions to Sadat that might keep the negotiations on track. But Begin was having none of it. When the three leaders met again at 10.30 a.m. on the third day of the summit, Begin insisted on ferociously dissecting Sadat's peace proposal line by line. It seemed to Carter as if the two men were determined to goad each other, as arguments and accusations raged back and forth. Carter was dismayed. It seemed as if there were no areas where Israel and Egypt could reach agreement. Sinai in particular appeared to be a major obstacle, with Sadat demanding Israel's full withdrawal and the dismantling of the settlements and Begin steadfastly refusing to make any such concessions. In fact Israel was now pumping oil from captured oil wells in the Sinai Peninsula, which further enraged the Egyptians.

When the three leaders met again that evening, Sadat and Begin were still at each other's throats. The meeting broke up in confusion with both stating that there was no point in continuing negotiations any further. The summit was finished. Carter was appalled. He had gambled his political career on this summit and he pleaded with Sadat and Begin to stay for just one more day to see if any compromise could be reached. The two men reluctantly agreed and Carter threw a party that evening to try to break the ice, but it was clear that both Begin and Sadat were deeply unhappy and they spent most of the evening sitting in frosty silence.

As day four dawned, Carter learned that Sadat and his team were after all preparing to leave. Begin meanwhile was preparing to brief the international media on the reasons why the summit had failed, citing Sadat's 'unworkable' peace proposal as the root of the problem. Carter asked Sadat to delay his departure until later and he rushed to Begin's cabin and spent much of the day trying to persuade him to show some flexibility. Late in the afternoon he went to Sadat's cabin and suggested that the Americans and the Egyptians could draw up a bilateral agreement that excluded the Israelis. This innovation appealed to Sadat, who agreed to spend one more night at Camp David. Carter knew that he was walking a tightrope, but nevertheless he had postponed the collapse of the summit for another few hours.

In fact there were no meetings on the Saturday, enabling Carter and his team time to draw up the promised US–Egypt plan. But the animosity between Sadat and Begin had reached a stage where the two were literally no longer on speaking terms. When the negotiations began again on the Sunday, Carter had to meet each of the leaders individually in their cabins then relay what had been said back to the other party. This was shuttle diplomacy in action, but Carter was determined to keep the summit going and it was his skill as a mediator that prevented the collapse of the negotiations on repeated occasions. But by the Sunday morning, Begin was starting to panic. He realised that the Egyptians had presented their peace proposal at the start of the summit and now the Americans were about to table their own plan. Only Israel had offered nothing in return and could be accused of having arrived empty-handed. Begin gathered his team together and started to dictate an improvised proposal, although in effect his document amounted to nothing more than a step-by-step rebuttal of everything the Egyptians had suggested.

Carter had another idea up his sleeve. He realised that claustrophobia was beginning to affect his foreign guests and he therefore planned an excursion to get them out of the compound for a few hours. He decided to take the Israelis and Egyptians to the Gettysburg National Military Park that morning, in the hope that Sadat and Begin might absorb lessons from the American Civil War that could be applied to their own dilemma. But Begin instructed four of his team to remain behind and told them to complete his rebuttal document, pack all of their bags and arrange for El Al flights back to Tel Aviv. For him, the summit was effectively over. On arrival at the famous battlefield, Carter, whose great-grandfather had fought on the Confederate side there, proceeded to recount the history of one of the bloodiest battles in American history. Everyone was startled when a reflective Begin, who was standing alone, away even from his own Israeli colleagues, suddenly began to recite the words of Lincoln's historic Gettysburg address. He knew it by heart. Perhaps, Carter thought, this could be turning point. Perhaps Begin had at last realised what peace could mean for Israel.

Back at Camp David, Carter and his team presented Begin, Weizman and Dayan with the American proposal. The Israelis were appalled, with Weizman referring to the document as 'seventeen pages of high explosive!'[5] Nevertheless, Begin asked for time to consider the document and Carter and his team met with them again later that evening. Their heated discussions went on until 3 a.m., with Carter at one point shouting in frustration: 'Listen, we're trying to help you bring peace to your land.'[6] Day seven of the Camp David summit witnessed a vigorous exchange of documents between the Americans and the Israelis, as Carter and his team tried to incorporate Israeli demands and objections into their own proposal. Their exertions were viewed with great suspicion by the Egyptians, and finally Sadat exploded in rage and said that he had concluded Begin had never had any intention of signing a peace deal. In these circumstances there was no point in remaining any longer at Camp David. They would leave the next day.

Carter had estimated that the summit would take no more than three or four days, but day eight dawned and still there was no sign of a breakthrough. Indeed Sadat and Begin were becoming more intransigent with each passing hour. Their hatred of each other seemed unfathomable. Both were determined to leave Camp David that very day, although Boutros-Ghali had warned Sadat that such a course of action could seriously undermine his leadership, and Dayan had warned Begin that leaving the summit empty-handed would be disastrous for Carter and could therefore wreck US–Israeli relations. In desperation, Carter scribbled another proposal on how to settle the problem of Sinai. He showed it to Sadat, who made a couple of minor changes, both of which favoured Israel, and agreed to the remainder. Carter now informed Begin that he would table a new proposal the following day and he even invited each side to send a delegate to help with the final drafting, effectively side-lining Sadat and Begin. But when Begin got hold of the American draft he raced round to Carter's cabin and in a lengthy and withering session, rejected it line by line. Carter was furious. He accused Begin of being totally unreasonable. Once again it seemed as if the summit was over.

Day nine saw Carter commence a negotiating session with members of Sadat's and Begin's teams that stretched into an 11-hour marathon. It was becoming increasingly clear that the success or failure of the Camp David summit hinged on one major issue – Sinai. The day ended with Carter trying to meet with Sadat, but the Egyptian president said he needed further time to think and refused his request for a late-night meeting. When Carter saw Sadat emerging from his cabin next morning for his usual brisk walk, he rushed to join him, and as they strolled around the tree-lined grounds, the two presidents spoke at length about the horrors of the American Civil War, Vietnam and the need for lasting peace. It was a philosophical encounter. But Carter realised that time was running out. He had been absent from the White House for far too long already. Eleven days had passed without any meaningful progress. He was facing defeat. His Camp David initiative would be portrayed in history as an international fiasco.

Later that morning Cyrus Vance told Carter that Sadat and his dele-gation had demanded a helicopter so that they could leave. Carter rushed over to Sadat's cabin, and sure enough found the Egyptian leader packed up and ready to go. Carter angrily confronted him, reminding him that his abrupt departure would rupture US–Egyptian relations. He added, poignantly, that it would also end their personal friendship. He demanded to know why Sadat was so determined to break these valuable ties and he promised that if Sadat decided to stay, he would back the Egyptian demand for a withdrawal of Israel from Sinai and the dismantling of the Israeli settlements. Sadat finally capitulated. Once again Carter had saved the day. Now he turned his attention to Begin, warning him that the summit had to end on the Sunday, two days hence and that he was scheduled to make a major speech in Congress when he would tell the world that the negotiations had failed because of Begin's intransigeance over Sinai.

This ultimatum from Carter jolted the Israeli delegation into action. Weizman telephoned General Ariel Sharon, renowned as an iconic Israeli military commander and hawk, who was greatly admired by Begin. Sharon was also the architect of the Sinai settlement programme. Weizman pled with Sharon to persuade Begin to compromise on Sinai, and a few hours later Begin told his startled delegation that he had received a call from General Sharon and that the general had told him that if the Sinai settlements were the only remaining obstacle blocking a peace deal with Egypt then he saw no military disadvantage in allowing them to be removed. This breakthrough could provide the political cover that Begin needed to seek such a compromise, but still he hesitated.

It wasn't until day 12 that the first glimmer of light began to appear in the negotiations. Carter and Begin and their respective teams talked right into the small hours, wrestling with the most difficult questions such as recognition of the rights of the Palestinian people and the dismantling of the Sinai settlements which they agreed would be subject to approval by the Knesset in Jerusalem. As the meeting broke up at around 1 a.m. on day 13, Carter was convinced that he had secured an historic peace deal between Egypt and Israel. Once again Carter joined Sadat for his morning stroll and informed him of the breakthrough with Begin. He assured Sadat that the Knesset would approve the removal of the Israeli settlements in Sinai if Begin did not stand in its way. He said that Begin had also agreed to a freeze on the building of any new settlements in Gaza or the West Bank. Sadat was exhilarated and immediately agreed that he was prepared to sign a treaty containing these proposals.

Carter decided to set up a special ceremony at the White House at 3 p.m. that day, where the three leaders would sign the peace treaty. But his plans were almost upended when Begin was shown a side-letter that the Americans had prepared as an annex to the treaty which mentioned the status of Jerusalem. Although the side-letter was not intended to have any legal status that might affect the treaty, it had been demanded by Sadat. In the letter, Carter reiterated the US position on Jerusalem, namely that America did not recognise the city as Israel's capital and that they regarded east Jerusalem as 'occupied territory'. Begin was outraged. He exploded in anger and said that he would refuse to sign any treaty that had such a side-letter attached to it. It was an impossible impasse for Carter. If he scrapped the letter, Sadat would walk out; if he kept it, Begin would walk out. The US president could hardly believe that he had got this close to signing an historic peace deal, only to see defeat snatched from the jaws of victory.

Carter told Begin that he was prepared to change the side-letter to say that the US position on Jerusalem was as stated by their ambassadors to the UN General Assembly on 14 July 1967 and to the UN Security Council on 1 July 1969, rather than repeating in full the actual speeches of the two ambassadors. While this slight alteration made no significant difference to the thrust of the letter, it surprisingly convinced Begin. He told Carter that he would sign. This was it. Camp David was finally over. An agreement that had seemed so unlikely right up until the very last moment had now been secured. That afternoon, the three leaders sat together at a desk in the East Room of the White House and signed two agreements: Framework for Peace in the Middle East and Framework for the Conclusion of a Peace Treaty between Egypt and Israel. Carter, Sadat and Begin all appeared to be exhausted. Some of Sadat's delegation had refused to attend the signing ceremony, convinced that their leader had committed an historic error. Sadat's Foreign Minister Mohamed Kamel, who had accompanied Sadat throughout the 13 days of negotiations at Camp David, resigned.

Six months later, President Jimmy Carter invited Anwar Sadat and Menachem Begin to the White House for a formal signing of the peace treaty and a State banquet to celebrate their historic agreement. Palestinian protesters had gathered to shout abuse outside the White House, but inside Jimmy Carter was able to say: 'During the past thirty years, Israel and Egypt have waged war, but for the past sixteen months these same two great nations have waged peace. Today we celebrate a victory – not of a bloody military campaign, but of an inspiring peace campaign.'

In his speech President Sadat said: 'President Carter, Prime Minister Begin, dear friends, only a few hours ago we laid down a solid foundation for a lasting peace in the Middle East. We did so in a determined effort to heal the wounds of the past and usher in a new era of love and fraternity. At long last cousins will be able to revive the traditions of the glorious past when they lived side by side in peace and harmony.'

Prime Minister Begin in a final toast to the assembled dignitaries said: 'I raise my glass to President Carter, President of the United States of

America, the mighty democracy which saved the world twice from the danger of tyranny, militarism, and totalitarianism, and which is still the guarantee for human liberty; and to President Sadat, whom I met for the first time in Jerusalem. And since then – as it is true, it comes from my heart – I have a deep sentiment for him. And under any circumstances, I will guard it in the depths of my heart.'

Two months after this historic banquet, Begin and Sadat met again in the town of El Arish in the Sinai Peninsula, where they signed an agreement formally transferring control of Sinai back to Egypt.

On 6 October 1981, as Anwar Sadat inspected the annual victory parade held to celebrate the time when Egypt had captured a small part of the Sinai Peninsula from Israel at the start of the Yom Kippur War, an Egyptian army officer assassinated him. It was the culmination of simmering tension in the Arab world where many believed that the state of Israel should be annihilated and that the peace agreement between Egypt and Israel had been a grave error. But Sadat left behind an enduring legacy. Both he and Begin had been awarded with the Nobel Peace Prize in 1978. Sadat was the first Muslim ever to become a Nobel laureate. Thirteen tension-filled days at Camp David that culminated in a lavish White House state banquet, brought peace to the former warring nations of Egypt and Israel that has lasted, sometimes uneasily, to this day.

But while peace between Egypt and Israel has survived, sometimes tenuously, it has proved to be the exception rather than the rule in the Middle East. Constant tension over Palestine, the rise of Islamic fundamentalism in Iran, two Gulf Wars, the so-called Arab Spring and the subsequent overthrow of a series of dictators, have left behind a searing cauldron of violence and bloodshed. The bloody civil war in Syria and ferocious battles against the murderous Daesh or Islamic State terrorists in cities across the Middle East provided the backdrop to the presidency of Barack Obama and to the arrival of Donald Trump as America's 45th President.

MENU

Columbia River Salmon in Aspic

Roast Sirloin of Beef with Seasonal Vegetables

Hazelnut Gianduja Mousse

Louis Martini Pinot Chardonnay
Paul Masson Cabernet Sauvignon
Almaden Blanc de Blancs

COLUMBIA RIVER SALMON IN ASPIC

SERVES 6–12

1 whole salmon, 2.5–2.75kg, scaled and gutted
2 onions, chopped
5 bay leaves
200ml champagne vinegar
750ml dry white wine
sea salt to taste
1 tsp cracked black pepper
1 packet of aspic powder
1 whole cucumber, channelled and sliced on
mandolin into neat whole 2mm slices
250g mayonnaise
3 lemons cut into 12 wedges

Place the salmon in a fish kettle. Add the onion, bay leaves, vinegar and wine and a good pinch of salt and black pepper. Add water until fish is covered by 1cm of liquid. Cover with a lid, or tin-foil, and bring to the boil on the stove. Once it is boiling, turn off the heat and allow the fish to stand in the water until cool. Carefully remove the salmon and place onto a board. Carefully scrape off the skin and place on a large flat serving dish that fits in the fridge; leave in the fridge until chilled.

Make aspic as directed by packet, cool down till just thickening then brush the salmon with this and place on cucumbers from the head to the tail overlapping in the form of fish scales. Once this is done, pour over the aspic and place in fridge to set. (If the aspic has set, just lightly warm, cool and then pour over.) Serve with mayonnaise and lemon wedges and crisp green salad.

WINE

Louis Martini Pinot Chardonnay – a Sparkling Brut Pinot Chardonnay from the Napa Valley in California.

ROAST SIRLOIN OF BEEF
WITH SEASONAL VEGETABLES

SERVES 6

2kg sirloin beef, French-trimmed by your butcher
10 garlic cloves, finely chopped
7 sprigs thyme, chopped
50ml rapeseed oil
10g of black peppercorns, crushed

FOR THE GRAVY

2 garlic cloves
2 bay leaves
6 sprigs thyme
750ml port
750ml red wine
600ml beef stock
100g redcurrant jelly

Heat oven to 200°C/400°F/gas 6. For the beef, mix the garlic, thyme and rapeseed oil with some black pepper. Rub over the beef and leave for at least 1 hour; the longer the better. Season the beef with salt and place in a roasting tin. Roast in the oven for 30 minutes, then turn the heat down to 180°C/350°F/gas 4 and cook for 10–15 minutes per 450g depending on how you like your meat – 10 minutes per 450g will give you rare meat and 15 minutes will give you meat that is cooked through.

When the beef is cooked, take it out of the roasting tin and allow it to rest somewhere warm, loosely wrapped in foil, for 30 minutes. Pour off and reserve any resting juices.

To make the gravy, place the roasting tin on a high heat with the garlic, bay and thyme; add the port; scrape with a wooden spoon to loosen any debris from the tin and bubble until almost completely reduced. Pour in the red wine and reduce by three-quarters before adding the stock and the redcurrant jelly. Bring to the boil and season to taste. Pour reserved resting juices back into the tin and boil down until it is to your taste. Finally, pour the gravy through a sieve into a warm jug. Carve the meat and serve with the gravy.

VEGETABLES

½ cauliflower
2 carrots
100g garden peas, shelled
100g broad beans, shelled
200g French beans
3 small leeks
salt
pepper
butter

Wash the vegetables and peel if necessary. Slice, chop or shred the vegetables as appropriate. Boil them in separate saucepans. Once cooked take each one out and shock in iced water to stop cooking; once cold, drain each vegetable.

To serve, mix all your vegetables together. Put a pot of water on to boil that will hold all the vegetables. Once boiling, place the vegetables in the pot and bring back to the boil, then drain. Place back in the pot, season with salt and pepper and add butter to taste; toss and serve.

WINE

Paul Masson Cabernet Sauvignon from the Sonoma County in California – a medium-bodied, fruit-driven red wine with a glorious red amber glow, rich, dark fruit notes of blueberry and blackberry as well as earth, dust, mocha and cedar.

HAZELNUT GIANDUJA MOUSSE

SERVES 6

800g gianduja milk chocolate
100ml water (for the syrup)
300g sugar
6 medium eggs
4 leaves gelatine, soaked in cold water
40ml water (for softening the gelatine)
250ml cream, whipped to ribbon stage

Heat the water and sugar to 118°C. While the sugar is on the boil, place eggs in a mixer and whip on high speed. Then slowly pour the water and sugar mix into the eggs, reducing the speed of the whisk to medium. When all the sugar syrup has been added, return the whisk to higher speed and whip until thick. Place the chocolate in a heat-proof bowl that will fit over a pan with simmering water; don't let the water touch the bowl or it will cook the chocolate. Melt the gianduja. Once melted, pour this into the egg mixture. This is now called a sabayon. Squeeze out the soaked gelatine and add to the gianduja sabayon mix. Fold in whipped cream. Pipe into glasses and pop into fridge to set. Take out for 30 minutes before you serve.

WINE

Almaden Blanc de Blancs – a sparkling Brut California wine.

ENDNOTES

CHAPTER ONE

1 McLynn, Frank, *The Jacobite Army in England. 1745. The Final Campaign* (John Donald, 1988) pp. 128–9.
2 'Memoirs of the life of the late Right Honourable Duncan Forbes, Esq; of Culloden; Lord-President of the Court of Session of Scotland' (London: printed for the author, and sold at his shop, opposite to Mercer's Street, Long Acre, 1748).
3 Jacqueline Riding, *Jacobites – A New History of the '45 Rebellion* (Bloomsbury Publishing, 2016).
4 Ibid.
5 Based on Prince Charles' household accounts during the 1745–6 campaign.
6 Jacqueline Riding, *Jacobites – A New History of the '45 Rebellion* (Bloomsbury Publishing, 2016).
7 Ibid.
8 Ibid.
9 Ibid.
10 A tombstone can be seen in Dunlop Kirkyard dated 1732 and the inscription reads: 'This is the burial place of John Dunlop of Overhill and Barbara Gilmour, his spouse and his children. Barbara was the originator of that brand of cheese known all over the world as Dunlop Cheese.'

CHAPTER TWO

1 Docent Manual, Carlyle House, Alexandria.
2 Ibid.
3 Letters of Col. John Carlyle, Docent Manual, Carlyle House, Alexandria.
4 Ibid.
5 Docent Manual, Carlyle House, Alexandria.
6 James D. Munson, (*Col. John Carlyle, Gent, 1720–1780* (Northern VA Regional Park Authority, 1986).

7 Letter dated May 14, 1755, Fort Cumberland, from George Washington to Mrs George William Fairfax.

8 *Historical Biographies, Nova Scotia: William Shirley (1694–1771)*. Available at: http://www.blupete.com/Hist/BiosNS/1700-63/Shirley.htm

9 Letters of George Washington, Docent Manual, Carlyle House, Alexandria.

10 Recipe taken from Gadsby's Tavern, 138 North Royal Street, Alexandria.

11 Ibid.

12 Letter from General Braddock to His Majesty's Ministers (The Docent Manual, Carlyle House, Alexandria).

13 *Pennsylvania Gazette*.

14 George Washington, July 18, 1755, letter to his mother. Similarly, Washington's report to Governor Dinwiddie. Charles H. Ambler, *George Washington and the West* (University of North Carolina Press, 1936, pp. 107–9).

15 Letters of George Washington (The Docent Manual, Carlyle House, Alexandria).

16 Ibid.

17 David M. Kennedy and Thomas A. Bailey, *The American Spirit: United States History As Seen by Contemporaries*, vol. 1 (Wadsworth Cengage Learning, 2010, p. 110).

CHAPTER THREE

1 Lucia Cinder Stanton (2012), *Those Who Labor for My Happiness – Slavery at Thomas Jefferson's Monticello* (University of Virginia Press, 2012).

2 In 1824, at the age of 67, Lafayette was invited back to America by President James Monroe and Congress, where he undertook a grand ceremonial tour, fêted throughout as a great hero of the War of Independence. He made a particular point of visiting Monticello to meet with his old friend and former president Thomas Jefferson and Jefferson's successor as president, James Madison.

3 Charles A. Cerami, *Dinner at Mr Jefferson's* (John Wiley & Sons, 2008). Cerami explains that because there was no definitive record of what was served at the dinner, the food the guests ate is based on the book *Dining at Monticello: In Good Taste and Abunndance* by Damon Lee Fowler (Thomas Jefferson Foundation, 2005) and to a personal luncheon given to Fowler by the president of Monticello, Daniel Jordan. In addition, Cerami based his wines on a book entitled *Thomas Jefferson on Wine* by John Hailman. I have followed Cerami's menu and wine list exhaustively.

4 He was probably America's first great wine expert and possibly even a bit of a wine bore. 'There was, as usual, a dissertation upon wines,' John Quincy Adams noted in his diary after dining with Jefferson in 1807: 'Not very edifying.'

5 James M. Gabler, *Passions – The Wines and Travels of Thomas Jefferson* (Bacchus Press, 1995).

CHAPTER FOUR

1 David King, *Vienna 1814* (Broadway Paperbacks, 2008).
2 Ibid.
3 According to the French lawyer Lucien Tendret (1825–96).
4 In the days before refrigeration, cream, unless eaten straight away, was allowed to sour naturally and become thicker, richer and slightly acid. It made the lightest scones and fluffiest pancakes, and gave just the right balance of acidity and creaminess to countless sauces. Today it is more often replaced by crème fraîche.
5 Paul Ramain, *Les Grand Vins de France* (Laffitte reprints, 1931, pp. 70–71).

CHAPTER FIVE

1 Max Hastings, *Catastrophe: Europe Goes to War 1914* (William Collins, 2013).
2 Menu taken from Vladimir Dedijer's book *Sarajevo 1914* (Simon and Schuster, 1966). The original menu is kept in the Kriegsarchiv, Vienna.
3 Edwin Kesiter Jr, *An Incomplete History of World War I* (Pier 9, 2007).

CHAPTER SIX

1 Legend has it that a strange horse-like beast had been seen in the loch, usually in bright sunlight in the early morning, when there was not a ripple on the water. These mythical beasts have become known as the Kelpies and have recently been immortalised in giant 30-metre-high sculptures by Andy Scott at the eastern entrance to the Forth and Clyde Canal in Falkirk, Scotland.
2 Stronachie Distillery produced a traditional Highland-style whisky for four decades until it finally closed in 1928, beset, like many other small distilleries, with problems of rising coal and grain prices. Only the ruins of the original distillery in Forgandenny village in Perthshire remain. But during its 40-year life its popular whiskies were distributed by A.D. Rattray Ltd who are still going strong and managed recently to purchase one of only four bottles of 1904 Stronachie Special Reserve Malt left in existence. They took a small sample from this bottle and used it to replicate the flavours and profile of this exceptional whisky, matching it finally to a single malt from the Benrinnes distillery in Aberlour on Speyside.

CHAPTER SEVEN

1 John Toland, *Adolf Hitler* (Ballantine Books, 1976).
2 Ibid.
3 Ibid.
4 David H. Lippman, *World War II Plus 75 – The Road to War* (Apple Wapple Productions, 2014).
5 Ibid.
6 The Nizkor Project *Nazi Conspiracy & Aggression Volume 1 Chapter IX – Aggression against Austria.*
7 Ibid.
8 David H. Lippman, *World War II Plus 75 – The Road to War* (Apple Wapple Productions, 2014).
9 John Toland, *Adolf Hitler* (Ballantine Books 1976).
10 William Manchester, *The Caged Lion – Winston Spencer Churchill 1932–1940* (Sphere Books, 1988).
11 John Toland, *Adolf Hitler* (Ballantine Books, 1976).

CHAPTER EIGHT

1 Robert Payne, *The Rise and Fall of Stalin* (Pan Books, 1968).
2 Alan Bullock, *Hitler and Stalin – Parallel Lives* (Harper Collins, 1991).
3 Frances Perkins, *The Roosevelt I Knew* (Viking Press, 1946).
4 Robert Payne, *The Rise and Fall of Stalin* (Pan Books, 1968).
5 Cita Stelzer, *Dinner with Churchill: Policy-Making at the Dinner Table* (Short Books, 2011).
6 Elliott Roosevelt, *As He Saw It* (Duell, Sloan and Pearce 1946).
7 David Dilks (ed.), *The Diaries of Sir Alexander Cadogan OM 1938–1945* (Cassell, 1971).

CHAPTER NINE

1 Philip Short, *Mao – A Life* (Hodder & Stoughton, 1999).
2 Jang Chung, *White Swans: Three Daughters of China* (Touchstone, 2003).
3 J. Guillermaz, *The Chinese Communist Party in Power, 1949–1976* (Westview Press, 1976).
4 Philip Short, *Mao – A Life* (Hodder & Stoughton, 1999).
5 Ibid.
6 Jung Chang and Jon Halliday, *Mao – The Unknown Story* (Jonathan Cape, 2005).
7 Ibid.

8 Ibid.

9 Philip Short, *Mao – A Life* (Hodder & Stoughton, 1999).

10 Ibid.

11 Winston Lord, *Moments in U.S. Diplomatic History – Nixon Goes to China* (Association for Diplomatic Studies & Training).

CHAPTER TEN

1 Jimmy Carter explained in a newspaper article in January 2013 that he had severed his ties with the Southern Baptist Convention after six decades as a practising Christian, due to losing his faith after recognising that almost all religions regarded women as inferior to men.

2 Lawrence Wright, *Thirteen Days in September* (Oneworld Books, 2014).

3 Ibid.

4 Ibid.

5 Ibid.

6 Ibid.